POLICE
PERSONNEL
MANAGEMENT

POLICE
PERSONNEL
MANAGEMENT

PAUL B. WESTON

Professor, Criminal Justice
California State University, Sacramento

PHILIP K. FRALEY

Associate Personnel Analyst
California State Personnel Board

PRENTICE-HALL, INC., ENGLEWOOD CLIFFS, N.J. 07632

Library of Congress Cataloging in Publication Data

Weston, Paul B
  Police personnel management

  Bibliography: p.
  Includes index.
  1.-Police—United States—Personnel management.
2.-Supervision of police personnel—United States.
3.-Collective bargaining—Police—United States.
I.-Fraley, Philip K., joint author. II.-Title.
HV7936.P47W47   658.3'7'36320973   79-9276
ISBN 0-13-683631-3

Prentice-Hall Series in Criminal Justice
James D. Stinchcomb, **Editor**

Editorial/production supervision: Esther S. Koehn
Cover design: RL Communications
Manufacturing Buyer: John Hall

© 1980 by Prentice-Hall, Inc., Englewood Cliffs, N.J. 07632

Printed in the United States of America

10 9 8 7 6 5 4 3 2 1

Prentice-Hall International, Inc., *London*
Prentice-Hall of Australia Pty. Limited, *Sydney*
Prentice-Hall of Canada, Ltd., *Toronto*
Prentice-Hall of India Private Limited, *New Delhi*
Prentice-Hall of Japan, Inc., *Tokyo*
Prentice-Hall of Southeast Asia Pte. Ltd., *Singapore*
Whitehall Books Limited, *Wellington, New Zealand*

To
Mary Ellen

Contents

III

CAREER DEVELOPMENT 83

6

Basic Training and Probation 87

7

Personnel Information System 101

8

Employee Development Programs 113

V

EMPLOYEE SUPPORT AND RETENTION   165

13

Job Structure and Salary Planning   169

14

Labor Relations   179

15

Collective Bargaining   191

16

Police Union Contracts   205

Preface

This book aims to develop the role of police personnel management in finding, hiring, and keeping police employees who can and will work at above-average levels, and get meaning and satisfaction in doing it. The authors believe that effective personnel management is on the threshold of its full utilization in the management of the human resources of police agencies.

Police Personnel Management has six major segments and 18 chapters. It fully describes and discusses the present dimensions and future trends of police personnel management. Chapter Objectives introduce each chapter. Chapter Reviews end each chapter with a summary of the chapter's content, a critique of the chapter, questions for discussion and review, and a workbook project stressing an important area of the chapter and the real world of local and state police agencies.

The authors wish to thank James D. Stinchcomb, Virginia Commonwealth University, for his prepublication review and suggestions; Ms. Mary Ellen Fraley for her legal and labor relations research; Jay F. Atwood, Program Manager of the California State Personnel Board, for his counsel and advice, and the many friends and associates who helped in the preparation of this text.

Paul B. Weston
Philip K. Fraley

POLICE
PERSONNEL
MANAGEMENT

I

OVERVIEW

Overview   Personnel managers in police agencies
are responsible for managing human
resources. The basic role of police personnel managers is to fill job vacancies
with men and women who will do satisfactory or better work and get meaning
and satisfaction from doing it. Since police employees are usually hired at
entrance level, this means employees must be developed to handle jobs of increasing difficulty and greater responsibility. It also means that working
conditions and terms of employment should contribute o the retention of
employees, and not lead to job dissatisfaction and resignation.

Police personnel managers can achieve meaningful and significant improvements in upgrading employees, but they must "sell" their programs to
the chief of police and/or the line commanders with direct authority over the
work force.

On-the-job relationships of the police personnel manager are

1. Direct authority of the chief of police over line commanders (work force
   generally) and the personnel manager
2. Staff authority of personnel manager through the chief of police to line
   commanders and through them to the work force
3. Liaison between the central personnel unit* and the police agency
4. Representative of the police agency in various contacts with representatives of a police union, that is, organized employees' association (see
   Figure I-1)

Within the scope of the above relationships, the police personnel manager has overall responsibility for determining just how many job vacancies
exist or can be expected. It is relatively easy to count existing vacancies, and to
project vacancies that will occur due to pending retirements, but the personnel
manager must seek the active help of line commanders in determining how
population growth and other demands will be reflected in work force
increases.

---

* Most governmental units at city, county, and state levels have a personnel unit which provides
  direction and guidance to a personnel program serving police, fire, health, and other agencies.

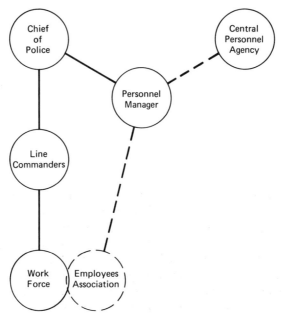

Figure 1-1
Relationships in Police Personnel Management

While the chief of police will normally seek this information for budgeting, police personnel planners should have some indications of need well ahead of the coming fiscal year. Ideally, the process of filling vacancies with qualified personnel will be an ongoing one, with the personnel manager acting out the role of an air-traffic controller and "stacking" qualified personnel in preparation for job openings.

1 Introduction

Chapter Objectives

- to trace the origin and history of personnel management in business and government
- to identify and describe the function of personnel management in police agencies

Since the turn of the century, most business concerns have made use of the theory and practice of personnel management to direct and control the human resources that figure so prominently in production. And for the past forty or fifty years, this has been true of police administration as well.

Every supervisor, middle manager, and executive of a police agency merges the elements of personnel management with the direct supervision and management of operations personnel, but each should ideally have the support of a specialist in personnel management. This specialist must have the skill and knowledge, and the time, to develop plans and implement programs for hiring job applicants who are most likely to perform at above-average work levels and find job satisfaction in a police career.

High crime rates and a continuing incidence of public disorders have warranted an increasing number of police officers to cope with crime and public order problems. At the same time, economic conditions have resulted in an upward trend in the cost of providing police services throughout the United States.

Since the major portion of police budgets is allocated for salaries, the effective management of the human resources of police agencies assumes increasing importance. Greater effectiveness in the utilization of an agency's human resources is a core area of personnel management, and a response to the rising cost of police services.

Historical Development   At the turn of the century, the function of personnel management consisted primarily of hiring, "time keeping," and terminating employees. Initially, supervisors relinquished the time-keeping task to a clerk, who then became a "personnel specialist." This time-keeper was soon assigned other responsibilities related to hiring employees and maintaining personnel records. A strong social welfare movement within the same period led to the position of "welfare secretary" in major industrial organizations. These jobholders may have supposed the employer's motivation to be of an altruistic nature, but more probably it stemmed from a generalized fear of labor unions. This was the first employee services position and emphasized the supply of health, safety, and other services to the work force.

Prior to World War I the expanded role of time-keeper was joined with the work of a welfare secretary into the concept of personnel management. In or about 1912, personnel management was formally identified as a subdivision of management. The first college-level course to emerge in this area was given at the Tuck School of Dartmouth College in 1915. By 1919 a dozen or more colleges were scheduling courses in personnel management. Within the span of a quarter century, the time-keeper and welfare secretaries were relics of the past and personnel management was fully recognized as a field of professional management.[1]

The scientific management theory of Frederick W. Taylor was an early approach to the management of employees and their work. He began his study of workers in 1885 and published his *Principles of Scientific Management* in 1911. While Taylor believed that special incentives must be given to workers in order to ensure their hard work, innovative action, and good will, his theoretical framework established new "personnel management" roles for management:

> Under scientific management the "initiative" of the workmen (that is, their hard work, their good will, and their ingenuity) is obtained with absolute uniformity and to a greater extent than is possible under the old system; and in addition to this improvement on the part of the men, the managers assume new burdens, new duties, and responsibilities never dreamed of in the past. The managers assume, for instance, the burden of gathering together all of the traditional knowledge which in the past has been possessed by the workmen and then of classifying, tabulating, and reducing this knowledge to rules, laws, and formulae which are immensely helpful to the workmen in doing their daily work. In addition to developing a *science* in this way, the management take on three other types of duties which involve new and heavy burdens for themselves.
>
> The duties are grouped under four headings:
>
> First. They develop a science for each element of a man's work, which replaces the old rule-of-thumb method.

[1] Herbert J. Chruden and Arthur W. Sherman, Jr., *Personnel Management* (4th ed.; Cincinnati, Ohio: South-Western Publishing Co., 1963), pp. 14–15.

Second. They scientifically select and then train, teach, and develop the workman, whereas in the past he chose his own work and trained himself as best he could.

Third. They heartily cooperate with the men so as to insure all of the work being done in accordance with the principles of the science which has been developed.

Fourth. There is an almost equal division of the work and the responsibility between the management and the workmen. The management take over all work for which they are better fitted than the workmen, while in the past almost all of the work and the greater part of the responsibility were thrown upon the men.[2]

Douglas McGregor was a contributor to many aspects of management theory and practice during the period following World War II. In a 1957 essay, "The Human Side of Enterprise," he pointed out that workers seek more than wages, and that any carrot-and-stick theory of motivation is no longer effective once a worker's basic needs have been satisfied. McGregor believed that the real concern of "human relations" was the realization of individual potential through proper guidance and an exchange of information within the organizational framework. His "Theory Y" statement delineates an area of responsibility for personnel management; the alignment of employees' personal goals with the objectives of the employer.

The broad dimensions of Theory Y are

1. Management is responsible for organizing the elements of productive enterprise—money, materials, equipment, people—in the interest of economic ends.
2. People are *not* by nature passive or resistant to organizational needs. They have become so as a result of experience in organizations.
3. The motivation, the potential for development, the capacity for assuming responsibility, the readiness to direct behavior toward organizational goals are all present in people. Management does not put them there. It is a responsibility of management to make it possible for people to recognize and develop these human characteristics for themselves.
4. The essential task of management is to arrange organizational conditions and methods of operation so that people can achieve their own goals *best* by directing *their own* efforts toward organizational objectives.[3]

Scientific management began by using time-and-motion studies to aid management in understanding the worker in relation to his or her task; it went on, however, to establish new guidelines for management's responsibility to employees. With McGregor's Theory Y the two halves of the worker-management equation were brought together. Employees' personal goals and

[2] Frederick Winslow Taylor, *Scientific Management* (New York: Harper and Brothers, 1947), pp. 36–37. Reprinted by permission.

[3] Warren G. Bemis and Edgar H. Schein (eds.), *Leadership and Motivation: Essays of Douglas McGregor* (Cambridge, Mass.: M.I.T. Press, 1966), p. 15. Reprinted by permission.

employers' organizational objectives were both affirmed in this new concept of human relations.

Shortly after McGregor's work became known, George Strauss and Leonard Sayles questioned the assumption that it is management's responsibility to create working conditions under which employees voluntarily work toward organizational objectives. They also questioned a second assumption, namely, that the needs of an employer and the needs of individual workers necessarily coincide.

Strauss and Sayles suggest a reality-oriented trade-off in which management accepts the responsibility for providing reasonable levels of satisfaction for both employer and employee (see Figure 1–1):

> A new approach called paths-goals analysis suggests that employees will be motivated to produce only if they perceive that production is a *path* toward a *goal* that they value, or more explicitly, that high production will lead to a reward that will satisfy a need important to them—and further, that the satisfaction from this effort is sufficiently great (equitable) to make the effort worthwhile.[4]

Figure 1-1
Paths-Goals Analysis

Source: Reprinted by permission from George Strauss and Leonard Sayles, *Personnel: The Human Problems of Management*, 3d ed. (Englewood Cliffs, N.J.: Prentice-Hall, Inc., 1960).

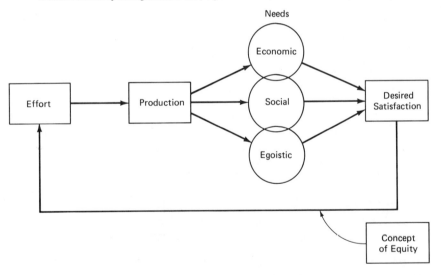

Thus, the origins of personnel management may be traced to scientific management, a philosophy oriented toward human relations, and a basic concept of equity in the employer-employee relationship.

---

[4] George Strauss and Leonard Sayles, *Personnel: The Human Problems of Management* (3rd ed.; Englewood Cliffs, N. J.: Prentice-Hall, Inc., 1960), p. 135.

Personnel Management Defined

The theory and practice of personnel management is primarily concerned with people, the crucial human resources of an employer.

While definitions are frequently inadequate, a classic and adequate definition describes personnel management as

> The field of management which has to do with the functions of procuring, developing, maintaining, and utilizing a labor force, such that the
>
> 1. objectives for which the company is established are attained economically and effectively;
> 2. objectives of all levels of personnel are served to the highest possible degree; and
> 3. objectives of the community are fully considered and served.[5]

This definition highlights the responsibility of management toward its human resources and spells out this charge in four distinct managerial areas.

Procurement is the process of recruiting and selecting the type of employee most likely to contribute toward achieving the organizational goals. More specifically, the prospective employee should either possess the skills required for the given job or be capable of learning those skills within a reasonable time.

Development is an ongoing program which gives the employee an opportunity to enhance skills and find job satisfaction through training, job placement, and career planning. Compensation continues to be an essential element in the development of personnel, despite the fact that most people view work as more than a source of income.

Maintenance is the art of retaining personnel who are generally satisfied and who also demonstrate this attitude in their work. It may also be thought of as a reasonable reconciliation of the interest of both employee and employer.

Utilization refers to the matching of an individual to a given task. The employer's objective should be to make job assignments that are responsive to the skills and interests of workers as well as to organizational objectives.

Each of the above functions is supportive of the others so that an organization which utilizes all four techniques will be making optimal use of its human resources.

Any complete definition of personnel management must also include the topic of labor relations. By so doing it extends the field from interpersonal relationships to intergroup relationships—from individual desires and grievances to group needs and achievements. Integrating labor-management relations with the traditional functions of procurement, development, maintenance, and utilization of employees encourages a coordinated ap-

---

[5] Michael J. Jucius, *Personnel Management*, 6th ed. (Homewood, Ill.: Richard D. Irwin, Inc., 1967), pp. 2–3.

proach to personnel management that helps managers deal with day-to-day problems on the basis of a more global approach.[6]

Civil Service *and the* *Merit Principle*	The law provides that all employees of any government agency, except such exempt classes as elected officials, some executives, and consultants, are

civil service employees. These personnel are not only appointed but also promoted on the basis of competitive examinations that taken together constitute a merit system.

The strengths of the merit principle are its assurance of equal opportunity, its potential for attracting the best-qualified applicants to public service, and its proven ability to develop a career-oriented work force to serve all members of a community regardless of changes in political leadership.

The guiding principles of personnel management in the field of public service are based on these strengths, but go beyond the procurement and maintenance functions to developing and utilizing a well-trained, satisfied, resourceful, and productive work force. This growth of the personnel management role in civil service calls for an increasing emphasis on the human aspects of management and the creation of an atmosphere in which employees are motivated to work through positive incentives and are able to derive genuine satisfaction from their jobs.[7]

Civil service has succeeded in establishing the fact that any "right" to public employment belongs first to the most worthy. In the past, those who secured employment in the public sector through the assistance of local politicians were never identified as the most efficient or most worthy candidates. For this reason, and also because it has foreclosed political domination of individual police officers, the merit system is to be applauded. Today one can genuinely say that, on the whole, police agencies in the United States are being upgraded—not only because better-qualified applicants are being appointed, but also because these new appointees do not owe any gratitude to a local politician during their term of employment.

All civil service programs are not oriented toward reform or toward providing a community with high-quality services, however. Political pandering, corruption of executives, and bureaucratic rigidity have been among the characteristics of some state, county, and municipal civil service commissions or personnel boards.

In 1940, one of the country's leading experts on police management, Bruce Smith, reported the growth of the civil service movement in relation to municipal policing with mixed feelings:

[6] Dalton E. McFarland, *Cooperation and Conflict in Personnel Administration* (New York: American Foundation for Management Research, 1962) pp. 24–36.

[7] Charles Cooke, *Biography of An Ideal: The Diamond Anniversary History of the Federal Civil Service* (Washington, D.C.: U.S. Government Printing Office, 1959), pp. 121–122.

Practically all the leading municipal police forces of the country are now subject to the control of either state or municipal civil service commissions. In some of the larger cities, such as Detroit and St. Louis, where efforts have been made to bar such extradepartmental controls, the results in terms of honest and effective personnel management certainly have not been inferior to those achieved in most of the civil service-controlled forces. On the other hand, it must be conceded that rarely is either type of merit system pursued with any marked degree of enthusiasm in our large police forces. Routine examination of applicants, the deadening influence of fixed official hierarchies, and tenure-of-office acts that place police employees beyond the reach of all ordinary disciplinary measures, have operated to reduce both the present and the future effectiveness of many police units.

All told, civil service commissions control the police forces of about three-fourths of our cities, and the proportion is rising. Thus the time is not far distant which shall see the last of the independent police merit systems reduced to a numerically negligible factor. Thereafter the future of municipal police service will be in the hands of state or local civil service commissions, operating without competition as to methods or results from police forces lying outside such controls, and without much prospect of a return to administrative independence in personnel matters.

Based upon the past record of civil service control—the political pandering, the personal corruption, and the bureaucratic rigidity so commonly noted among its characteristics—there is little in the prospect to lend hope for better things in municipal police administration. Two possibilities, however, will always be present: (1) a reform in the civil service regime, such as is taking place in a few centers; (2) an increasing disposition on the part of police administrators to lead the way toward new personnel selection techniques that square with the realities of police duty. While the evidence of such impending changes in attitude and functioning is none too impressive, it seems safe to conclude that, whatever the future of our municipal police forces, the civil service system will exercise a great influence for better or for worse.

If one is to be guided by results rather than academic argument, it would appear that the best personnel administration is achieved by civil service commissions which are organically close to the police department. State-administered civil service control, as exemplified in Massachusetts, has yielded the least desirable results in terms of personnel selection, promotion, and discipline. In contrast, local civil service, aided in technical matters by the state Civil Service Commission, has produced superior results in New York State; while purely local civil service control as in Virginia has produced several outstanding police departments. That local personnel control may be abused is apparent, but where it is aided by technically qualified personnel administrators as in New York State, the flexibility attained has more than compensated for theoretical weaknesses.[8]

Despite Bruce Smith's misgivings about the civil service system, the period from 1940 to the present has seen the extension of such programs to a

[8] Bruce Smith, *Police Systems in the United States* 2nd ed., revised by Bruce Smith, Jr. (New York: Harper & Row, 1960), pp. 127–128. Reprinted by permission.

majority of the police agencies in America. Most importantly, a decision of the U.S. Supreme Court may have thrown out the last vestige of political control over police employees.

In *Elrod* v. *Burns*, 427 U.S. 347 (1976), various employees of the Cook County (Chicago, Illinois) Sheriff's Office were discharged or threatened with discharge solely because they were not affiliated with or sponsored by the local Democratic party. They sought injunctive relief in the courts to prevent or reverse such action by the newly elected Democratic sheriff. Ultimately, the U.S. Supreme Court addressed the question of whether public employees who allege they were discharged or threatened with discharge solely because of their partisan political affiliation have a claim for deprivation of constitutional rights secured by the First and Fourteenth Amendments. The Court's decision was that a non-policy-making, nonconfidential government employee may not be discharged from a job that he or she is satisfactorily performing, solely on the basis of his or her stated political beliefs.

Police Personnel
Management

Police personnel management is oriented toward the objectives of a public employer at one of several levels—municipal, county, state, or federal. Within the scope of an employing agency's objectives, the police personnel function is comparable to that in business and commerce. The tasks of procuring, developing, maintaining, and utilizing a labor force in the public versus the private sector differ only in relation to the special problems encountered in each area.

To summarize, then, the role of police personnel management is to work within an overall administrative structure that is responsive to the functions, goals, and objectives of the particular employing agency; to fill these jobs with men and women who will do the work well and get meaning and satisfaction from doing it; and to support these workers in achieving both personal and agency goals and objectives.

Chapter Review

Summary

Before World War I, personnel management was a rather insignificant subdivision of business administration. However, several events contributed to its rapidly expanding role in the production equation. Frederick W. Taylor's scientific management theory was the first attempt to understand workers from a psychological outlook; Douglas McGregor's Theory Y extended this understanding and broadened management's role in promoting it. Finally, George Strauss and Leonard Sayles reemphasized the worker's responsibility toward his/her employer and introduced the basic concept of equity in employer-employee relationships.

Personnel management is defined broadly as the managing of an organization's human resources by developing relationships with individual employees and with employee groups (labor-management relations). For public employees, it is inextricably bound up with civil service regulations and the merit principle. Finally, personnel management is especially valuable in the administration of police agencies precisely because these agencies' main function is the provision of services, a task no computer has yet been able to handle adequately.

Critique   Police chiefs may assume the role of personnel manager (as is common among many executives in the private sector), or they may downgrade the personnel management function by placing responsibility for many personnel programs on overburdened staff personnel or uninformed line personnel. The full benefit of personnel management to all concerned (employee, employer, community) is seriously diminished when a police executive underestimates the importance of this function to the smooth operation of a police agency.

Questions for Discussion and Review

1. Describe Strauss and Sayles's concept of equity.
2. Define personnel management.
3. What major events in the first quarter of this century are illustrative of the link between the American labor movement and personnel management?
4. What are the strengths of the civil service system? Its weaknesses?
5. What is the role of personnel management?
6. List five examples of personnel management in business and commerce; in police agencies.

Workbook Project   List the annual increase/decrease in the number of police employees in your local police agency for a ten-year period. For the same period, list the annual increase/decrease in salaries for such employees. Compute percentage increase or decrease for the ten-year period.

2

Personnel Planning

Chapter Objectives

- to develop a basic understanding of personnel planning
- to examine how police personnel managers can match candidates to job openings on an organization-wide basis
- to explore the limitations of civil service regulations regarding hiring and promotions

Personnel planning in police agencies as in private enterprises, is a balancing of the agency's demand for workers with specific skills against the total supply available in the labor market and within the organization. The objective of all such planning is to provide qualified candidates to meet the future staffing needs of the police agency.

Police personnel management is a dynamic system that is more than the sum of its subsystems of employee procurement, development, maintenance, and utilization. The interaction among these subsystems is in fact the vital element in the equation—the flow of human resources into, upward, and out of the employing agency.

Police Officer:
Job Role and Tasks

Police officers are employees who are responsible for such basic police functions as responding to calls for help and enforcing observed violations of law. In county governments, the term deputy sheriff may be used instead, but in either case this group constitutes the sworn versus the civilian contingent of a police agency.

The skills requirement for employment in a police agency is dependent on two a priori conditions:

1. hiring is usually at the entrance level
2. the role of "patrol officer" is considered the core of the more generalized duties of police officer

The major route into a police organization is employment as a recruit police officer. Of course, there are some lateral entry routes allowing transfers from other police agencies at various job levels above recruit officer, but these transferees invariably entered the system at the recruit level.

Each recruit officer must possess the necessary qualifications to serve, at least initially, as a patrol officer. He or she must also be prepared to carry out these duties during emergencies, when an "all hands" mobilization requires every police officer regardless of rank or assignment to support the regular patrol force.

The National Advisory Commission on Criminal Justice Standards and Goals describes police patrol as "the prime police function" and sets the following standard for the role of patrol officer:

> Every police chief executive immediately should develop written policy that defines the role of the patrol officer, and should establish operational objectives and priorities that reflect the most effective use of the patrol officer in reducing crime.
>
> 1. Every police chief executive should acknowledge that the patrol officer is the agency's primary element for the deliverance of police services and prevention of criminal activity.
> 2. Every police chief executive should insure maximum efficiency in the deliverance of patrol services by setting out in written policy the objectives and priorities governing these services. This policy:
>   a. Should insure that resources are concentrated on fundamental police duties;
>   b. Should insure that patrol officers are engaged in tasks that are related to the police function;
>   c. Should require immediate response to incidents where there is an immediate threat to the safety of an individual, a crime in progress, or a crime committed and the apprehension of the suspected offender is likely. Urban area response time—from time a call is dispatched to the arrival at the scene—under normal conditions should not exceed 3 minutes for emergency calls, and 20 minutes for nonemergency calls;
>   d. Should emphasize the need for preventive patrol to reduce the opportunity for criminal activity; and
>   e. Should provide a procedure for accepting reports of criminal incidents not requiring a field investigation.
> 3. Every police chief executive should insure that all elements of the agency, especially the patrol and communications elements, know the priority placed upon each request for police service.
> 4. Every police chief executive should implement a public information program to inform the community of the agency's policies regarding the deliverance of police service. This program should include provisions to involve citizens in crime prevention activities.[1]

[1] The National Advisory Commission on Criminal Justice Standards and Goals, *Report on Police* (Washington, D.C.: U.S. Government Printing Office, 1973), p. 191. Reprinted by permission.

The above standard defines the role of a patrol officer in terms of a number of tasks including speedy response to crimes in progress and other crime-related radio messages and preventive patrol to reduce the opportunity for criminal activity.

A 1967 publication of the President's Advisory Commission on Law Enforcement and the Administration of Justice[2] states that the object of patrol is to disperse police officers in such a way as to eliminate or reduce the opportunity for misconduct and to increase the likelihood that a criminal will be apprehended while he/she is committing a crime or immediately thereafter; and to afford protection to individuals who are likely to be victimized or are in some other way prey to harm—the down-and-out drunk, the mentally ill, or the naive patrons of vice activity who may be subjecting themselves to the risk of robbery or worse.[3]

The basic role-and-task requirements of patrol officers were put into perspective in recent years by increasing numbers of women applicants. The key question prior to full acceptance of women as police officers was whether they could serve effectively in the patrol officer's role.[4]

In the Police Foundation's study of women as patrol officers, evaluation of individuals was based on "patrol skills," which were, however, not rank ordered. Nonetheless, the list is informative as it specifies common tasks of a patrol officer:

1. Questioning a rape victim
2. Writing reports
3. Arresting prostitutes
4. Settling family disputes
5. Getting information at crime scenes
6. Handling disorderly persons
7. Cruising around and observing
8. Handling traffic accidents
9. Handling victims of an armed robbery
10. Dispersing a group of noisy juveniles (ages 9–12)
11. Handling threatening situations where someone has a knife or gun
12. Handling a down-and-out drunk[5]

A similar study conducted by the California Highway Patrol in 1974 was designed to evaluate the performance of women as traffic officers on the state level. This study developed a rank ordering of the tasks of a state traffic officer that revealed a close relationship between duties of traffic work and the general

[2] *Task Force Report: The Police* (Washington, D.C.: U.S. Government Printing Office, 1967).

[3] *Task Force Report*, pp. 1 and 13.

[4] Peter B. Bloch and Deborah Anderson, *Policewomen on Patrol: Final Report* (Washington, D.C.: Police Foundation, 1974), pp. 1–7.

[5] Bloch and Anderson, *Policewomen on Patrol*, p. 39. Reprinted by permission.

role of patrol officer. The top-ranked tasks were making high-risk (felony) vehicle stops and arresting dangerous suspects.[6]

A New York City Police Department field study made in the 20th Precinct (a moderately active center-city area with a variety of police problems) not only categorizes the patrol officer's tasks but also lists (1) the frequency of occurrence of each category of reported incidents, (2) the total time spent on each activity, and (3) the average time spent per incident. Table 2-1 ranks reported incidents on the basis of total service time required of the patrol officer; Table 2-2 ranks reported incidents by frequency of occurrence.[7]

Women in Policing

The traditional cultural belief that women as a class are incapable of demonstrating the skills required to be patrol officers has been rejected. Women now constitute an important part of the labor market available for police employments. Thousands of female students are working on degree programs leading to undergraduate and graduate degrees in criminal justice and related academic disciplines and thousands of others are seeking employment with various agencies but temporarily postponing their education efforts. Police personnel specialists can plan not only on recruiting applicants qualified for the entrance level position, but also on retaining these women officers as future employees with an excellent potential for career development.

The Police Foundation report cited in the last section[8] firms up the thrust of federal regulations and court decisions that sex is no longer a bona fide occupational qualification for police patrol work.

The advantages and disadvantages of women patrol officers are summed up in this report as follows:

> The hiring of women enlarges the supply of personnel resources, may reduce the cost of recruiting and may assure that police personnel will be more representative of both the racial and sexual composition of the city. Because citizens generally support the concept of equal employment opportunity for women, women officers may improve police-community relations. Also, women are less likely to become involved in serious unbecoming conduct which can damage community relations.
>
> Another advantage gained by a police department in the hiring of women for patrol work is that it brings the department into compliance with Federal law. Title VII of the Civil Rights Act of 1964, as amended in 1972, prohibits state and local agencies from employment discrimination based on sex, except when sex is a bona fide occupational qualification. The courts have limited "bona fide occupational qualifications" to two narrowly

[6] *Women Traffic Officer Project: Final Report* (Sacramento, Calif.: California Highway Patrol, 1976), pp. 29–30.

[7] *Police Training and Performance Study* (Washington, D.C.: U.S. Department of Justice, Law Enforcement Assistance Administration, National Institute of Law Enforcement and Criminal Justice, 1970), p. 15.

[8] Bloch and Anderson, *Policewomen on Patrol.*

Table 2-1
Incidents in the 20th precinct, New York City Police Department, ranked in order of total time spent per incident, 1967–68

Incident type	Number of incidents	Total time (in minutes)	Average time (in minutes)
1. Sick	4,552	202,143	44.4
2. Other	5,629	162,310	28.8
3. Other misdemeanors	1,190	106,034	89.1
4. Dispute	3,582	106,016	29.6
5. Burglary	2,518	104,881	41.7
6. Unfounded	5,132	102,881	20.7
7. Dead on arrival	402	60,126	149.8
8. Injured	1,170	46,063	41.1
9. Intoxicated person	1,555	41,830	25.9
10. Disorderly groups	1,693	37,780	22.3
11. Robbery	512	33,476	65.4
12. Auto accident	547	32,943	60.2
13. Alarm of fire	1,013	30,483	30.0
14. Felonious assault	309	26,982	87.3
15. Auto accident—injury	286	25,334	88.6
16. Larceny from auto	514	17,579	34.2
17. Malicious mischief	435	16,261	37.4
18. Utility trouble	378	14,502	38.4
19. Narcotics	59	13,582	230.2
20. Auto larceny	104	12,556	120.7
21. Grand larceny	235	11,598	49.4
22. Other felonies	64	9,559	149.4
23. Motor vehicle recovered	73	7,221	98.8
24. Traffic violation	270	7,201	27.1
25. Vehicles mechanical trouble	201	7,201	35.8
26. Accidental alarm	264	6,873	26.0
27. Grand larceny— pocketbook snatch	130	6,366	48.9
28. Auto safety check	126	4,175	33.1
29. Prowler	121	3,549	29.3
30. Dangerous condition	81	3,510	43.0
31. Found persons	46	2,802	60.9
32. Auto accident— serious injury or death	13	2,587	199.0
33. Arrest—serving summons	81	2,480	30.6
34. False alarm of fire	86	1,865	21.7
35. Property recovered	35	1,848	52.8
36. Homicide	6	1,744	290.6
37. Rape	29	1,622	55.9
38. Weapons	9	1,298	144.2
39. Missing persons	24	1,096	45.7
40. Prostitution	7	1,090	155.7
41. Attempted suicide	13	1,056	81.2
42. Gambling	7	813	116.1
43. Traffic court warrants	40	713	17.8
44. Suicide	6	607	101.2
45. Alcohol Beverage Control violation	5	160	32.0

Table 2-2
Incidents in the 20th precinct, New York City Police Department, ranked in order of frequency of occurrence, 1967-68

Incident type	Number of incidents	Total time (in minutes)	Average time (in minutes)
1. Other	5,629	162,310	28.8
2. Unfounded	5,132	102,881	20.0
3. Sick	4,552	202,143	44.4
4. Dispute	3,582	106,016	29.6
5. Burglary	2,518	104,881	41.7
6. Disorderly groups	1,693	37,780	22.3
7. Intoxicated person	1,555	41,830	25.9
8. Other misdemeanors	1,190	106,034	89.1
9. Injured	1,170	46,063	41.1
10. Alarm of fire	1,013	30,483	30.0
11. Auto accident	547	32,943	60.2
12. Larceny from auto	514	17,579	34.2
13. Robbery	512	33,476	65.4
14. Malicious mischief	435	16,261	37.4
15. Dead on arrival	402	60,216	149.8
16. Utility trouble	378	14,502	38.4
17. Felonious assault	309	26,982	87.3
18. Auto accident injury	286	25,334	88.6
19. Traffic violation	269	7,201	27.1
20. Accidental alarm	264	6,873	26.0
21. Grand larceny	235	11,598	49.4
22. Vehicle mechanical trouble	201	7,201	35.8
23. Grand larceny—pocketbook snatch	130	6,366	48.9
24. Auto safety check	126	4,175	33.1
25. Prowler	121	3,549	29.3
26. Auto larceny	104	12,556	120.7
27. False alarm of fire	86	1,865	21.7
28. Arrest—serving summons	81	2,480	30.6
29. Dangerous condition	81	3,510	43.0
30. Motor vehicle recovered	73	7,211	98.8
31. Other felonies	64	9,559	149.4
32. Narcotics	59	13,582	230.2
33. Found person	46	2,802	60.9
34. Traffic warrants	40	713	17.8
35. Property recovered	35	1,848	52.8
36. Rape	29	1,622	55.9
37. Missing persons	24	1,096	45.7
38. Auto accident—serious injury or death	13	2,587	199.0
39. Attempted suicide	13	1,056	81.2
40. Weapons	9	1,298	144.2
41. Prostitution	7	1,090	155.7
42. Gambling	7	813	116.1
43. Homocide	6	1,744	290.6
44. Suicide	6	607	101.2
45. Alcohol Beverage Control violation	5	160	32.0

defined situations. One is where the nature of the job requires a male or female, as in some acting or modeling jobs. The other is where members of one sex are clearly better qualified for a job and an employer has made reasonable attempts to develop selection criteria which would permit the hiring of qualified members of both sexes. Some police departments have already discovered that it is difficult for them to persuade the courts that discrimination based on sex is justified by police work requirements.

The attitudes of male officers and police supervisors impose a burden on a police management which wants to treat men and women equally in all respects. Many men do not believe that women can perform as well as men, and they tend to be protective toward women. Unless management develops countermeasures, they may find that women are given stationhouse assignments, such as clerical duty, more often than are men. They may also find that some men will insist that women remain in a police car while they handle traffic stops; some women will be happy to accept this less-active role. If the protectiveness of male officers is not counteracted, women will not have a full opportunity to demonstrate their capability. Serious personnel problems also may arise among male officers who will complain that women are not doing equal work but are receiving equal pay.

The tendency of men to be protective toward women also may make it difficult to fire incompetent policewomen during their probationary period. While there is no indication that this difficulty occurred during this experiment, the attitudes that were uncovered suggest that it may occur elsewhere. Care should be taken during the probationary period to assure that all officers, of either sex, satisfy performance standards. Unsatisfactory officers should be fired.

It has been noted that the performance of men and women was similar. They responded to similar types of calls for police service while they were on patrol. They saw similar proportions of citizens who were dangerous, angry, upset, drunk or violent. They were observed to obtain similar results in handling angry or violent citizens.

Citizens showed similar levels of respect and generally favorable attitudes toward officers of both sexes. There were no differences between male and female officers in their levels of respect and generally favorable attitudes toward citizens.

Despite the observed similarities of performance, male officials and officers retained serious reservations—which they held before the experiment began about the ability of women to handle violent situations. Because the sample of situations in which violence actually occurred is small, empirical evidence cannot entirely refute these views. However, because of the small size of the sample, the possibility also exists that women are more effective than men in avoiding violence by defusing potentially violent situations.

The principal differences in the performance of men and women are these:

Women made fewer arrests and gave fewer traffic citations;
Men were more likely to engage in serious unbecoming conduct;

Women were somewhat more likely to be assigned to light duty as the result of injuries, but injuries did not cause them to be absent from work more often than men.[9]

The overall evaluation of the differences in performances between male and female police officers can be graphically shown as in Figure 2-1.

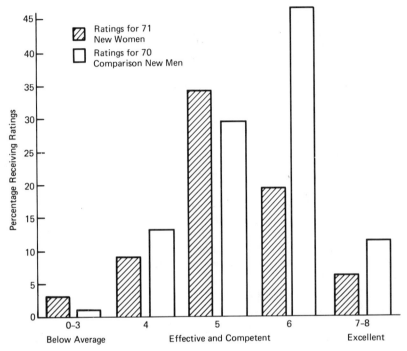

Figure 2-1
Overall Evaluation Ratings—Men versus Women

Source: Reprinted by permission from Peter B. Bloch and Deborah Anderson, *Policewomen on Patrol: Final Report* (Washington, D.C.: Police Foundation, 1974), p. 2.

Civilian
Employees

Civilian employees of police agencies need not enter at the basic level of patrol officer, and since they do not take the same oath as the police officer group, are termed "unsworn" personnel.

Civilians have traditionally borne the lion's share of clerical and typing positions, as well as service occupations such as janitor. However, current practices evidence a definite trend toward greater use of civilians for such tasks as communications, identification, and detention. A 1975 study[10] examined

[9] Bloch and Anderson, *Policewomen on Patrol*, p. 30. Reprinted by permission.

[10] Alfred I. Schwartz, Alease M. Vaughn, John D. Waller, and Joseph S. Wholey, *Employing Civilians for Police Work* (Washington, D.C.: U.S. Department of Justice, Law Enforcement Assistance Administration, National Institute of Law Enforcement and Criminal Justice, 1975).

the utilization of personnel in thirteen police departments of various sizes across the country. Its findings, summarized in Table 2–3, show not only *increased* utilization of civilians by police agencies but *more varied* utilization.

Table 2–3
Civilian Employment on Thirteen Municipal Police Departments

Cities Visited	Civilians as a Percent of All Police Department Employees	Civilians in Communications, Identification and Detention (combined) as Percent of All Civilian Employees
Detroit, Michigan	12%	21%
Jacksonville, Florida	35	25
Atlanta, Georgia	13	42
Denver, Colorado	18	19
Oakland, California	28	45
Huntsville, Alabama	42	16
New Haven, Connecticut	25	10
East St. Louis, Illinois	45	11
Kansas City, Kansas	28	22
Compton, California	39	20
Scottsdale, Arizona	31	13
High Point, North Carolina	32	40
Pittsburg, California	16	20

Reprinted by permission from Alfred I. Schwartz et al., Employing Civilians for Police Work (Washington, D.C., U.S. Department of Justice, 1975); p. 60, table 1.

The major objective in employing civilians is to free police officers for assignment to more critical police tasks. Secondary justifications include cost savings (salary and training) and the potential for improved service to both the public and police field personnel, who usually consider such clerical positions as confining and demeaning to the role of a police officer. Civilians without this hangup are much more likely to perform well in "station duty" positions.

Job descriptions for positions in communications, identification, and detention units include the following specific duties:

1. Communications	Receives messages
	Transmits messages
	Prepares reports
	Operates switchboard
	Secretarial/clerical duties
2. Identification	Receives and catalogs evidence
	Takes photographs and fingerprints
	Verifies fingerprints
	Testifies in court
	Performs clerical duties
	Operates teletype

3. Detention	Processes prisoners
	Transports prisoners
	Oversees welfare of prisoners
	Serves as witness
	Operates computer
	Performs clerical duties[11]

Clearly, police personnel planners no longer question whether civilians should be hired; rather, they begin by analyzing those tasks in their agencies that can be handled by civilian employees, and then proceed to list the job requirements for each position in terms of skills, knowledge, and abilities.

There is no real dispute that the practice of assigning police officers to record-keeping and clerical duties is unsound from the viewpoint of economy and efficiency. There also is growing acceptance among police officials that communications, identification, and detention tasks can be performed equally well—and much less expensively—by civilian employees. In fact, civilians are being hired for an ever wider range of positions, from clerks and typists to technicians and specialists.

The growing range of positions for which civilians are now deemed suitable promotes upward job mobility among both groups of police employees. It also permits personnel planners not only to diversify job assignments but also to prepare all personnel for tasks involving responsibility and leadership potentials.

Career *Development* One of the major responsibilities of personnel planners is to outline a formalized career development system. In police agencies, the planner must design a system around several nationwide policies, including up-the-ranks promotion and hiring at the entry level; provision of equal opportunity to women applicants for the position of police officer; and the increasing number of civilian employees, particularly in a paraprofessional capacity.

A major objective of career development is a work force in which the total available skills inventory of all employees meets the total skills demand of the agency (see Figure 2-2).

Police employees' benefits—seniority, promotion, and pension equities—and the minimal opportunity they have for lateral transfer without loss of these rights both contribute to a relatively stable labor pool. For this reason, it is ideally possible to relate the knowledge, skills, and abilities of employees to employees' attributes and interest, on the one hand, and to agency needs, on the other. This statement applies to all jobs and tasks, from entrance level position to that of police chief.

The skills inventory of the total work force is the available human resources of the police agency. While it may sometimes be supplemented by

[11] Schwartz et al., *Employing Civilians*, pp. 7-9.

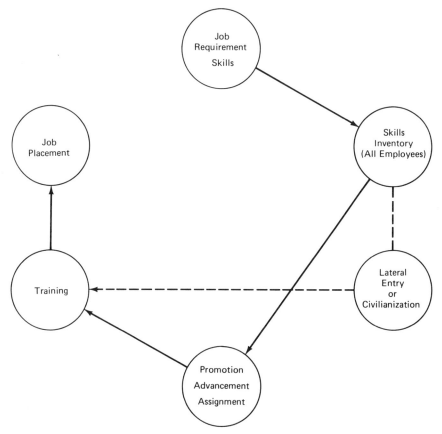

Figure 2-2
Career Development: Jobs and Skills

lateral entry or by increased employment of civilians, police personnel planners must usually seek to fill positions of greater difficulty and responsibility from within the ranks.

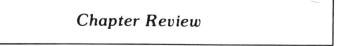

Chapter Review

Summary   The job of patrol officer is not only the entry level position for "sworn personnel," it also constitutes the basic core of all police work. Two recent changes in hiring policy are the acceptance on an equal basis of women applicants for police officer and the increased use of civilians not only in clerical but also in various specialist capacities.

The major thrusts of personnel planning are employing individuals with a potential for upward job mobility and using the career development process to prepare such men and women for better and more difficult jobs. Every police agency needs a labor pool of potential applicants for all current and future job openings above the level of patrol officer. The test of superior personnel planning is how accurately this labor pool reflects the needs of the employing agency.

Critique   Small and rapidly expanding police agencies have problems in developing from within their own labor pool qualified applicants for higher-level positions such as police chief or detective, or special investigatory officer. The policy of entry level hiring severely restricts personnel managers in any talent search for qualified applicants for jobs above the patrol officer level. At the same time, workers may actively seek to advance within the agency by developing certain skills, yet may be unable to put these skills to use simply because there are no job openings.

In order to be effective, police personnel planners must be able to hire qualified applicants for jobs above the patrol officer level from outside police agencies or other sources. However, such a modification of existing regulations would demand one of two things: (1) planners must either demonstrate the inadequacy of agency employees to fill the openings, or (2) they must initiate an "open" talent search in which the job opportunity exists for employees and outside applicants on a truly competitive basis.

Questions for Discussion and Review

1. Define personnel planning.
2. Why is sex no longer a bona fide occupational qualification for the position of patrol officer?
3. Distinguish between "sworn" and "unsworn" personnel. Is this distinction necessary? Desirable?
4. How does the policy of hiring at the entrance level handicap police personnel planning? The policy of patrol officer as the basic role of sworn personnel? The policy of hiring from the ranks?
5. What are the advantages of employing civilians in police agencies?
6. What is the role of career development in personnel planning?

Workbook Project   Prepare a list of jobs (by job title and description) above the level of patrol officer in your local or state police agency.

3 Equal Employment Opportunity

Chapter Objectives

- to examine the contemporary social and legal climate of employment opportunities
- to define and clarify the meaning of equal opportunity in employment
- to illustrate how the concept of equal protection applies to individuals of various colors, races, creeds, or countries of national origin

The most powerful factors in achieving the socioeconomic goals of equal employment opportunity are civil rights legislation and judicial decisions interpreting and enforcing both these statutes and the basic constitutional guarantees of equal protection under the law.

Police officials have long supported the civil service system with its competitive examinations as the best means of excluding political influence from hiring and promotion decisions. Unfortunately, the actual tests and/or the administration procedures associated with them have in many cases inadvertently discriminated against minority persons and women. Proof of this *de facto* discrimination is the overwhelming number of white males in upper-level positions in police agencies throughout the nation.

Both statutory law and legal precedent provide guidelines for preventing discrimination in employment. An agency's strengths and weaknesses in providing equal employment opportunity can be identified through statistical study of the racial and ethnic backgrounds, and the sex of persons hired and employees transferred, advanced, or promoted.

Equal employment opportunity begins with a recruiting and selection process that is free of cultural bias and utilizes job-related tests to determine the most qualified applicants. Whether it has in fact been attained can only be determined by a self-study that spells out the numbers of women and minority group applicants who have been hired, transferred, or promoted or advanced in any way.

Legislation The Fourteenth Amendment to the U.S. Constitution, ratified in 1868, explicitly states: "No state shall deny to any person within its jurisdiction the equal protection of the laws."

The baseline for equal employment opportunities is Title VII of the Civil Rights Act of 1964, as amended by the Equal Employment Opportunity Act of 1972 (Title 42, U.S. Code, Sections 2000e–2, *et. seq.*). Extracts of importance to police personnel managers in Title VII are:

> It shall be unlawful employment practice for an employer—(1) to fail or refuse to hire or to discharge any individual, or otherwise to discriminate against any individual with respect to his compensation, terms, conditions, or privileges of employment, because of such individual's race, color, religion, sex, or national origin; or (2) to limit, segregate, or classify his employees or applicants for employment in any way which would deprive or tend to deprive any individual of employment opportunities or otherwise adversely affect his status as an employee, because of such individual's race, color, religion, sex, or national origin.

Exemption

> Notwithstanding any other provision of this subchapter, it shall not be an unlawful employment practice for an employer to hire and employ employees . . . on the basis of his (her) religion, sex, or national origin in those certain instances where religion, sex, or national origin is a bona fide occupational qualification reasonably necessary to the normal operation of that particular business or enterprise.

> Nothing contained in this subchapter shall be interpreted to require any employer . . . to grant preferential treatment to any individual or to any group because of the race, color, religion, sex, or national origin of such individual or group on account of an imbalance which may exist with respect to the total number or percentage of persons of any race, color, religion, sex, or national origin employed by any employer . . . in comparison with the total number or percentage of persons of such race, color, religion, sex, or national origin in any community, State, section, or other area, or in the available work force in any community, State, section, or other area.

A U.S. District Court decision shocked the nation's police establishment by mandating ratio hiring of a stated percentage of black troopers in the Alabama state police force. This class action suit was sponsored by the NAACP in an effort to open up state police jobs to blacks.

The court's comments on the validity of the NAACP's claim of discrimination are as follows:

> Plaintiffs have shown without contradiction that the defendants have engaged in a blatant and continuous pattern and practice of discrimination in hiring in the Alabama Department of Public Safety, both as to troopers and supporting personnel. In the thirty-seven-year history of the patrol

there has never been a black trooper and the only Negroes ever employed in the department have been nonmerit system laborers. This unexplained and unexplainable discriminatory conduct by state officials is unquestionably a violation of the Fourteenth Amendment.[1]

The thrust of the court's decision on hiring practices of state police forces is found in these four enjoinders to Alabama police officials:

1. Hire and permanently employ one Negro trooper for each white trooper hired until approximately twenty-five per cent of the Alabama State trooper force is comprised of Negroes.
2. To find and hire the necessary qualified black troopers.
3. Make a special recruitment effort to fully advise the Negro citizens of Alabama of this employment opportunity.
4. New hiring lists are to be compiled and utilized for black troopers.[2]

In a subsequent decision, however, another U.S. District Court declined to impose a quota system to remedy past discrimination in the employment practices of the Mississippi Highway Patrol. In *Morrow* v. *Dillard*, Morrow brought suit on behalf of himself and others similarly situated against W. K. Dillard, Commissioner of the Mississippi Department of Public Safety (DPS). In discussing the question of whether the need for an increasing number of black troopers on the Mississippi Highway Patrol (MHP) necessitated a temporary quota hiring system or racial hiring ratio, the court commented:

This Court is of the opinion that this case is one in which the drastic remedy of quota hiring is not dictated or necessary *at this time*; rather, in view of the other affirmative hiring relief prescribed herein, the more extensive recruiting program and the administering of a now agreed-upon job-related test, it is reasonably foreseeable that an increase in the number of blacks on the MHP and in the DPS as a whole will be immediately effected. The DPS will be ordered to submit to this Court a plan which effectuates the requirements set forth in this Opinion and to immediately implement that plan with a view of achieving the required result now.[3]

Police promotional opportunities were the subject of alleged employment discrimination in the case of *Allen et al.* v. *The City of Mobile* (Alabama). This was a class action suit on behalf of black police officers seeking injunctive relief against alleged denial of equal protection of the laws in relation to the promotional examination for police sergeant. In this case the court declined any scheme of preferential treatment for the black police

[1] NAACP v. Allen, 340 F. Supp. 703 (1972).
[2] NAACP v. Allen, 340 F. Supp. 703 (1972).
[3] Morrow v. Dillard, 412 F. Supp. 494 (1976).

officers, holding that equal protection does not entitle any group (minority or majority) to superior or preferential employment rights:

> This Court will not in the name of Constitutional law render a judgment initiating a new paternalism under the guise of compensatory rectification or preferential treatment. Neither will this Court insult the Negro plaintiffs' intelligence, disparage their initiative, their sense of responsibility, or their ability to render quality service as qualified and valued workmen by a decision which gives preferential treatment.
>
> This decree does not attempt to formulate "instant" qualifications for any job for any person. Its purpose is to provide that all persons, white and black, be brought up to the starting line in the race for jobs and compete under equal rules. Let those who by ability, or those who are willing to pay the price by dent of dedicated hard work, or those who are willing to scratch and scramble, or those who by reason of motivation, inspiration or ambition be given the opportunity, unshackled, to outdistance—and they will—the more talented but less motivated, and move up into places of leadership and responsibility.[4]

While a quota or ratio may be justified in some circumstances, it is an acknowledgement of the integrity of police personnel management generally that courts consider quotas or ratios as a "drastic remedy" not required when the same goals can be achieved in both hiring and promotion by a more extensive recruitment program and by job-related and racially neutral testing.

A case in point is *Washington* v. *Davis*, in which the Court rejected petitioners' claim of discrimination in violation of Fifth Amendment rights (due process); the provisions of Title 42, U.S. Code, Section 1981 (civil rights); and local law (District of Columbia).

The petitioners were rejected applicants for police officer positions in the Metropolitan Police Department, Washington, D.C. They failed a basic entrance test (Test 21). The Court held that:

> (a) Though the Due Process Clause of the Fifth Amendment contains an equal protection component prohibiting the Government from invidious discrimination, it does not follow that a law or other official act is unconstitutional *solely* because it has a racially disproportionate impact regardless of whether it reflects a racially discriminatory purpose. [Pp. 239–245.]
>
> (b) The Consitution does not prevent the Government from seeking through Test 21 modestly to upgrade the communicative abilities of its employees rather than to be satisfied with some lower level of competence, particularly where the job requires special abilities to communicate orally and in writing; and respondents, as Negroes, could no more ascribe their failure to pass the test to denial of equal protection than could whites who also failed. [Pp. 245–246.]
>
> (c) The disproportionate impact of Test 21, which is neutral on its face, does not warrant the conclusion that the test was a purposely discriminatory

---

[4] Allen et al v. City of Mobile (Alabama), 331 F. Supp. 1134 (1971).

device, and on the facts before it the District Court properly held that any inference of discrimination was unwarranted. [P. 246.]

(d) The rigorous statutory standard of Title VII [Civil Rights Act of 1964] involves a more probing judicial review of, and less deference to, the seemingly reasonable acts of administrators and executives than is appropriate under the Constitution where, as in this case, special racial impact but no discriminatory purpose is claimed. Any extension of that statutory standard should await legislative prescription. [Pp. 246–248.]

(e) Statutory standards similar to those obtaining under Title VII were also satisfied here. The District Court's conclusion that Test 21 was directly related to the requirements of the police training program and that a positive relationship between the test and that program was sufficient to validate the test (wholly aside from its possible relationship to actual performance as a police officer) is fully supported on the record in this case, and no remand to establish further validation is appropriate. [Pp. 248–252][5]

The concept of discrimination and the phrase "equal protection of the laws" may be susceptible to varying interpretations, but the Fourteenth Amendment's guarantee of equal protection cannot mean two different things when applied to individuals of different races or colors. This is the import of the U.S. Supreme Court's decision in the case of *Regents of the University of California* v. *Bakke*. Bakke claimed "reverse discrimination" because the Medical School of the University of California at Davis used explicit racial quotas to deny his application for admission; specifically, applicants who were not Negro, Asian, or Chicano were totally excluded from a specific percentage of the seats in the entering class in the medical school of the University of California at Davis. In *Bakke* the majority opinion of the Court recognized a university's interest in promoting ethnic diversity among students admitted to its various programs, but stated that an admissions program focused solely on ethnic diversity would hinder rather than further the attainment of genuine educational opportunity. The Court's opinion held up the admissions policy of Harvard College as an "illuminating example" for achieving educational diversity:

In Harvard College admissions the committee has not set target quotas for the number of blacks, or of musicians, football players, physicists or Californians to be admitted in a given year . . . But that awareness [of the necessity of including more than a token number of black students] does not mean that the Committee sets the minimum number of blacks or of people from west of the Mississippi who are to be admitted. It means only that in choosing among thousands of applicants who are not only "admissible" academically but have other strong qualities, the Committee, with a number of criteria in mind, pays some attention to distribution among many types and categories of students . . .

In such an admissions program, race or ethnic background may be deemed a "plus" in a particular applicant's file, yet it does not insulate the

[5] *Washington* v. *Davis*, 426 U.S. 229 (1976).

individual from comparison with all other candidates for the available seats. The file of a particular black applicant may be examined for his potential contribution to diversity without the factor of race being decisive when compared, for example, with that of an applicant identified as an Italian-American if the latter is thought to exhibit qualities more likely to promote beneficial educational pluralism. Such qualities could include exceptional personal talents, unique work or service experience, leadership potential, maturity, demonstrated compassion, a history of overcoming disadvantage, ability to communicate with the poor, or other qualifications deemed important. In short, an admissions program operated in this way is flexible enough to consider all pertinent elements of diversity in light of the particular qualifications of each applicant and to place them on the same footing for consideration, although not necessarily according them the same weight. Indeed, the weight attributed to a particular quality may vary from year to year depending upon the "mix" both of the student body and the applicants for the incoming class.

This kind of program treats each applicant as an individual in the admissions process. The applicant who loses out on the last available seat to another candidate receiving a "plus" on the basis of ethnic background will not have been foreclosed from all consideration for that seat simply because he was not the right color or had the wrong surname. It would mean only that his combined qualifications, which may have included similar nonobjective factors, did not outweigh those of the other applicants. His qualifications would have been weighed fairly and competitively and he would have no basis to complain of unequal treatment under the Fourteenth Amendment.[6]

The U.S. Supreme Court's decision in *Bakke* offers new guidelines for police personnel managers in dealing with any instance of discrimination, reverse or otherwise.

Implicit in the *Bakke* doctrine, however, is that the individual rights guaranteed by the Fourteenth Amendment are not absolute when confronted by a "substantial state interest," and a demonstrated and substantial state interest may be legitimately served by a properly devised equal employment opportunity program involving the competitive consideration of race and ethnic origin.

Self-Study by Employer

An essential first step prior to implementing an equal employment opportunity program is a comprehensive and detailed examination of current agency-wide employment practices as these impinge on the employment, transfer, and promotion of women and members of minority groups.

[6] Regents of the University of California v. Bakke, 98 S. Ct. 2733 (1978).

Police personnel managers are in an excellent position to record, analyze, and appraise the findings of such a self-study. To be realistic and effective, the study must carefully examine past and present practices, as well as the composition of the present work force. Minority persons are defined as

1. blacks
2. individuals with Spanish-surnames (Mexicans, Puerto Ricans, Cubans, and Latin Americans)
3. Orientals
4. American Indians, including Eskimos and Aleuts[7]

To facilitate the examinations, the personnel planner may find the acronym COINS, a useful classificatory device:

C = Caucasions; whites and nonminority persons (includes Pakastanis and East Indians)
O = Orientals (includes persons of Filipino descent)
I = Indians (American)
N = Negroes
S = Spanish-surnamed Americans[8]

For each of these categories, plus the classification "Women," the study seeks to compile information on employee status with respect to

1. Applicant flow from filing of job application to permanent appointment
2. Current work force
3. Promoted employees (supervisors/managers)
4. Employees "advanced" to rank involving a merit salary increase
5. Employees who have requested a geographical, shift, or work transfer (no salary increase involved) and those actually transferred
6. Disciplined employees; internal justice actions and sanctions
7. Terminated employees

Identifying the presence or absence of discriminatory employment practices requires first of all accurate record keeping. If each (prospective) employee's sex and ethnic background is noted (by means of the COINS distribution, for example), then that person's progress through the organization can be followed and data collected. Applicant flow should be traced from the application itself (accepted or rejected) through the selection process to permanent employment. Collected data should reveal the

---

[7] Jacque K. Boyer and Edward Griggs, *Equal Opportunity Employment Development Manual* (Washington, D.C.: U.S. Department of Justice, 1974), p. 23.

[8] Boyer and Griggs, *Equal Opportunity Employment,* pp. 23-24.

percentage distribution by sex and race at each stage of this recruiting-selecting-hiring process (see Figure 3-1).

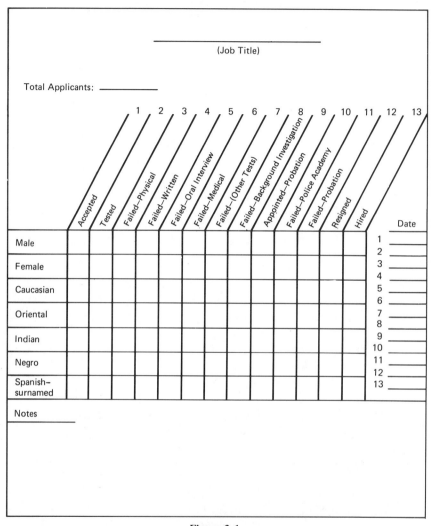

Figure 3-1
Applicant Flow Chart
A percentage distribution by sex and race can be developed for the success/failure ratio at each stage of the overall recruiting-selection-hiring process.

The composition of the current work force by sex and ethnic background should be outlined according to the job titles used by the employer. It is a simple tally of the distribution at each job level (see Figure 3-2).

Compiling data on promotions to various supervisory and management positions is slightly more complex, since the personnel planner must

	Total	Male	Female	C	O	I	N	S
Authorized Strength: _____								
Total Employees: _____				(Date)				
Patrol Officer								
Sergeant								
Lieutenant								
Captain								
Deputy Chief								
Detective								
Detective Sergeant								
Detective Lieutenant								
Specialist								
Patrol Generalist								
Civilian—Clerical								
Civilian—Other								

Figure 3-2
Work Force Chart
Sex and race (COINS) distribution by job in total work force.

determine whether employees placed on the eligible list were actually promoted or whether their names remained on the expired list. The bottom line in this category should give the actual number of successful candidates, not the number who passed the examination.

In most police departments, advancement with a salary increase refers to job mobility from patrol officer to detective; in larger departments, however, this may signify promotion to "generalist" positions within the patrol division. Data on advancements should include not only the initial advancement, but also each salary step on the way to the maximum. Also, since many of these advancements are not permanent (no job tenure is conferred), data should indicate any reductions in salary or the return of detectives to the patrol division. These data should be entered on a chart similar to that shown in Figure 3–1.

Transfer data should be divided into geographic, shift, and work transfers and then further subdivided into requests made and requests actually granted. Job title is generally not a relevant factor in evaluating transfer policy, but if the personnel planner feels some purpose may be served by such an analysis, data can be arrayed by job title.

Data on disciplinary actions and sanctions should refer only to those personnel actions that are a part of the employee's permanent personnel file.

Charts for entering such data will differ from agency to agency, but the basic data to be entered should be listed by sex and race, and should reveal the event upon which the disciplinary action was based (absent without leave, lost service firearm, or use of unnecessary force, for example) and the penalty assessed (reprimand, suspension, dismissal). This particular data array will reveal any unusual trends with regard to discipline and the sex/race of employees.

Termination data are linked to the information on disciplinary actions and penalties because such data compare the number of women and minority group employees dismissed in relation to male and majority group (Caucasian) employees. Of course, a complete listing also contains voluntary terminations (resignations), retirements, and disability terminations—with or without disability pensions. A chart for arraying these data would account for the total number of employees by sex and race (available from Work Force Chart); employees terminated for cause (dismissals available from chart of disciplinary actions and penalties); resignations; retirements, and disability terminations. As with all previous comparisons, these data can be developed into percentages or ratios reflecting the sex or race factor.

The bottom line in any review of equal employment opportunity is the comparison of the percentage distribution of women and minorities in the work force and the percentage of women and minorities in the "target population" from which an employer could be reasonably expected to search out job applicants.

An analysis of the employment practices of an employing agency should relate the facts disclosed in the self-study to the employing agency's past performances as well as to the goals of its equal employment opportunity program. The purpose of analyzing such data is to identify discrimination or the disparate effect of the processes by which applicants are recruited, selected, hired, promoted or advanced, transferred, disciplined, and terminated. (See Figure 3–3.)

Equal Employment *Opportunity Program* An equal employment opportunity program should be responsive to the facts disclosed by an employer's self-study, and its stated goals should be to provide equality of job opportunity and to compensate for any past discrimination.

In order to ensure a higher percentage of women and minority group members in the various job levels of a police agency, the personnel officer should undertake a testing and evaluation process that is job-related and free of cultural bias. Similar objective criteria should also apply to the process of granting or denying requests for transfers to more desirable work or advancement in grade (without formal promotion).

In police agencies in which past discrimination has been evident and widespread over a lengthy period, an equal employment opportunity program

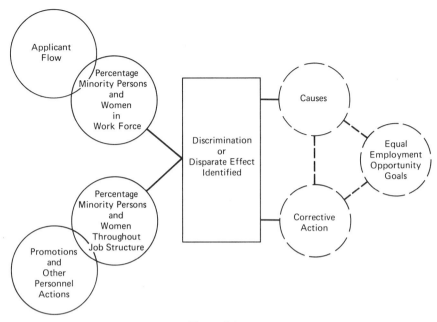

Figure 3-3
Identification of Discrimination

must consider action such as racial hiring and/or promotion quotas. When limited preferential treatment is necessary to overcome the overt results of past inequality in job opportunities, then the guidelines of *Bakke* can be utilized to achieve the necessary goals for minority persons and women. The U.S. Supreme Court, in *United Steelworkers of America* v. *Weber* (1979), approved of temporary job preference programs for minorities to remedy manifest racial imbalance in employment.

The diversity among candidates that the *Bakke* decision has termed furthering a "compelling state interest" encompasses a far broader array of qualifications and characteristics than merely the applicant's race or sex. Each candidate must be considered in terms of a wide range of pertinent characteristics, and the weight given to a particular qualification may vary from year to year depending upon the desired mix of successful candidates.

Following the selection guidelines of *Bakke* should allow the employing agency to overcome, within some reasonable time period, the effects of past discrimination. In terms of ratios, this means raising the percentage distribution of women and minority group persons to equal their percentage distribution in the local labor market.

Determining the "best qualified" candidates for various jobs in a police agency is still best accomplished by means of a test program, but to ensure equal treatment of all candidates these tests must be professionally validated as free of cultural bias and job-related. In past years, when the number of candidates was large and projected job openings were small, personnel technicians raised the level of difficulty of tests to avoid generating an eligible list out of proportion to the expected job openings. But in many cases, what they were actually testing was test-taking ability, not a projection of the applicant's on-the-job performance. The goals of an equal opportunity testing program are twofold: (1) to ensure equal opportunity to all applicants to achieve the "best-qualified" designation; and, counterbalancing this, (2) to affirm the merit concept of civil service as transcending race, religion, sex, or national origin.

Chapter Review

Summary   Legislation and case law forbid discrimination in employment; however, ratio hiring and promotion may temporarily produce unequal employment opportunities. The High Court's attitude toward this situation has been ambivalent, but it has usually sought less drastic remedies. In *Bakke*, for example, the Court opened the gates for employers to take into consideration a wide number of factors in selecting and promoting workers; at the same time, however, it affirmed that an applicant's qualifications should be "weighed fairly and competitively" to ensure equal protection under the Fourteenth Amendment.

Self-study of past and present hiring and promotion practices and procedures will indicate the extent of discrimination in a police agency. A corrective action program can then be devised to rectify the faults found in this self-study and, through job-related tests free of cultural bias, ensure equal employment opportunity to all persons. In affect, then, self-studies should help employers avoid any imposed hiring or promotion quotas.

Critique   The only compelling evidence of equal employment opportunity is the fact that there is a significant number of minority group persons and women among those who are hired, transferred, advanced, or promoted. For this reason police personnel managers are confronted with the near-impossible task of "working backward" to arrive at test practices and procedures that are likely to achieve these results. In tangential opposition is the doctrine of the *Bakke* decision and the belief among contemporary police officials and employees that "politics" should be kept out of police hiring and promotion practices and procedures.

1. Is there an implicit guarantee against job discrimination in the Fourteenth Amendment?

2. Identify the essential elements of Title VII.

3. Trace the trend in judicial action in equal opportunity employment cases.

4. What is the doctrine of the *Bakke* case?

5. What are the goals of an employer's self-study?

6. Should a corrective action program to insure equality in employment be responsive to an employer's self-study? How responsive?

7. Can a corrective action program likely to include a higher percentage of minority persons and women among new and promoted employees be free of bias against other applicants and employees? Explain.

Workbook Project

Research recent writings in the area of equal employment opportunity and list five references for and against preferential hiring of minority persons and women in police agencies.

II

PERSONNEL PROCUREMENT

Personnel Procurement   Procurement in police personnel management may be defined as the process of recruiting, selecting, and hiring men and women who will work at satisfactory or better levels in police jobs and find satisfaction both with working conditions and the work itself. In fulfilling the procurement function, the police personnel manager serves two masters—job applicants and the line managers of the police agency.

Personnel procurement begins with the premise that within the total labor force there is a target group of persons who can be interested in police employment and who have the necessary basic qualifications. The goal is to develop job applicants from this target group in some relationship to the number of existing and projected job openings. The method involves a three-step selection process: (1) to screen applicants through job-related and racially neutral tests; (2) to establish an eligible list that ranks candidates according to some rational standard(s); and (3) to hire the best qualified individuals (see Figure II-1).

Figure II-1
The Procurement Funnel
At each state a lesser number of individuals
moves toward acceptance as recuirts.

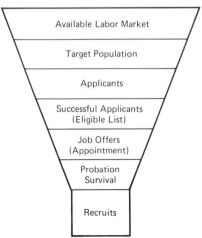

Available Labor Market

Target Population

Applicants

Successful Applicants
(Eligible List)

Job Offers
(Appointment)

Probation
Survival

Recruits

Police personnel managers seeking to fill a specialist or management-level position may find that the skills and/or ability levels of present employees leave something to be desired. If so, the pending examination should be viewed as a talent search, and applications should be received from those who desire a lateral transfer from another agency, as well as from individuals with no police experience but otherwise well qualified for the job opening. As noted previously, any overtones of political selection must be avoided; all hiring must be on the basis of competitive testing that accurately mirrors the job requirements.

4 Recruiting

Chapter Objectives

- to define and describe the initial stage of human resource management—finding well-qualified candidates for current and projected job openings
- to relate job requirements to recruiting methods that will yield an adequate number of qualified job applicants

The police personnel manager's objective in recruiting is to find those persons who have an interest and an aptitude for police work and to attract a significant percentage of them to apply.

People differ in their knowledge, skills, abilities, interests, personalities, and needs. Once a general occupational area has been chosen, an individual will usually make a final decision on the basis of personal values and the strength of his/her self-concept.

Economic pressures often influence occupational decision, as does the job market, though social factors can also figure prominently. Police salaries, the guaranteed annual wage of police employment, and the very real value of certain fringe benefits may be important deciding factors. On the other hand, some individuals may be swayed by the overt or covert disapproval of family and friends to reject police employment, a phenomenon that can be observed especially among blacks and Hispanics.

To date, no survey has recorded the number of individuals who may be interested in police work, but there are indications that the target population is increasing. There has been a tremendous growth during the past decade in criminal justice education at both two- and four-year colleges and a high percentage of these students have chosen degree programs that could lead to police careers. The pressure police agencies have felt as public employers to implement equal employment opportunity practices will undoubtedly attract an increasing number of qualified minority group applicants. In addition, the apparent interest of women in police work, and their demonstrated capability in the field, is likely to change the self-concept of many women and open this segment of the labor force to police recruiting.

Police personnel managers should seek help in recruiting from the "central" personnel agency. This is the personnel unit with responsibility for all employees of a city, county, or state. Because of their experience in serving other departments in government, the officials and technicians of this agency can offer assistance in planning and developing an effective recruiting program. In some jurisdictions, police agencies must actually rely on the central agency to supply applications. In any case, the basic responsibility for a successful recruiting program rests with the chief of police and ultimately with the designated police official in charge of personnel management.

Standards for Police Employment

Applicants for entrance to police agencies must meet a generalized set of job-related minimum requirements. At one time these standards varied from community to community and from state to state, but in recent years various police and "peace officer" standards commissions have established uniform statewide standards that have in some cases been adopted by entire groups of states.

This trend toward uniformity resulted in the 1973 publication entitled *Report on Police* by the National Advisory Commission on Criminal Justice Standards and Goals (NACCJSG). One section of the report, "State Mandated Minimum Standards for the Selection of Police Officers," calls for state commissions to set hiring standards and cites guidelines to be followed:

1. The commission should be composed of representatives of local law enforcement agencies and other areas of criminal justice and government.
2. The commission should establish minimum standards for
   a. Age
   b. Physcial health, strength, stature, and ability
   c. Personality profile
   d. Character
   e. Compensating factors (to overcome minor deficiencies)
   f. Education
3. The commission should insure that standards are met by inspecting for local compliance, and certifying as competent to exercise police authority only those police officers who have met the mandated standards.[1]

To enumerate NACCJSG's recommendations in the second item:

1. Recruitment age standards should specify both minimum and maximum ages to reflect the physical demands placed upon a police officer and the retirement liability of the employing agency.

[1] National Advisory Commission on Criminal Justice Standards and Goals, *Report on Police* (Washington, D.C.: U.S. Government Printing Office, 1973), p. 334.

2. Physical requirements and the dimensions of a personality profile should be based upon the physical and emotional demands of police work.
3. Character standards should be chosen so as to reflect public demands for trust and confidence and be equal to the awesome responsibilities of police officers.
4. Compensating factors should be weighed against certain minor deficiencies, particularly in areas such as age, height, or weight.
5. Educational requirements should be commensurate with the mental skills and knowledge necessary to perform the police function.

Educational standards for police officers have been upgraded both to reflect the national trend toward more specialized higher education and to acknowledge the need for broadly educated personnel who are able to handle the diverse duties and responsibilities of police officers.

The National Advisory Commission on Criminal Justice Standards and Goals recommends an escalating educational standard for police entry level positions from the successful completion of one year of college to completion of degree requirements at a four-year college or university and suggests that this final standard be operational in all police agencies no later than 1982.[2]

In *Upgrading the American Police*, Charles B. Saunders, Jr., stated the case for eventually requiring all police personnel to complete the baccalaureate degree:

> Low educational attainment may not necessarily reflect on an individual applicant's intelligence, although it is likely to signal other problems of personal or social adjustment. In a time when the preponderant majority of the population completes four years of high school and goes on to college, however, the generally low educational level of the nation's police has critical implications. Unless educational standards for selection rise substantially higher than the steadily rising level of schooling for the general population, the police manpower situation can only grow worse as departments increasingly draw their recruits from the bottom half of the population in terms of ability.[3]

Unfortunately, most police agencies do not require applicants for the entry level position to have more than a high school diploma. Table 4–1 presents data from an extensive study of personnel practices in municipal police agencies conducted in 1976 by the International City Managers Association.[4] Only 4 percent of the cities reporting require "some" college education; another 4 percent require an associate degree (two years), but only 0.1

---

[2] NACCJSG, *Report on Police*, p. 369.

[3] Charles B. Saunders, Jr., *Upgrading the American Police* (Washington, D.C.: The Brookings Institution, 1970), pp. 43–44. Reprinted by permission.

[4] James R. Mandish and Laurie S. Frankel, *Personnel Practices in the Municipal Police Service*, Urban Data Service Reports Vol. 8, No. 13 (Washington, D.C.: International City Managers Association, December 1976), p. 4.

Table 4-1
Minimum Educational Requirement for Initial Appointment to the Police Private Position

Classification	No. of cities reporting (A)	Some high school No.	Some high school % of (A)	High school diploma or equivalent No.	High school diploma or equivalent % of (A)	Some college no degree No.	Some college no degree % of (A)	Associate degree No.	Associate degree % of (A)	Bachelor's degree No.	Bachelor's degree % of (A)	No formal educational prerequisites No.	No formal educational prerequisites % of (A)
Total, all cities	1,574	22	1.4	1,410	89.6	58	3.7	56	3.6	2	0.1	26	1.7
Population group													
1,000,000 and over	4	0	0.0	3	75.0	0	0.0	0	0.0	0	0.0	1	25.0
500,000–999,999	18	0	0.0	16	88.9	1	5.6	0	0.0	0	0.0	1	5.6
250,000–499,999	27	1	3.7	22	81.5	4	14.8	0	0.0	0	0.0	0	0.0
100,000–249,999	77	0	0.0	67	87.0	4	5.2	5	6.5	1	0.5	1	1.3
50,000– 99,999	195	2	1.0	168	86.2	12	6.2	12	6.2	0	0.0	0	0.0
25,000– 49,999	391	2	0.5	341	87.2	14	3.6	22	5.6	0	0.0	12	3.1
10,000– 24,999	862	17	2.0	793	92.0	23	2.7	17	2.0	1	0.1	11	1.3
Geographic region													
Northeast	440	12	2.7	406	92.3	8	1.8	3	0.7	0	0.0	11	2.5
North Central	489	3	0.6	435	89.0	15	3.1	26	5.3	0	0.0	10	2.0
South	364	7	1.9	331	90.9	14	3.8	8	2.2	1	0.3	3	0.8
West	281	0	0.0	238	84.7	21	7.5	19	6.8	1	0.4	2	0.7
Metro status													
Central	293	3	1.0	261	89.1	16	5.5	7	2.4	0	0.0	6	2.0
Suburban	868	10	1.2	765	88.1	32	3.7	43	5.0	2	0.2	16	1.8
Independent	413	9	2.2	384	93.0	10	2.4	6	1.5	0	0.0	4	1.0
Form of government													
Mayor-council	580	11	1.9	527	90.9	11	1.9	17	2.9	1	0.2	13	2.2
Council-manager	869	9	1.0	766	88.1	44	5.1	39	4.5	1	0.1	10	1.2
Commission	71	1	1.4	65	91.5	3	4.2	0	0.0	0	0.0	2	2.8
Town meeting	31	1	3.2	29	93.5	0	0.0	0	0.0	0	0.0	1	3.2
Rep. town meeting	23	0	0.0	23	100.0	0	0.0	0	0.0	0	0.0	0	0.0

Note: Percentages may not add to 100% because of rounding.

Source: James R. Mandish and Laurie S. Frankel. Personnel Practices in the Municipal Police Service, p. 6. Reprinted by permission.

percent demand a bachelor's degree. However, 90 percent of the respondents in this study required a high school diploma or its equivalent.

Educational requirements—even the almost ubiquitous high school diploma—have been cited time and again as discriminating against socially disadvantaged persons, usually members of minority groups. It is alleged that these candidates are otherwise qualified and that their lack of schooling is the result of socioeconomic pressures.

A U.S. District Court refused to void the requirement of a high school education or its equivalent in order to remedy past racial discrimination in the Mississippi Highway Patrol (MHP). The court's reasoning involved three considerations: (1) blacks and whites had an equal opportunity to obtain a high school education in the Mississippi school system, (2) states have a right and a duty to prescribe minimum preemployment qualifications for police officers; and (3) a high school education was necessary to complete police recruit training and such training was vital to satisfactory levels of work performance in the MHP.

In the following excerpt, the court examines at length the viability of this educational requirement:

> The plaintiffs challenge as racially discriminatory the statutory laws of the State of Mississippi which require that applicants for the position of a Mississippi Highway Patrolman must possess a high school education or its equivalent. It is undisputed that the patrol accepts a GED completion certificate in lieu of a high school diploma. The plaintiffs contend in their Memorandum of Law filed in support of their Motion for Supplemental Injunctive Relief and Proposed Decree that based upon 1970 census data half of the white residents of Mississippi completed more than 12.1 years of school and half of the blacks have not completed more than 7.5 years of school; that 52.6% of Mississippi whites 25 years old and over have completed a high school education whereas only 15% of blacks and other races 25 years of age and over have a high school diploma; that 49.2% of Negro males between the ages of 20 and 49 years of age have not completed high school whereas only 15% of white males between the ages of 20 and 49 years have not done so, and rely on *Johnson* v. *Goodyear Tire & Rubber Co.*, 491 F.2d 1364 (5th Cir. 1974) to support their contention that Mississippi's statutory educational requirement has a racially discriminatory impact and thus is unconstitutional.
>
> No statistics have been cited to this Court and we are unable to find any which accurately reflect the percentages of white males and black males in Mississippi between the ages of 23 and 36 who are thus qualified by age, Miss.Code Ann. §45-3-9 (Supp. 1975), to become members of the patrol and who have a high school education or its equivalent (which is and has been equated to the statutory educational requirement). In any event, this Court takes judicial notice of the fact that within the last ten years and at the present, blacks have the same educational opportunity as whites in Mississippi and hopefully and apparently are taking advantage of this once denied right which has now been secured for them. Furthermore, this Court

is confident that a quality high school education is equally obtainable by blacks and whites in this State. Certainly, there has been no showing in this record that this educational requirement has produced a racially discriminatory impact by denying blacks the right to apply for or become Mississippi Highway Patrolmen, such as was found to exist by the Court in *Johnson* v. *Goodyear Tire & Rubber Co., supra.*[5]

In other cases judicial opinion can be seen moving toward requiring the completion of an associate (two-year) program for entrance employment. In *Castro* v. *Beecher*, 459 F. 2d 725 (1972), for example, it was noted that a high school education was a bare minimum for the successful performance of the role of police officer in Boston; and in upholding the Akron (Ohio) Police Department's requirement of a high school diploma or G.E.D. equivalency, the court found a significant relationship between educational attainment and job performance as a police officer [*Arnold* v. *Ballard*, 390 F. Supp. 723 (1975)].

One approach to higher educational standards has been to introduce "educational incentives" into the career development system. Programs that reward both preemployment and in-service educational efforts have been well accepted by rank-and-file employees, and have in many cases become part of formal police contracts. Rewards range from paying the costs of tuition and books for those engaged in job-related studies to percentage salary increases for blocks of semester (or other) units representing various educational achievements. Usually these incentives apply to courses in the criminal justice area. Table 4–2 reveals that over half of the municipalities responding to a nationwide survey provided some educational incentives at the college level, with this percentage rising to 73 percent in cities located in the West.[6]

The most effective device for increasing the general educational level of police officers over the past decade has been the Law Enforcement Education Program (LEEP) of the Law Enforcement Assistance Administration, U.S. Department of Justice. Under this program, grants-in-aid are available to in-service criminal justice personnel for tuition and to preservice students for tuition and other expenses related to attending a college or university. Loans to preservice students are automatically stricken from the books if these individuals go on to complete several years employment with a criminal justice agency. So far, participation by police personnel in criminal justice courses through the LEEP program has outstripped participation by personnel from other areas, for example, courts and corrections. As a result, the impact of LEEP upon the nation's police services is being recognized.

The *National Manpower Survey of the Criminal Justice System*, mandated by the Safe Streets Act of 1973 and conducted by the National Planning Association, notes that educational assistance under the LEEP program appears to have contributed significantly to a recent increase in numbers of college-educated police officers. In assessing the results of LEEP, however, it recommends a shift in emphasis from general upgrading of the police force to a

---

[5] *Morrow* v. *Dillard*, 412 F. Supp. 494 (1976), pp. 499–500.

[6] Mandish and Frankel, *Personnel Practices in the Municipal Police Service*, p. 4.

Table 4–2
Incentives for Education Beyond High School

Classification	No. of cities reporting (A)	Cities providing incentives		Incentives provided only for police-related course work	
		No. (B)	%of (A)	No.	%of (B)
Total, all cities	1,576	865	54.9	561	64.9
Population group					
1,000,000 and over	4	1	25.0	1	100.0
500,000–999,999	19	10	52.6	3	30.0
250,000–499,999	28	14	50.0	7	50.0
100,000–249,999	76	45	59.2	26	57.8
50,000– 99,999	200	133	66.5	76	57.1
25,000– 49,999	393	233	59.3	144	61.8
10,000– 24,999	856	429	50.1	304	70.9
Geographic region					
Northeast	437	252	57.7	179	71.0
North Central	495	242	48.9	167	69.0
South	359	162	45.1	109	67.3
West	285	209	73.3	106	50.7
Metro status					
Central	295	169	57.3	101	59.8
Suburban	872	529	60.7	352	66.5
Independent	409	167	40.8	108	64.7
Form of government					
Mayor-council	582	248	42.6	173	69.8
Council-manager	870	542	62.3	333	61.4
Commission	70	29	41.4	20	69.0
Town meeting	32	26	81.3	18	69.2
Rep. town meeting	22	20	90.9	17	85.0

Source: James R. Mandish and Laurie S. Frankel, *Personnel Practices in the Municipal Police Service*, p. 11. Reprinted by permission.

more selective, quality-oriented program designed to improve competencies of managerial-level personnel and of professional staffs in planning, research, evaluation, and education.[7]

Target Population The target of a police recruiting program is the total number of potential applicants in the available labor market; that is, all those who would meet entry level requirements, given the necessary motivation.

The lifting of preemployment residence requirements, the removal of sex as a qualification, and the modification of traditional age, visual acuity, and

[7] *The National Manpower Survey of the Criminal Justice System: Executive Summary* (Washington, D.C.: Law Enforcement Assistance Administration, U.S. Department of Justice, 1978), p. 18.

height requirements, all mean that larger target groups can be assembled, with the major constraint being the statewide minimum standards.

In many police departments, the lower and upper age limits now range from approximately 21 to 34 years.[8]

Eyesight qualifications vary among municipalities, but the trend has been to allow for correction by glasses, with some agencies accepting 20/200 vision when corrected with glasses or contact lenses.[9] The traditional 20/20 requirement for police jobs has been under attack for many years, particularly in view of the fact that our military services had long since adopted more lenient standards.

Height has been one qualification that America's police leadership has been slow to relinquish. However, recent trends point toward an easing of this requirement in order (1) to increase the size of target populations for police recruiting, and (2) to guard against a minimum height requirement disqualifying a disproportionate number of women and minority group persons.

In determining the minimum height requirements for women state traffic officers, personnel technicians of the California Highway Patrol realized that the prior all-male recruiting standard of five feet eight inches would reduce the target population of potential women candidates to an unacceptably low number. After some deliberation, a minimum height of five feet six inches was set for the first group (pilot project) of women candidates. The rationale for adopting this cutoff figure was that candidates shorter than five feet six inches could not reach the ground with both feet while sitting astride a motorcycle, could not safely back a patrol car without unbuckling the seat belt, and were less visible than taller persons when directing traffic at an intersection.[10]

In developing a target population from the available labor force, police personnel managers must seek out men and women between the minimum and maximum ages who are in good physical health with the potential strength and agility required by the job. These individuals should also have good to excellent character references and display a mental attitude that will permit them to withstand the normal stresses of police work. In addition, their educational achievements should reflect mastery of certain skills and factual information that will promise satisfactory or better performance.

Affirmative Action:
Recruiting of Women
and Minority Persons

Equal opportunity employment concepts and requirements demand an affirmative action program with an outreach designed to reach blacks and Hispanics. When a substantial racial or ethnic minority population resides within the jurisdiction of the recruiting police agency, the goal of such a

---

[8] Terry Eisenberg, Deborah Ann Kent, and Charles R. Wall, *Police Practices in State and Local Governments* (Washington, D.C.: Police Foundation, 1973), p. 18.

[9] Eisenberg et al., *Police Personnel Practices.*

[10] *Women Traffic Officer Project: Final Report* (Sacramento, Calif.: California Highway Patrol, 1976), p. 18.

program should be to achieve a ratio of minority group employees that mirrors the makeup of the population served by the agency.

In any recruiting program directed toward attracting large numbers of minority applicants, the following methods are suggested:

1. Recruitment advertising and material depicting minority group police personnel on the job, and placing emphasis on the community service role of police
2. Active cooperation of the minority news media as well as the general news media
3. Liaison with local minority community leaders to encourage referral of minority applicants
4. Recognition of special abilities such as the ability to speak a foreign language, strength and agility, or other factors in compensation of minor deficiencies
5. Assignment of minority police officers to this affirmative action recruiting
6. Regular personal contact by police recruiters with minority applicants from initial application to determination of employability[11]

The present surge of interest among women in police employment, and the concurrent growth in their self-confidence to deal with the full range of police field duties, apparently needs little more from police recruiters than assurances of fair treatment in preemployment tests, in police academy training and during the probation period, and in future equal opportunities for upward job mobility. In many instances, potential women applicants are working at jobs below their skill competence level, and once made aware of police employment as a career, become eager members of the target population.

As we noted earlier, probably the major stumbling block to women becoming sworn personnel has been the necessity of patrol duty as a first step in the career development system. However, police administrators who in the past denied this assignment to women are now remedying this situation at local levels.

Among the reassurances that most women candidates seek, either explicitly or implicitly from a recruiting police agency are that

1. selection procedures will facilitate the employment of women
2. all recruits, including women officers will be assigned to the full range of patrol duties
3. selection, training, and salary policies will neither favor nor discriminate against women

[11] NACCJSG, *Report on Police*, p. 329. Reprinted by permission.

4. career paths for women will allow each individual to attain a position classification commensurate with his/her particular degree of experience, skill, and ability

5. there will be no separate organizational entities composed solely of policewomen—except those identified by function or objective, such as female jail facility

The ban against discrimination in employment on account of sex places on an employer the burden of proving by means of factual evidence that all or substantially all women would be unable to perform safely and efficiently the duties of the job involved.[12] With respect to police agencies, two reports are relevant here. One, a study of the work of women patrol officers in Washington (D.C.) Metropolitan Police Department, indicates women can perform at satisfactory levels as patrol officers. The other, a California Highway Patrol pilot project, found that women were qualified to perform the full range of police duties as traffic officers.[13]

College Recruiting

College students, particularly those majoring in criminal justice, constitute an important part of the target population, yet there is presently a severe deficit in the number of employees with college backgrounds. College education is desirable not only for police officers, but also a as prerequisite to the development of police managers and specialists.

One of the major problems in recruiting college students for police employment has been convincing many of these potential candidates that the recruiting police agency was ready to make it worth their while—that is, that there was a tangible advantage in pay and promotional opportunities for candidates with a college degree. High school graduates and college students—even school dropouts in some cases—have had to take the same test and usually no credit was given for a college degree when assignment as a detective or promotion to supervisor was sought.

Over the years, however, the college graduate's ability to secure high marks on entrance examinations and to move upward rapidly in a progressively successful career pattern has vindicated the true value of higher education. And the increasing numbers of students enrolled in criminal justice degree programs, along with a rise in the number of schools and colleges offering this degree, supports the contention that police employment is a viable job choice.

In the private sector, college recruiting consists basically of a campus interview with students who have notified the college or university placement office of their career interests. An effective campus interview has been described as a meeting in which the student interviewed finds an employer who

---

[12] *Weeks* v. *Southern Bell Telephone & Telegraph Co.*, 408 F. 2nd 228 (1969); *Rosenfeld* v. *Southern Pacific Company*, 293 F. Supp. 1219 (1968).

[13] Peter B. Bloch and Deborah Anderson, *Policewomen on Patrol: Final Report* (Washington, D.C.: Police Foundation, 1974); California Highway Patrol, *Women Traffic Officer Project.*

has the work and career opportunities he or she desires and is able to arrange employment with the recruiting firm. Most recruiters conducting campus interviews have the authority to make decisions on whether interviewees have "the stuff " to justify further action. At the same time, they screen out those students they deem unacceptable and rank order promising candidates, attempting to persuade particularly strong applicants to come with the firm.[14]

Police recruiters cannot conduct campus interviews along these lines. In fact, the "interviews" they conduct are little more than sales pitches as to the benefits of police work generally and the attractive features of employment with their particular agency. They cannot hire, nor can they single out promising students for special hiring treatment. All they can do is to repeat when the next examination will be held and to emphasize that it is a competitive, non-discriminatory test designed to put those who succeed on the second step toward an offer of employment.

However, police recruiters can contact placement officers, vocational counselors, and members of the faculty of criminal justice at nearby colleges and universities for aid in informing interested students not only about examination schedules but also about current projections of job vacancies. This recruiting device can also be extended to more distant colleges and universities through mail contacts or ego-building visits to administrators and faculty.

Another device that will be beneficial to both recruiters and potential candidates for police employment is the student worker program. This program provides part-time employment for college students from ages 17 to 25 who have shown a sincere and prior interest in a police career. Police student workers should be full-time students (twelve or more academic units) and should be limited to a twenty-hour work week with the police agency. They should be assigned duties that prepare them for future work as regular police officers, but should not have the authority of a regular police officer or be authorized to carry firearms.[15] Of course, the basic assumption of these programs is that a certain number of the "apprentices" will go on to employment as police officers by taking and passing the regularly scheduled civil service examination.

Lateral Entry Recruiting Another potential target population for recruiters is the group of young officers from other police agencies who are dissatisfied with their present employment in some ways, most often because they find their advancement blocked by a lack of vacancies at higher levels. Since there is some evidence that experienced police officers tend to transfer from larger to smaller organizations, small police agencies would do well to focus some attention on this target population.[16] Needless to say, all

[14] George S. Odiorne and Arthur S. Hann, *Effective College Recruiting* (Ann Arbor, Mich.: The Bureau of Industrial Relations, University of Michigan, 1961), pp. 107–127.

[15] NACCJSG, *Report on Police*, p. 326.

[16] Eisenberg et al., *Police Personnel Practices in State and Local Governments*, pp. 27 and 74.

transferees must pass the regular competitive civil service test at the appropriate level.

In many states, successful completion of the standardized police "basic training" at any of the authorized police academies in the state automatically exempts the new recruit from the agency-directed initiation program and allows the officer to assume patrol duty after only a short briefing period. This is a significant advantage to the employing agency in terms of both time and money, for it means a few days of orientation versus the normal ten to sixteen weeks of basic recruit training.

A growing number of police agencies are attempting to make a lateral entry at the police officer entry level as attractive as possible. Many base the transferee's starting salary on previous full-time police experience; also, depending on prior experience, the employee may be credited with certain seniority benefits, including a certain amount of leave, vacation benefits, and equal chance for promotion.

The roadblock to this type of lateral entry has always been the loss of pension rights vested in a particular employing agency. Although personnel managers are aware of the need for "portable" pensions, pension systems continue to be developed locally, and the transfer of retirement credits and funds is difficult or impossible. However, police officers with only a few years in one pension system may seek employment elsewhere, particularly where police recruiters can arrange for these officers to "buy in" equal pension credit at the time of hiring. When a member of a pension system terminates, the funds contributed by the employee are usually returned with interest. The "buy-in," therefore, represents a transfer of funds from one pension system to another.

At one time lateral recruiting was termed "raiding," and a good number of police chiefs and sheriffs had unwritten agreements among themselves not to raid when recruiting. Today, however, both police officers and personnel managers are coming to recognize the professional rights of officers to seek employment elsewhere. A survey by the International City Management Association has revealed lateral transfer at entrance levels is now a "two-way street" between large and small police agencies: 67 percent of the large city (one million and over population) police agencies reporting made lateral transfer attractive by hiring at salary rates above the minimum step and 55 percent of the smaller police agencies (cities in the 10,000 to 24,999 population class) did likewise.[17]

New Sources of Applicants

A major goal of police recruiters is to develop new sources of job applicants from among the target population. This means seeking out individuals for whom police employment might mean a positive trade-off. Several factors come to mind that could influence a

[17] Mandish and Frankel, *Personnel Practices in the Municipal Police Service*; 1976, p. 6.

person's decision-making process. For example, educational deficiencies and/or lack of family resources may prevent the individual from finding employment in a preferred field, or perhaps entry into the chosen occupation requires the intercession of influential relatives or family friends. Assuming that the individual is assured entry, (s)he may be faced with a trade-off between satisfying such short-term wants as money, challenge, and adventure versus securing the longer range of benefits of status, job security and meaning, and career development potential (see Figure 4-1).

In many instances, individuals who had never planned on police work as a career are won over because the advantages of police employment outweigh its disadvantages and because the recruiting police agency offers them what they want out of the employee-employer relationship.

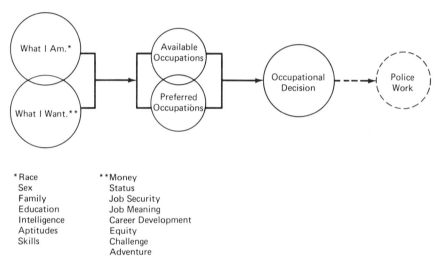

* Race	**Money
Sex	Status
Family	Job Security
Education	Job Meaning
Intelligence	Career Development
Aptitudes	Equity
Skills	Challenge
	Adventure

Figure 4-1
Compromise between Preferred and Available Occupations

Recruiting Methods   Advertising the contents of an examination notice has been a basic recruiting method for many years (see Figure 4–2). Such advertising should stress those aspects of the job that will attract potential applicants, including:

a forty-hour work week

full pay while in training

monthly salary range at entrance and upon attaining full seniority

overtime pay and its rate

additional compensation for special skills (motorcycle, helicopter duty, member of bomb squad, and so on)

Figure 4-2
Oakland, California, Examination Notice

amount of paid holidays and vacation
provision for sick leave
coverage under a health insurance and retirement plan
incentive pay for educational achievements

Of course, factors that exclude certain candidates should be spelled out clearly in the job requirements section of the examination notice.

Police recruiters may also advertise in the help-wanted sections of local newspapers. Although this method is relatively inexpensive, it reaches only the unemployed, and limited space does not permit a full presentation of the attractive features of police employment.

CITY OF OAKLAND
INVITES APPLICATIONS FOR

POLICE OFFICER

(CONTINUOUS TESTING)

MONTHLY SALARY RANGE: $1390, $1443, $1493, $1544, $1595 (Applicants with Police experience may be considered for employment above the first salary step.)

THE POSITION: The Oakland Police Department wants able, ambitious men and women who desire to build a worthwhile career in the professional police field. After receiving over five months of training at Oakland's Police Academy, a Police Officer performs a variety of assignments, including district patrol, criminal investigation, juvenile control, community relations, traffic enforcement and plain clothes work. Promotions are made by competitive examinations from within the Department.

BENEFITS:

1. **UNIFORM AND EQUIPMENT ALLOWANCE:** $100 initial allowance and, in addition to the initial allowance, the Officer receives an annual allowance of $218.

2. **HEALTH PLAN:** Members are offered a choice of two Health Plans. The City will pay 100% of the least expensive premium or make substantial contribution towards the alternate plan.

3. **DENTAL INSURANCE:** Dental insurance is provided for all Police Officers. Dependents may be covered at the Officer's expense. Effective July 1, 1977, the City will pay the cost for both the employee and dependents.

4. **VACATIONS:** Annual paid vacations range from three to four weeks per year depending on length of service.

5. **HOLIDAYS:** Officers are compensated for eleven holidays per year.

6. **SICK LEAVE:** A liberal plan continues your earnings when illness keeps you off the job. Sixty (60) days at full pay and sixty (60) days at half pay are provided per illness.

7. **EDUCATIONAL PROGRAMS:** The City provides cash tuition reimbursement to Officers completing approved college courses and additional pay for Officers (after probation) with A.A. (1%), Bachelor's (4%) and Master's degrees (5%) from accredited universities and colleges. Officers also may be sent to the FBI Academy and other schools for specialized training at the City's expense.

8. **RETIREMENT:** Retirement benefits are provided through the Public Employee's Retirement System (PERS). These benefits include retirement as early as age 50 with 50% of salary, basic and special death benefits, and disability retirement. The mandatory age for retirement, with maximum benefits is age 60.

REQUIREMENTS FOR APPLICATION:

Education: High school graduate or GED with a total score of 262.

Vision: Uncorrected 20/100, corrected to 20/20 in one eye and 20/30 in the other with no color vision deficiencies.

Age: 21 - 32 years. To age 35 with 2 years college or 2 years police experience. Candidates will be removed from the eligible list upon reaching their 35th birthday.

Weight: Must be proportional to height.

Driver's License: Possession of a valid unrestricted license by date of hire.

THE EXAMINATION:

The examination will consist of three parts which will be weighted as follows: The written and physical performance test will be qualifying and the oral examination will be 100%.

College seniors and graduates with a major in a law enforcement related field may request a waiver of the written examination by submitting a copy of their college transcripts for review.

The examination will be conducted on a continuous basis and held in Oakland only. Applicants who do not qualify may repeat the examination after 12 months.

AN AFFIRMATIVE ACTION EQUAL OPPORTUNITY EMPLOYER

Figure 4-2 (cont.)
Examination Notice Interior Highlights Benefits and Requirements

Television "spots" are vastly superior to either of the first two methods, principally because they can visually detail some of the attractive areas of police employment. One East Coast city developed a powerful recruiting device with a film of police officers in action, with the officers shown representing a good ethnic cross-section of the city's population. A Southern city emphasized the field work nature of police employment.

Radio advertising reaches a larger audience than help-wanted ads but lacks the "immediacy" of television. Since timing is crucial in both radio and TV advertising, personnel planners should consult local advertising executives as to the best time to run such promotional devices.

Newspaper display advertising is another valid recruiting method. The higher costs of such displays vis-a-vis classified advertising are justified for several reasons: (1) they often supplement the written copy with attractive art work that engages the reader's attention for the factual presentation, (2) they permit the agency to list many of the benefits of police employment, and (3) they reach more than just the unemployed segment of the population.

Of course, an agency may use more than one form of advertising simultaneously. However, the entire advertising format should be coordinated so that applicants will be clear about when applications are available and when the completed applications must be filed.

Publicity differs from advertising both in terms of the direct costs and the time frame. Although publicity involves no out-of-pocket cost, it is not "free" in the sense that the police recruiter must expend some time and effort to arrange for the public notice. However, publicity may be utilized at almost any time, and certainly well ahead of the expected date upon which an examination is to be announced. Both radio and TV offer excellent opportunities for public relations personnel to advertise the challenging nature of police work. The traditional avenue of publicizing an event is the press release, but guest appearances of police personnel on "talk" shows offer a much greater potential.

Printed materials range from informative pamphlets to blown-up display advertising. This is a low-cost recruiting method that reaches the walk-ins, call-ins, and write-ins, and those who read any notice posted in a conspicuous place. People who seek information about police work are likely candidates, and large-sized posters fastened to bulletin boards in public libraries, college administration buildings, and other public buildings will probably attract sufficient candidates to justify the cost involved.

Direct-mail advertising has been little used in police recruiting, but is definitely worth trying on an exploratory basis. If the necessary contacts have been made with members of the criminal justice faculty at nearby colleges and universities, names and addresses of graduating criminal justice majors may be obtained. This is one of the most potentially fruitful mailing lists. Other lists might be developed from past applicants who failed some portion of the selection process, but whose basically strong background warrant their trying again for the position; from applicants for employment at other nearby police agencies not reached for hiring; and from members of various local social service organizations.

Dimensions of the Recruiting Program The aim of every police recruiting program is to identify an adequate number of potential new employees to fill personnel needs as they exist or develop. Accordingly, the size of an agency's target population depends on both its personnel needs and its selection procedures.

Because the possible yield from any recruiting campaign depends largely on the state of the local labor market, police recruiters must keep a careful record of past experiences, which can then be adjusted to account for various short-range influences. Similarly, recruiters should be able to estimate the yields from each of the various recruiting methods based on past experiences. Evaluating each recruiting method necessarily involves careful record keeping. In most instances, police agencies will want to institute the practice of querying new employees as to how they learned about the job and the examination. An alternative, but less accurate method to compare recruiting techniques is to examine the agency's past recruiting budgets. Planners will then get some idea of how much was spent on each method in relation to its impact.

Obviously, the costs of a recruiting campaign will be related to the projected size of the target population—it costs more to reach a larger group of potential applicants. Money can be saved, however, if by yield analysis personnel planners can distinguish between better and poorer recruiting techniques.

When, despite all efforts, a recruiting program fails to secure an adequate number of qualified candidates, some adjustment to the selection process is in order. Police personnel managers commonly do one of two things: lower the percentage of items the applicant must answer correctly in order to pass, or schedule another examination sooner than was originally projected.

At the other extreme is the instance of recruiting too many applicants. Again, the personnel planner cannot afford to discount the cost factor in what may be a difficult selection process. But since police agencies in America operate in a democracy, a police recruiter has a duty to consider the applications of all persons meeting the minimum qualifications established in an examination notice.

Chapter Review

Summary The target population of police recruiting should be that sector of the available labor market likely to yield sufficient qualified applicants to meet the agency's present and ongoing needs for new employees. In recent years,

several developments have enlarged the yield of any target population: dropping local residence requirements; modification of age, eyesight, and height requirements; removal of sex as a bona fide occupational qualification; and the implementation of equal employment opportunity legislation. Job re- simultaneously. However, the entire advertising format should be coordinated so that applicants will be clear about when applications are available and when the completed applications must be filed.
quirements necessarily continue to limit this yield, but college recruiting, lateral entry expansion, and new sources of applicants have given recruiters greater leeway.

All recruiting materials feature the contents of the examination notice. Advertising and publicity are combined to direct the attention of potential applicants to attractive aspects of the job and to solicit applications. The dimensions of a police recruiting program expand in terms of both variety of methods used and their intensity in order to procure an adequate number of applicants, and all submitted applications are considered on their merits.

Critique

The failure of researchers to set out a clear set of criteria for the position of police officer has long handicapped police recruiting. Searching for the "best possible individual" can be described as a groping for candidates likely to deliver above-average performance in the multidimensional role of police officer. A collateral failure has been the unwillingness of American police officials to establish professional standards that would adequately compensate those individuals who had successfully completed two or four years of college work in a degree program such as criminal justice or a related area.

Questions for Discussion and Review

1. Summarize police entrance standards.

2. What police entrance standards dards indicate that the profession is being upgraded?

3. Should a police recruiting program search out women applicants? Minority applicants? Why?

4. Justify a recruiting program that seeks out college students or graduates.

5. What are the problems of recruiting college students?

6. What factors diminish the size of a target population? Expand it?

7. Outline the elements of an examination notice likely to attract job applicants.

8. What recruiting methods are most likely to produce an adequate yield from the target population?

9. What methods are likely to yield an adequate number of minority candidates?

Workbook Project   Develop a "profile" of the ideal police candidate, listing qualifications and characteristics you believe important to future job performance as a police officer.

5 The Selection Process

Chapter Objectives

- to stress the selection process as a key event in the future operational effectiveness of the employing police agency
- to show how each stage of the selection process operates to (1) screen out undesirable job applicants and (2) identify the best qualified applicants

The selection process consists of a number of evaluation concepts along with necessary implementation techniques. The goal of the selection process is to screen out undesirable candidates and to identify those who appear to be most qualified for the position in question.

Personnel managers in a police agency can expect considerable guidance from the central personnel agency in designing the various stages of the selection process. Technicians of state, county, and municipal personnel units are skilled in job analysis, the development of selection procedures, and scoring tests. In some jurisdictions they preempt that area by law or custom.

The selection process, as outlined in Figure 5–1, has several major stages:

1. Test preparation—job analysis and establishing selection criteria to indicate potentially successful job performance
2. Preemployment tests—written examination, personal qualification interview, and tests of strength, endurance, agility, and physical and mental health; also a background (character) investigation
3. Probationary employment—evaluation of grades in police academy and on-the-job performance for a period of six to eighteen months

Several criteria must be met by any job applicant selection process:

1. The process should assess those qualities actually needed on the job
2. It should not discriminate with respect to race, ethnic origins, or sex

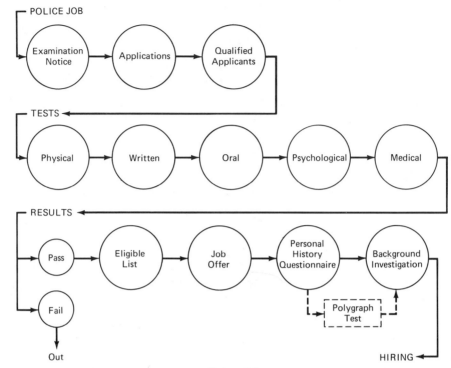

Figure 5-1
Police Selection Process

3. Applicants should understand and accept the overall selection process as an equitable one

4. No portion of the selection process should threaten or demean any applicant[1]

Obviously, the critical dimensions of on-the-job police performance must be the baseline for designing tests to use in evaluating job applicants.[2] The essential elements of the police selection process are:

1. The selection process shall include:

    a. A physical test (strength and agility)

    b. A written test of mental ability or aptitude

    c. An oral interview

    d. A psychological examination

[1] Roger H. Hawk, *The Recruitment Function* (New York: American Management Association, 1967), pp. 88–89.

[2] Marvin D. Dunnette and Stephan J Motowidlo, *Police Selection and Career Assessment* (Washington, D.C.: Law Enforcement Assistance Administration, U.S. Department of Justice, 1976), p. xv.

e. A medical examination

f. An in-depth background investigation

2. All tests shall be job-related and nondiscriminatory.

3. Qualifying and ranking scoring of tests shall be in accordance with a system validly and reliably predicting police officer performance; minimum qualifying scores should validly and reliably predict performance warranting hiring.

4. No delay between initial application filing and final determination of employability (that is, no more than eight weeks).

5. Applicants are promptly notified of the results of each major stage in the selection process.

6. The selection process is cost effective.[3]

The Job Application The bridge between the recruiting and the selection process is the job application. Application forms should be short and simple. Lengthy and complex application forms may intimidate potential candidates whose writing skills are below average. Later, when successful applicants are certified for employment and prior to conducting a background investigation, a pre-employment questionnaire can be used to fill in the missing data.

The major segments of an application form are the applicant's name, address, and social security number; his/her place and date of birth and citizenship; and requests for specific information that would automatically disqualify the applicant, for example, height, weight, or uncorrected vision.

Many application blanks now provide space for the applicant to tell how (s)he learned of the job opening. Such data are helpful to police recruiters in estimating yields from various recruiting methods.

Job applications are reviewed to determine if the applicant satisfies the basic job requirements as specified in the examination notice. Those candidates who do not qualify are notified promptly, and the area of their deficiency is specified in the notice. Notices to qualified applicants usually include the date and time for the scheduled written/physical examination.

Job Analysis A basic job analysis should identify the
and Job Relevance duties of a job on two dimensions—
importance and frequency—and then relate these dimensions to the SKA factor: skills, knowledge, and abilities essential to perform the job. Any data collected should accurately reflect what job incumbents do, how often they perform a specific function, and the SKA levels necessary to complete the task successfully. The overall

[3] National Advisory Commission on Criminal Justice Standards and Goals, *Report on Police* (Washington, D.C.: U.S. Government Printing Office, 1973), pp. 337, 350, 498.

description of a job that appears in the examination notice is based on this job analysis, as are the training curricula of all recruit training programs.

Collecting job analysis data about police positions should involve several fact-finding techniques. The ideal method employs all of the following:

1. Individual interviews with job incumbents
2. Group interviews with job incumbents
3. Individual and/or group interviews with direct supervisors one level above job incumbents
4. A sampling of job incumbents by questionnaire or daily logs to formulate a list of day-to-day tasks
5. On-the-job observations of successful and unsuccessful performance

Time and money can be saved through selective interviews and sampling of tasks to determine what SKA factors are essential to the job being studied. Interviews focus on those tasks the participants consider important and frequently performed. For each task sampled, the participants are queried on the knowledge, ability, and skills necessary to perform it adequately. For the purpose of linking the SKA factors, *skill* refers to the *ability to use knowledge competently and readily.*

The costs of developing a job analysis and appropriate job-related selection procedures can be reduced if the criteria are roughly equivalent from one municipality or other jurisdiction to another. Job analysis findings and conclusions as to selection procedures can be shared throughout the occupation, modified as necessary by local conditions, and then used by other employers in the occupation.[4]

The problems associated with job-related selection procedures have resulted in a call for occupation-wide job criteria, particularly with respect to the entry level position of police officer. The National Advisory Commission on Criminal Justice Standards and Goals has recommended that a group composed of police practitioners and behavioral scientists develop job-related mental ability and aptitude tests, as well as personality inventories in order to identify qualified applicants. In essence, the report calls for a comprehensive analysis of police tasks and the development of criteria based on scientifically validated tests, or test models and personality "norms," that will reliably determine whether an applicant is qualified, intellectually and in terms of interpersonal skills, to perform the tasks of a police officer.[5]

Research in nine cities, with almost two thousand police participants, has led to the development of a career index to be used in evaluating both job applicants and officers being considered for promotion. The "Patrol Officer Career Index" section consists of a battery "inventory" of tests and a scoring system designed to evaluate entry level candidates on the three major func-

[4] Eugene J. Rouleau and Burton F. Kreim, "Using Job Analysis to Design Selection Procedures," *Public Personnel Management,* September–October 1975, pp. 300–304.

[5] NACCJSG, *Report on Police,* p. 348.

tions of a patrol officer—public contact, overall performance, and cooperation. Researchers note a high correlation between the "predictor scales" and
actual on-the-job performance, but the authors note that their work is still in
the formative stage; in their own words, "It provides, at this stage, merely a
crude 'feel' for what we may hope for in using the combined predicators."[6]

In the final analysis, any job analysis or selection procedure should be
strictly accountable to the following checklist:

1. The job analyst has used professionally acceptable data collection techniques to identify job tasks.
2. (S)he has identified measurable applicant characteristics linked to
   predicting satisfactory job performance.
3. (S)he has devised selection procedures whose measures are as job-related
   as possible.
4. All findings and inferences are logical and persuasive.

In sum, would a jury of ordinary citizens conclude the analyst had reasonably
inferred job requirements and selection procedures direct from the job
analysis data and findings?[7]

Technicians skilled in psychometrics have devised three types of tests to
predict an applicant's performance of a specific job—the criterion-related test,
the construct validity measure, and the content validity measure. In
Bridgeport Guardians v. *Bridgeport Civil Service Commission*, the court discussed these three measures in relation to the plaintiffs' arguments that the
written test of the Bridgeport (Connecticut) Police Department was not job-
related:

> Determining the utility of an exam, however, requires some consideration of
> the standards applied in the field of psychological testing. Three approaches
> are used. (a) The preferred approach is criterion-related or predictive
> validity. Criteria are identified which reflect successful performance of the
> job, and test scores are then correlated with the performance ratings for the
> pre-determined criteria. A high correlation demonstrates that the test is a
> useful predictor of the quality of the applicant's job performance. (b)
> Construct validity involves an identification of what the psychologists call
> "constructs," and what laymen would probably call characteristics or traits,
> that are believed to be important to successful job performance. A test is
> then given which purports to measure the degree to which the applicant pos-
> sesses the required characteristics. (c) Content validity involves the direct
> measurement of knowledge or skill needed for successful job performance.
>
> Unlike the examinations to which they are applied, these "tests" are not
> readily susceptible to passing or failing grades. All of them have shortcom-
> ings. Criterion-related validation requires measurement of the employee's
> job performance. If the task is typing, speed and accuracy can be readily and

---

[6] Dunette and Motowidlo, *Police Selection,* pp. 50–51.

[7] Rouleau and Kreim, "Using Job Analysis," p. 303.

accurately measured. But with jobs of more complexity, especially those requiring exercise of judgment, there is not likely to be agreement on which criteria are truly indicative of successful job performance, nor has the art of evaluation acquired such precision that measurements of job performance can always be readily or accurately made. Who is to say what aspect of a policeman's work is to be measured—crimes solved, crimes prevented, or people assisted—and what measurements are to be used for job performance characteristics such as compassion, dedication and discretion? Construct validation similarly invites dispute as to which characteristics are the significant ones to be tested for, to what degree the applicant should possess these characteristics and what measurements are valid. Content validation also poses problems concerning which fields of knowledge should be tested for and how much knowledge of a field should be required; moreover, this approach injects the uncertainty as to whether a person found to have an appropriate amount of knowledge of appropriate fields will actually perform on the basis of that knowledge when confronted with the realities of his work assignment.[8]

Equal Employment Opportunity Tests

No test can be used that has an adverse effect on the hiring of minority persons unless that test can be shown to be demonstrably related to actual job performance. This criterion of job relevance applies not only to written tests but also to personal qualification interviews; to specific physical and educational requirements; and to any "screening" techniques an agency may use.

In *Griggs* v. *Duke Power Company*, the U.S. Supreme Court developed this "demonstrably job-related" doctrine. The facts of the case and the Court's holding are:

Facts:

Negro employees at respondent's generating plant brought this action, pursuant to Title VII of the Civil Rights Act of 1964, challenging respondent's requirement of a high school diploma or passing of intelligence tests as a condition of employment in or transfer to jobs at the plant. These requirements were not directed at or intended to measure ability to learn to perform a particular job or category of jobs. While §703(a) of the Act makes it an unlawful employment practice for an employer to limit, segregate, or classify employees to deprive them of employment opportunities or adversely to affect their status because of race, color, religion, sex, or national origin, §703(h) authorizes the use of any professionally developed ability test, provided that it is not designed, intended, or used to discriminate. The District Court found that respondent's former policy of racial discrimination had ended, and that Title VII, being prospective only, did not reach the prior inequities. The Court of Appeals reversed in part, rejecting the holding that residual discrimination arising from prior practice was insulated from remedial action, but agreed with the lower court that there was no showing

---

[8] Bridgeport Guardians v. Bridgeport Civil Service Commission, 354 F. Supp. 778 (1973).

of discriminatory purpose in the adoption of the diploma and test requirements. It held that, absent such discriminatory purpose, use of the requirements was permitted, and rejected the claim that because a disproportionate number of Negroes was rendered ineligible for promotion, transfer, or employment, the requirements were unlawful unless shown to be job related.

Held: 1. The Act requires the elimination of artificial, arbitrary, and unnecessary barriers to employment that operate invidiously to discriminate on the basis of race, and, if, as here, an employment practice that operates to exclude Negroes cannot be shown to be related to job performance, it is prohibited notwithstanding the employer's lack of discriminatory intent.

2. The Act does not preclude the use of testing or measuring procedures, but it does proscribe giving them controlling force unless they are demonstrably a reasonable measure of job performance.[9]

The practice of using a general intelligence test as one part of the selection procedure has been common in police agencies throughout the United States, and police personnel technicians have long regarded intelligence test scores as related to applicants' projected performance. Now this attempt to upgrade the profession is being challenged by the criterion of job relevance.

When any test that operates to exclude blacks or some other minority group is shown to be not relevant to job performance it is prohibited. However, according to the Court's opinion in *Griggs*, an employer can still claim "business necessity" to justify retaining a test that does impact adversely on minority persons. The business necessity defense requires an employer to show a compelling and *overriding* business necessity for the particular qualification in contention. Second, the challenged test must effectively measure this given qualification; and finally, there must be no viable alternative tests to accomplish the business necessity claimed.

Another recent decision that has had an impact on the issue of the relevance of testing to job performance is *Washington* v. *Davis*. This case established that the ability of a police recruit to read was indeed related to job performance, albeit indirectly. As trainees, recruits must be able to understand the materials covered in police academy courses. Extracts from the concurring opinion of Justice John P. Stevens in *Washington* v. *Davis* highlight the need for an adequate reading ability in order to master a police training program:

> . . . Reading ability is manifestly relevant to the police function, there is no evidence that the required passing grade was set at an arbitrarily high level, and there is sufficient disparity among high schools and high school graduates to justify the use of a separate uniform test. Second, the same test is used throughout the federal service. The applicants for employment in the District of Columbia Police Department represent such a small fraction of the total number of persons who have taken the test that their experience is

---

[9] Griggs v. Duke Power Company, 401 U.S. 424 (1971).

of minimal probative value in assessing the neutrality of the test itself. That evidence, without more, is not sufficient to overcome the presumption that a test which is this widely used by the Federal Government is in fact neutral in its effect as well as its "purpose" as that term is used in constitutional adjudication.

The Court's specific holding on the job relatedness question contains, I believe, two components. First, as a matter of law, it is permissible for the police department to use a test for the purpose of predicting ability to master a training program even if the test does not otherwise predict ability to perform on the job. I regard this as a reasonable proposition and not inconsistent with the Court's prior holdings, although some of its prior language obviously did not contemplate this precise problem. Second, as a matter of fact, the District Court's finding that there was a correlation between success on the test and success in the training program has sufficient evidentiary support to withstand attack under the "clearly erroneous" standard mandated by Fed.Rul Civ.Proc. 52(a).[10]

The U.S. Supreme Court's action in this case tends to support the U.S. District Court's decision in *Morrow* v. *Dillard*, that the requirement of a high school education or its equivalent for police officers is not racially discriminatory, bears a demonstrable and significant relationship to job performance, and serves a compelling state interest.

Police personnel officers faced with a claim that a test, test procedure, or selection requirement discriminates against minority groups or women must show, and furnish legally sufficient supportive evidence, that the claim is groundless. This may be more difficult if *de facto* discrimination is shown to exist. For this reason, a generalized offer of proof that action has been taken to bar any discrimination against these groups may be helpful. Within the public service employment arena, a police personnel officer has the burden of proof in overcoming allegations that segments of the selection process discriminate against minorities or women.

Physical Performance Tests

The purpose of a physical performance test at the entry level is to determine the applicant's strength, endurance, and agility. The events in these tests vary considerably, but the "overkill" events of past years have been eliminated largely. For instance, the physical performance test in Oakland, California, calls for eight events to be performed in "obstacle course" fashion. The applicant must wear a belt simulating a police officer's gun belt and (1) run 300 feet; (2) scale a six-foot wall; (3) walk the length of a standard balance beam; (4) run 300 feet; (5) grasp and squeeze with a one-hand grip a strength-measuring device—75 pounds pressure is qualifying; (6) run 50 feet; (7) drag a 140-pound dummy 50 feet, and (8) place the 140-pound dummy on top of a two-foot high platform within two minutes and 30 seconds, including a 30 second rest after

[10] Washington v. Davis, 426 U.S. 229 (1976).

the grip strength test. Since sex is no longer a bona fide occupational qualification these tests have undergone significant modification to avoid discrimination against women applicants.

A future objective for physical performance tests is to base them on a prior determination of the amount of physical strength necessary to handle certain types of situations. However, certain estimates may have to be modified if the testing is not to have an adverse impact on women applicants; that is, they should not fail an unreasonable percentage of women applicants.

The Written Test

Most written examinations for the entry level position attempt to assess an applicant in two broad areas: (1) the dimension of cognitive functioning, including the individual's decisiveness, judgment, and skill in reading and writing; and (2) the noncognitive dimension of interpersonal skills, stability and flexibility under stress, self-confidence, and motivation.

Most written tests in the public employee area make use of multiple choice answers, primarily because the "objective" test minimizes arbitrary scoring procedures.

Written tests generally have a high potential for integrity. Basic security measures can protect the secrecy requirement of test material prior to an examination date; and identifying applicants by examination number rather than name during test scoring assures the integrity of the grading procedure. Thumb-printing and verification of the applicant's signature via the application form guard against substitutes taking the examination.

When examination plans include an oral interview to appraise an applicant's personal qualifications, the written test is usually limited to the cognitive areas (decisiveness, judgment, written communications, and reading comprehension).

Unlike the more subjective fiindings of oral interviews, written tests can achieve a high degree of correlation between information elicited and the actual cognitive aspects of job performance.

The Personal Qualifications Appraisal Panel (Oral Interviews)

This is a face-to-face confrontation between an applicant and a group of examiners assembled for the specific purpose of conducting interviews with a considerable number of job applicants. In many jurisdicitons these panels consist of (1) a personnel technician from the central personnel agency, (2) an assigned member of the department seeking employees, and (3) a member of the general public.

In theory, and hopefully in practice, these panels of examiners are nonpartisan and nonpolitical. Their sole assigned task is to evaluate the total individual in terms of education and experience vis-à-vis job preparedness. Each panel either selects a chairperson or delegates this responsibility to the representative of the personnel unit; the chairperson greets the applicant upon entering the place assigned for the interview, introduces him or her to the other members of the panel, and opens the questioning of the applicant.

Each of the examiners questions the applicant according to some general outline. Initially the applicant may be asked: "Why do you want to become a police officer?" "How are you better qualified for this job than other applicants?" As the interview develops, each examiner probes the interpersonal skills of the applicant in terms of stability and flexibility under stress, self-confidence, motivation, and so forth.

At one time the major objective of these oral interviews was to eliminate applicants who performed so poorly during the interview that the examiners considered them definitely unfit for police work. More recently, interviewers have been instructed to evaluate applicants against a generalized profile of the "ideal" applicant and also to take into account the performance of other applicants interviewed at the same time.

Scoring
Test Results

The written test score represents the number of questions answered correctly on a base of the total number of questions. However, the interview scores given by the appraisal panel represent a more subjective response to the total applicant. Their grading rationale might be described as intellectual, supplemented by a good deal of sensory and psychological feedback. Grades are usually expressed in terms of percentages to allow subsequent interfacing with written test scores.

Years ago, personnel technicians in civil service agencies rarely weighted interview grades more than five on a base of ten, and generally limited the interview's weight to three. Then, during the last decade, a trend emerged to give a greater weight to interview grades; in fact, one police test in California ranks applicants solely on interview scores, relegating the written test to a pass/fail qualifying examination.

Now the pendulum seems once again to be swinging in the opposite direction. As we have already noted, recent litigation upholds the criterion of job relatedness with respect to any employment test. Since it is certainly easier to demonstrate the validity of a written test than that of an oral interview, police personnel planners are reassessing their weighting system.

Cutoff pass/fail levels must also be defensible. The cutoff point must be chosen as a grade on each test below which applicants would be considered unqualified. Ideally, it is based on statistics of recent examinations and follow-up studies indicating job successes in relation to examination scores. Relatively high cutoff points are warranted in police examinations because of the serious consequences of error in many situations police officers encounter.

The integrity of the testing process requires the same cutoff point for all candidates. No federal law requires any adjustment for past racial discrimination in establishing this pass/fail point, and certaily different cutoff points for different ethnic groups is a concept in violent opposition to the merit system of civil service.

Psychological Screening   There are tremendous consequences when error in the selection process results in the employment of emotionally unstable or mentally ill applicants. Psychological screening of all applicants can identify and eliminate from the selection process applicants who are emotionally or otherwise unfit for the work of a police officer. At the least, psychological testing is warranted when a background (character) investigation of a candidate reveals behavior patterns or personality proven deleterious to normal on-the-job functioning.

It may be true that psychological testing techniques are difficult to correlate with on-the-job performance of police officers. Yet it is equally true that such testing is the only means by which grossly unfit applicants can be discovered and rejected. At stake is not only the welfare of fellow workers and the general public, but also the emotional well-being of the applicant.

Beyond this minimal use of psychological testing there is a definite potential in this field to identify applicant types and relate them to predictions of successful and unsuccessful patterns of job performance. A research project in the Chicago (Illinois) Police Department has successfully identified several "patrolman types," defining these groups of officers on a performance basis far more detailed than the usual job description of "patrol officer." Studies such as this indicate the possibility of specifying quite accurately the psychologial makeup of police officers.[11]

In their evaluation of psychological testing devices, the research staff in this study was motivated mainly by the practical aspects of testing large numbers of participants. In opting for a low-cost, easily administered and scored test battery, they reasoned that the following three factors were paramount.

1. Group administration of tests to subjects (as opposed to individual testing)
2. Paper-and-pencil tests (as opposed to test requiring special apparatus)
3. Objective scoring (scored directly with a prepared key)[12]

[11] Melany E. Baehr, John E. Furcon, and Ernest C. Froemel, *Psychological Qualifications in Relation to Field Performance: The Identification of Predictors for Overall Performance of Patrolmen and the Relation Between Predictors and Specific Patterns of Exceptional and Marginal Performance* (Washington, D.C.: Law Enforcement Assistance Administration, U.S. Department of Justice, 1968), pp. 223–224.

[12] Baehr et al., *Psychological Qualifications*, p. 56.

Of the eight "patolman types" identified in this study, five were rated adequate in job performance while the remaining three were termed either (1) poor performance, (2) poor performance with disciplinary problems, or (3) conflict performance with general disciplinary problems.[13]

The inherent promise of such research to police personnel technicians is the ability to eliminate from further consideration job applicants who are almost certain to perform poorly and to become disciplinary "problem" personnel.

Police personnel managers and representatives of the pertinent central personnel agency should mutually agree to the employment of a competent and qualified person to conduct this psychological screening. Specialists in the area of psychological testing can be found in virtually every geographical region, so there is no reason to settle for someone whose credentials are not up to par or whose professional competence is questionable. An additional consideration in hiring a psychological consultant is that he/she may be called upon as an expert witness to document the validity of test techniques and any decisions based on them.

The Medical Examination

Medical examinations of applicants are conducted under the direct supervision of a licensed, competent physician. These physicals should be as extensive as necessary to determine each applicant's health and physical fitness. They should identify (1) existing disease, (2) abnormalities, (3) physical abilities below established minimum levels, and (4) any condition likely to cause non-job-related illnesses, inefficiency, unnecessary accidents, or premature retirement as a result of disability.

Police work is an occupation in which premature retirement on account of job-related medical problems is not uncommon. Therefore, it is especially important that the physicians who conduct these medical examinations be knowledgable about job-related medical problems and attempt to identify (and reject) applicants most susceptible to such illnesses.

Polygraph Tests

The use of the polygraph (lie detector) test in the selection process has diminished to the vanishing point. Such tests have been sticken down morally and legally on the grounds that they invade an applicant's privacy, afford too great a license in failing applicants, encourage too much trust in the polygraph examiner, and show no relationship to on-the-job performance.

Currently the polygraph is used primarily as an investigative tool when conflict is discovered in an applicant's recall of events disclosed in a background investigation. Although the background investigator may recommend using a polygraph, the decision must be approved by the police

[13] Baehr et al., *Psychological Qualifications*, pp. 197–222.

personnel manager, and no polygraph test should be conducted unless the applicant consents to the test and its scope in writing.

A nationwide survey of all state, county, and municipal police agencies with fifty or more sworn persons revealed that the polygraph test was the most infrequently employed procedure for assessing aptitude and character of police applicants.[14]

The Background Investigation

As indicated earlier, the background investigation is really an investigation into an applicant's "character"—his/her personality configuration as revealed by educational and work experiences, and life style. In order to disqualify an applicant at this stage of the selection process, the personnel officer must show that certain of the applicant's behavior patterns and personality traits overtly indicate inability to perform satisfactorily as a police officer.

Since the maximum age at entrance to police work is usually in the low thirties, the fifteen-year coverage common to applicant investigations includes all of the applicant's past employment experiences as well as secondary—and sometimes primary—education.

A background investigation begins with the preparation of a "Confidential Employee Questionnaire" requested of applicants who are on the eligible list and have accepted a formal job offer. This form asks the applicant to supply detailed information as to date and place of birth, the location of present and past residences, education, employment, credit, and military service (if applicable), and to name several references and detail any adverse encounters with police, from arrests to citations for traffic violations (except parking).

The purpose of the background investigation is to verify information given by the applicant and to learn how the applicant has behaved as a student, employee, neighbor, and friend.

While many of the statements made by an applicant are easily verified by mail, the central premise of an effective background investigation is that the personal interview provides the most in-depth information about the applicant. In addition to interviewing those persons listed as references, effective background investigators will routinely make note of opinions given by an applicant's teachers, landlords, bankers, neighbors, former employers, supervisors, and co-workers. All interviews are face-to-face conversations whose purpose is to secure the most direct, firsthand information possible about the applicant. The suggested interview format is nonsuggestive and nondirective, but it is structured to save time and provide a basic orderliness.

Since background investigations are both costly and time-consuming, they have been made the last step in the selection process. This also confers on

[14] Terry Eisenberg, Deborah Ann Kent, and Charles R. Wall, *Police Personnel Practices in State and Local Governments* (Washington, D.C.: Police Foundation, 1973), p. 20.

them a "final say" status. For this reason, caution should be exercised before rejecting an applicant merely on the basis of some piece of derogatory information. If the information is of such a nature as to shed serious doubt on future job performance, then personnel technicians should seek to document it by obtaining evidence from at least two other sources.

Before recommending that an applicant be rejected, the work of all investigators should be reviewed by the police personnel unit. The job applicant should also be notified as to the basis of his/her disqualifications. Appeals from rejection because of certain background investigation findings are usually claims that (1) the alleged facts are untrue, or (2) the alleged facts do not justify rejection.

In the case of alleged discrimination against black police applicants by the Philadelphia Police Department, the agency supplied a list of negative or disqualifying factors that weighed heavily in its rejection decisions based on background investigations. The ten most frequently disqualifying factors that appeared in the federal court write-up are

1. Court-martial conviction
2. Military arrests
3. Illicit or immoral conduct
4. No valid driver's license
5. Alleged threats of violence to spouse, neighbors, fellow workers, and so on
6. Job termination for cause (fired)
7. Improper conduct of friends/relatives
8. Job problems (unemployment, short-term jobs)
9. Arrests
10. Juvenile police record[15]

The decision to reject an applicant on grounds such as those cited above and previously used by police agencies such as the Philadephia Police Department may be reversed upon court application to vacate the notice of disqualification. On the other hand, the applicant's past life should, upon investigation, demonstrate that (s)he is of good moral character. The 1976 case of *Metzger* v. *Nassau County* (New York) illustrates a reasonable rejection situation.

The memorandum of the court in this case states:

On November 18, 1972, petitioner took a competitive examination for a position as a Police Officer in the Nassau County Police Department. He passed the examination and was placed on the eligible list. An investigation into the petitioner's overall personal fitness was conducted.

The investigation revealed that, between November, 1970 and November 17, 1974, petitioner was guilty of eight traffic violations; that he

---

[15] Commonwealth of Pennsylvania v. O'Neill, 348 F. Supp. 1084 (1972).

had been arrested on an outstanding warrant and found guilty of speeding; and that his driving license was once suspended for a month. The investigation revealed that, during the same period, petitioner was involved in seven automobile accidents. In one of those mishaps petitioner's car collided with a youth on a bicycle. At that time petitioner received a ticket because his car was equipped with defective brakes. He pled guilty to that charge. The investigation also revealed, through interviews with his neighbors, that petitioner worked on cars in his driveway in a loud, noisy and disturbing manner, and that he drove his car through the neighborhood at excessive rates of speed. As a result of the investigation petitioner was disqualified from the eligible list by written notice dated June 17, 1975, on the grounds of "disrespect for the requirements and processes of law and an unsatisfactory reputation." Petitioner was afforded a hearing, where he was represented by counsel and given the opportunity to submit facts in opposition to the appellant's determination. After the hearing, appellant [Nassau County officials] adhered to their initial determination of disqualification.[16]

The New York Supreme Court, Appellate Division, held that petitioner Metzger's history of traffic violations and automobile accidents supported the determination that he had not demonstrated the requisite character to be eligible for the police position. The concluding paragraphs of the court's opinion state:

... The law in this area has been properly stated in *Matter of Haynes* v. *Brennan*, 16 Misc.2d 13, 14-15, 135 N.Y.S.2d 900, 902:

"It is well-settled law that the Civil Service Commission may inquire into the character and reputation of applicants for public employment and exclude from such civil service of the State or municipality any person it deems unfit to occupy a public position by reason of 'indolence, inadaptibility to the service, garrulousness, want of character, experience, tact, integrity, or a lack of proper disposition, or the existence of habits which would render him quite unfit to assume the duties of the position and yet not be actually incompetent.' "

Moreover, subdivision 4(par. [a]) of section 50 of the Civil Service Law provides:

"4. Disqualification of applicants or eligibles. The state civil service department and and municipal commissions may refuse to examine an applicant, or after examination to certify an eligible

"(a) who is found to lack any of the established requirements for admission to the examination or for appointment to the position for which he applies.

[16] Metzger v. Nassau County (N.Y.), 386 N. Y. S. 2d 890 (1976).

[3] Wide discretion is afforded to civil service commissions in determining the fitness of candidates. The exercise of that discretion is to be sustained unless it has been clearly abused (*Matter of Cowen v. Reavy,* 283 N.Y. 232, 28 N.E.2d 390). In fact, the unique role of the police officer has been recognized by the State Legislature in its enacting of former section 58 of the Civil Service Law. That section provides, in pertinent part:

"§58. Requirements for provisional or permanent appointment of certain police officers

"1. Notwithstanding any other provision of this law or any general, special or local law to the contrary, no male person shall be eligible for provisional or permanent appointment in the competitive class of the civil service as a police officer of any police force or police department of any county . . . unless he shall satisfy the following basic requirements:

* * * * * * *

"(d) he is of good moral character."

Under the circumstances herein, it is our view that appellants did not act arbitrarily or unreasonably in determining that petitioner did not demonstrate the requisite character to be eligible for the position of police officer and that appellants did not act arbitrarily or unreasonably in so determining (cf. *Matter of Vegas* v. *Schechter,* 13 Misc.2d 265, 178 N.Y.S.2d 67).[17]

Notification Procedures and Cost Considerations   It is a policy of most police personnel departments to notify applicants as soon as possible after each test (written, physical, oral, medical) has been scored. Applicants who successfully pass all of these tests are notified of their place on the eligible list when the list is published.

Some jurisdictions have written into their personnel policy special credit for veterans. Such legislation may grant veterans absolute preference, placing qualified candidates at the top of an eligible list, but more commonly it provides for an award of a certain number of percentage points added to the applicant's overall score.

The time lapse between final filing of applications and initial hiring from the new eligible list should be as short as possible, without at the same time neglecting the niceties of test preparation, delivery, and scoring. The important lesson for personnel planners to learn is that the selection process must run smoothly—that is, avoid unnecessary delays between stages—in order not to discourage or actually lose qualified applicants.

As noted earlier, certain stages of the selection process are less expensive than others. Planning for cost effectiveness demands, therefore, that the number of job applicants be significantly reduced prior to the high-cost

[17] Metzger v. Nassau County.

background investigation stage. Cost-effective planning will schedule either the written or the strength and agility test first, because of the low cost involved in administering these examinations. Whichever test is scheduled first is used as a qualifier for the other, and candidates who pass both go on to take the oral interview. These three examinations eliminate unfit candidates and reduce the number of successful applicants who will proceed to the more expensive psychological, polygraph, and medical tests leading up to the background investigation.

Chapter Review

Summary

The receipt and review of job applications is the first step in the selection process. Applicants who do not meet initial job requirements are rejected; those who do are scheduled for testing. Tests must be job-related—proven by job analysis to identify important and frequent duties and to measure the skills, knowledge, and abilities essential to effective performance of such duties. They must also be nondiscriminatory in the sense of affording all applicants equal employment opportunity. Tests that do have an adverse effect on minority group persons and women can only be retained in the face of overwhelming evidence that they constitute a "business necessity."

Applicants' achievements on physical performance and written tests, and in an oral interview, are scored objectively to determine each individual's qualifications in terms of the entire range. Psychological screening, a medical examination, a background investigation, and possibly a polygraph test identify undesirable and unfit applicants. Cost effectiveness structures the sequence of the various tests, and effective personnel management avoids undue delays between application and hiring to prevent discouraging qualified applicants.

Critique

The "well-qualified" job applicant is just as nebulous a concept as the "ideal" police officer candidate. Any research into the dimensions of the police officer's role or into a given set of performance objectives must first identify the qualifications, characteristics, skills, knowledge, and abilities that constitute successful performance. For years the police selection process has rejected a greater number of applicants than it has accepted, yet actual on-the-job performance of many police officers has left much to be desired. Some are unable to withstand the stresses of police work, and others are simply incapable of deriving meaning and satisfaction from their jobs. This raises the question of whether the selection process should be more rigorous, or whether the criteria and testing procedures themselves are invalid—that is, screen out the wrong applicants.

Questions for Discussion and Review

1. What is the role of job analysis in the selection process? Job relevance?
2. What is the usual sequence of the various tests in the selection process?
3. What are the strengths and weaknesses of oral interviews?
4. Why are medical examinations important? What is the role of psychological screening?
5. What is "arbitrary and capricious rejection" of applicants?
6. How is the selection process validated?
7. What is cost effectiveness in relation to the selection process?
8. What are the dual goals of the police selection process?

Workbook Project

List what you believe to be ten circumstances for rejecting applicants as a result of a background (character) investigation. Rearrange your list so that number 1 will be the reason most easily justified and number 10, the hardest to justify.

PERSONNEL PROCUREMENT

III

CAREER DEVELOPMENT

Career Development   Police agencies need employees who can perform a wide variety of professional, supervisory, managerial, and executive jobs at many different salary and status levels. Employees also have needs, and one of them is the recognition that accrues to an advancement, with its consequent raise in salary and the confrontation of a new and potentially more challenging job.

Government agencies that evidence high employee turnover would not be justified in funding costly career development programs, but police employees are certainly not transients. A very high percentage of police officers serve a lifetime with one employing agency.

The career development process begins when employees complete basic training and the probationary period. From this point on, upward job mobility will depend upon an employee's training, experience, and education as compared with similar records of competing candidates. Of course, personnel managers must continually update personnel data to provide line commanders with information about which employees are qualified by training, experience, and education for advancement or promotion. Employees themselves often initiate the process by requesting new jobs. A job-related selection process identifies the best-qualified candidates for new jobs (see Figure III-1 on the next page).

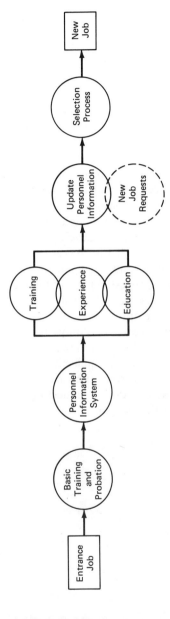

Figure III-1
Career Development Process

6

Basic Training and Probation

Chapter Objectives

- to stress the importance of basic training
- to emphasize the role of field training in the preparation of new recruits for regular duty
- to show that successful performance of regular duties by the end of the probationary period is the mutual goal of both the police recruit and the employing agency

Although practices vary from one jurisdiction to another, recruits generally remain "probationary police officers" until they have completed a ten- to sixteen-week period of basic training. Their temporary employment status usually specified by a contingency clause in the employment contract, conflicts with the fact that they are already covered by seniority rules. Another indicator of the new recruit's insecure status is the fairly common awareness among applicants that they can be "washed out" by poor grades on periodic tests or by a generally inadequate performance of duties.

For too many years this period of basic training and probation has been monopolized first by the "drill instructors" of police academies and later by line commanders who advise newly assigned recruits to forget whatever they learned in police academy. Police personnel managers have a duty and obligation to help their associates in police management recognize the interrelatedness of all the stages in recruitment and career development. It is no more than reasonable that the personnel unit participate in the basic training and probationary period, since this stage is the logical conclusion of the selection process it initiated. Even more importantly, it is the personnel unit that retains primary responsibility for the career development of all employees. Thus line managers must come to the realization that the basic training and probationary period is a crucial first step in the career development process.

Mandatory Minimum
Training Standards

Since mid-century most states have enacted legislation that mandates minimum basic training for new police officers. By specifying a minimum time period and certain broad curricular guidelines, the public is assured that police employees will meet certain professional standards.

The National Advisory Commission on Criminal Justice Standards and Goals recommends that every state enact legislation establishing

1. Mandatory minimum basic training for police
2. A state commission to develop training standards and faculty
3. Continuing financial support for statewide police training[1]

Mandatory statewide basic training assures the public that police officers throughout the state meet a common skills and knowledge level regardless of the community served or the size of a police agency. Such a base line can also serve as a starting point for future in-service educational programs.

A state commission composed of members representing the diverse police agencies throughout the state is vital to achieving the ultimate goal of statewide basic training, namely, to improve the capabilities and service potential of *all* police agencies in the state. Such a commission also serves a second purpose in that it helps overcome the fragmentation of police agencies that necessarily results from local control.

State financing of the cost of basic police training is warranted when the state mandates such training to ensure its citizens of quality police services. The cost of basic training is high, but it can never equal the cost in lives and property of intervention by untrained police personnel—or the cost of litigation resulting from such actions.

The basic training program should cover the subjects police officers need to learn to perform acceptably the tasks they will be assigned after graduation.

Basically, every basic training program must

1. Satisfy state standards for police training
2. Meet the stated needs of participating police agencies
3. Be job-related
4. Communicate expectations

In 1969 the National Sheriffs' Association *Manual on Training for Sheriffs*[2] was published. This book was prepared by association staff with the

National Advisory Commission on Criminal Justice Standards and Goals, *Report on Police* (Washington, D.C.: U.S. Government Printing Office, 1973), p. 384.

[2] Larry A. Giddings, Mark Furstenberg, and Henry J. Noble, *Manual of Training for Sheriffs* (Washington, D.C.: U.S. Government Printing Office, 1969).

assistance of a group of consultants with extensive backgrounds in police operations and administration or in criminal justice education. The job-related curriculum recommended in the *Manual on Training for Sheriffs* can be the basis for curriculum development in any policy agency in the United States. It includes the following areas of study:

1. Orientation (ethics, conduct, agency function, job meaning, training objectives, and learning and performance standards)
2. Introduction to law enforcement
3. Rules of evidence
4. State and local criminal codes
5. Administration of justice
6. Community relations
7. Criminology
8. Patrol procedures
9. Criminal investigation
10. Highway and street traffic supervision
11. Juvenile procedures
12. Defensive tactics
13. Chemical weapons
14. First aid
15. Civil process[3]

In 1970 the International Association of Chiefs of Police published the *Police Reference Notebook*.[4] This is a definitive text containing a wide range of material useful to instructors in basic police training school and to recruits. Because numerous source documents have been used in the past to supplement classroom lectures and field experience, this reference has proved especially useful.

While the arrangement of topics differs slightly from that presented in the *Manual on Training for Sheriffs*, there is general consensus on the following areas of study.

1. Introduction
2. Criminal justice
3. Basic law
4. Police procedures
5. Traffic control
6. Investigation

[3] Giddings et al., *Manual of Training for Sheriffs*, pp. 49–88.

[4] Thomas S. Crockett and James A. F. Kelly (eds.), *Police Reference Notebook* (Gaithersburg, Md.: International Association of Chiefs of Police, 1970).

7. Juveniles
8. Proficiency areas (firearms, defensive tactics, first aid, defensive driving, and so on)
9. Community relations
10. Reference material
11. Department orders
12. Department policy and procedures[5]

In 1974 the staff of Project STAR (System Analysis of Requirements for Criminal Justice Participants) released its conclusions as to the appropriate roles, tasks, and performance goals for participants in the criminal justice system and how these lead to certain expectations for training (as well as recruitment, selection, education, assignment, promotion, and evaluation). Among the criminal justice roles studied was that of police officer.

Project STAR's *Police Officer Role Training Program*[6] identifies three learning elements (knowledge, attitude, and skills) and relates these elements to the *behavior categories* of knowing, feeling, and doing and to the *performance areas* of role and job tasks (see Figure 6-1). Through a "role training program" Project STAR training aims at developing desired personal characteristics, attitudes, and behavior in students through an active involvement in the learning process. The focus of Project STAR's recommended training "modules" is broader than the aforementioned curricula of the National Sheriffs or the International Chiefs of Police; rather than merely conveying information, it involves students in the actual tasks of a police officer.[7]

Figure 6-1
Project STAR's Training Model

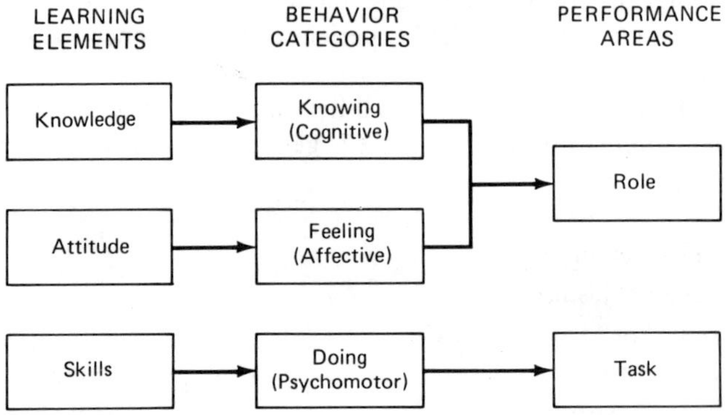

---

[5] Crockett and Kelly, *Police Reference Notebook*, pp. 1–B–1 to 1–B–70.

[6] Published jointly by Davis Publishing Company, Inc., of Santa Cruz, Calif., and Anderson Publishing Company of Cincinnati, Ohio.

[7] Project STAR, *Police Officer Role Training Program*, pp. 19–28.

In the future, police personnel managers should seek a curriculum and training program for their recruits that will familiarize them with the content inherent in the National Sheriffs' and Police Chiefs' training programs but employ an instructional stategy similar to Project STAR's *Role Training Program.*

Curriculum content must be linked to the achievement of training and performance objectives by quality control measures that will ensure an optimal learning environment. Such quality control measures include

1. *Physical facilities.* Classrooms and other places of instruction should equal the facilities of a college or university.

2. *Total basic training period.* The total number of weeks of basic training should be keyed to the scope of the selected curriculum, instructional strategy and methods, and learning and performance objectives.

3. *Instructional strategy and methods.* Innovative designing and planning can enhance recruit receptivity and participation not only during class but also in study and reflection at home.

   a. *Class size.* Classes should be small—25 recruits or less—and some provision should be made for breaking up such classes into smaller discussion groups.

   b. *Instructional Modules.* The division of a curriculum into segments is the principal key in achieving learning and performance objectives.

   c. *Instructional Methods.* This is the technique of instruction best suited to the instructional module or part thereof. It can range from discussion to lecture, and involve the use of audio visual aids or extensive participation of each recruit.

   d. *Testing and evaluation.* Valid and relevant tests should be established for each instructional module, and the performance of all recruits should be evaluated in terms of the learning and performance objectives established for that particular module. The achievement continuum should allow for a broad range of performances from excellent to poor.

   e. *Monitoring of faculty.* Observation reports should never call into question the basic academic freedom of faculty in any academic institution, but should offer instructors opportunities to learn from the critical appraisal of supervisors or associates the nature of their strengths and weaknesses in classroom teaching. Effective monitoring requires that a supervisor or associate observe the instructor for a full class period before rendering a critique of the instructor's performance. Only when an instructor fails to remediate his or her classroom performance according to the suggested criticisms should the individual be removed and assigned other duties.

   f. *Faculty renewal.* Instructors should be given field assignments to increase their expertise whenever time permits and circumstances warrant this transfer; they should also be allowed leave with pay to upgrade their academic achievements. In years past, during periods when no recruits were hired, the basic training school was temporarily closed and the faculty reassigned to previous duties. In more recent years, however, attempts have been made to keep a basic training school operating at least nine months of each year and to use the slack hiring period as a time for retraining and renewal of instructors.

The importance of basic training to recruits, their future on-the-job associates, the employing police agency, and the community warrants no less than an outstanding faculty for any police academy. A police training school should *not* be a dumping ground for problem field personnel or a haven for operations personnel unhappy with their patrol beats. The faculty of a basic training school should be selected on the basis of competence, a demonstrated interest in teaching, and a capability for effective teaching. Many states now require police instructors to demonstrate both professional expertise and satisfactory completion of an instructor training program. This should be a minimum requirement in any state, and all appointments to a police training school faculty should be based on a presentation of work experience, professional credentials, and educational achievements.

When qualified police personnel are not available, or when the instructional module suggests the use of civilian instructors, then similarly qualified individuals should be sought from other governmental agencies, colleges, and universities.

In the past, one of the central questions about methods of instruction related to "stress" versus "nonstress" training. Those who favored the stress approach justified its highly militaristic and authoritarian techniques by directly relating on-the-job performance of authority figures such as police officers to such training methods.[8]

Since most institutions of higher learning allow the individual student a good deal of freedom (with responsibility), it is reasonable to assume that the learning process may be handicapped, destroyed, or diverted to fringe areas in an authoritarian atmosphere. In addition, this type of recruit training has never been fully validated as necessary for coping with on-the-job stress after graduation, but there have been some signs that "stress" training can be used to discourage students from continuing in their new employment or to discriminate against students because of faculty prejudice or bias against minority persons and women. In short, graduation from a basic training school for police recruits should not be a *rite de passage*. Rather, it should indicate a recruit has successfully completed scheduled training qualifying him or her for duty in a field training program.

Field Training   After successful completion of basic training, a new recruit is assigned to a patrol unit for field training, which is really an extension of basic training. The

---

[8] This issue is discussed in Howard H. Earle, *Police Recruit Training—Stress vs. Nonstress; A Revolution in Law Enforcement Career Programs* (Springfield, Ill.: Charles C Thomas, Publisher, 1973), pp. 56–59.

purposes of field training are to teach the application of skills and knowledge learned in basic training, to supplement such training, and to aid the new recruit in developing appropriate attitudes toward the role of police officer and its tasks.

The basic relationship in the field training experience is that between the new recruit and the training officer. During this indoctrination period, the training officer "coaches" the newcomer, offering both companionship and on-the-job training. Thus, the value of field training is that the new recruit is not alone in attempting to transfer skills and knowledge learned in the classroom to actual practice under real-life conditions.

To the employer field training represents a safety valve that allows the agency to gauge individual performance on a trial basis. With proper supervision recruits will become aware of the explosive nature of certain situations and will avoid acting hastily or unfairly out of uncertainty or inadequacy. Death or injury to officers and social injustice to citizens are less likely to occur when police recruits first work as patrol officers under the supervision of an experienced officer.

The one-on-one field training does place the experienced officer in the role of supervisor. In most police agencies, the experienced officers are designated as training officers; and in some agencies the recruits and their training officers are grouped together in a training platoon.

Training officers should be selected with great care to make certain they have the capability to supervise the work of police recruits. An officer who lacks skills or knowledge, or has inappropriate attitudes toward day-to-day tasks can demoralize a recruit by negating a considerable portion of what (s)he has learned in basic training. Not only must a training officer have above-average skills and knowledge, but he or she must also believe in the police academy curriculum and instructors, and view field training as a meaningful experience for both recruits and training officers.

Currently the emphasis in field training is on observing and modeling the training officer's behavior. Each team of training officer and recruit is assigned a sector for patrol, and is expected to respond to radio messages and perform random (preventive, inspectional) patrol in the same manner as other patrol units. The trainer and recruit work as partners, each observing the other. Between tasks they discuss how various situations have been handled, and so provide feedback that will hopefully improve performance.

Of course, part of the supervisory role of the training officer is a formal evaluation of his recruit partner. In the past, each training officer was expected to follow a checklist in grading a recruit on the perfomance of a wide variety of specific tasks. This procedure has now been replaced by an overall rating of recruits' strengths and weaknesses as observed in the normal course of working a patrol sector.

In sheriffs' offices, where deputies are commonly assigned to one or two years' duty in a county jail, field training should precede the recruit's assignment; otherwise the probationary period could expire before the deputy has been evaluated on patrol duty.

To make certain police recruits have the necessary support of a training officer during the transition from basic training to patrol duty, the field training minimum should be four months.[9] Since basic training at a police academy also averages from three to four months, this allows recruits a period of seven to eight months to complete their basic training.

Probation

Probation signifies a proceeding to ascertain the truth or to determine character and qualifications. It is the final stage of the employee selection process. Neither the many tests of the preemployment selection process nor the evaluation of a recruit during basic training accurately measure the person's ability to perform well the full range of police duties over a considerable period of time. It is the probationary period that offers the employer a final opportunity in the selection process to detect recruits unable to cope with the actual demands of police work and eliminate these individuals prior to permanent employment.

In its 1967 report, the President's Commission of Law Enforcement and Administration of Justice recommended a probationary period of one year to eighteen months.[10] This concurs with the ten-week basic training and four-month field training minimums recommended in 1973 by the National Advisory Commission on Criminal Justice Standards and Goals.[11]

A one-year probationary period allows the employing agency more than six months to evalute the police recruit under actual working conditions, when the projected four-month field training experience is deducted from the total "apprenticeship." During the post-training period, the recruit either works alone or with a fellow officer, but always under the supervision of a superior officer.

Eighteen months of probation may be more time than is necessary to judge a recruit's fitness for employment and may be unfair to new employees. In addition, it is safe to assume that persons considering police employment may be deterred by this length of time during which they do not have tenure and serve at the employer's discretion. On the other hand, the one-year probationary period seems reasonable, particularly in light of time discounted for basic training and field training.

Some police personnel managers may argue that a long probationary period carries little threat to recruits, as merit civil service procedures require substantial evidence of incompetence or misbehavior to justify dismissal. In some jurisdictions the employing agency is even required to show documentation of cause just as it would if terminating a permanent employee. All this may be true, but it does not usually alleviate the employee's uneasiness about

[9] National Advisory Commission, *Report on Police.* p. 392.

[10] *Task Force Report: The Police* (Washington, D.C.: The President's Commission on Law Enforcement and Administration of Justice, 1967), p. 132.

[11] National Advisory Commission, *Report on Police*, p. 392.

probationary status and the very real fear of dismissal without any need to show a specific cause.

This fear, and its potentially undesirable influence on both job applicants and recruits, could be reduced by requiring a "due process" type of administrative hearing at which the police agency would offer evidence of just cause for dismissing a probationary employee and allow for both a defense by the recruit and an appeal from an adverse decision.

Under some circumstances dismissal proceedings against a recruit may be warranted during field training, at the completion of basic training, or even during the period of academic study. However, during the entire training period, instructors and training officers are expected to be supportive of recruits with problems. The trend is to retain such individuals and offer them remedial training. Remedial services have proven effective with recruits having difficulty because of personal problems, communication obstacles, and low training performance. Remedial services may extend from professional counseling to special instruction sessions.

Police managers often rationalize extensive remedial services on the theory of cost effectiveness: because it is expensive to recruit, select, and train a new officer, any termination must be for good and sufficient reasons. Some police managers also admit to considering the employee's feelings in the save-or-dismiss decision. They recall undertaking the considerable cost of buying uniforms and equipment and the worry about what they would do to recover these costs if they were terminated during their probationary period. Actually, in managing human resources neither factor is out of order—the welfare of both employer and employee must be considered in the save-or-dismiss decision.

Any decision to dismiss a recruit should be based on periodic reports of training officers and supervisors who have worked with the individual; such reports should document the deficiencies on which the dismissal action is based and should also describe the remedial services provided prior to the decision to dismiss.

A dilemma that often arises is whether a save-or-dismiss decision should be resolved in favor of the recruit or the employing agency. The only possible response is to develop some concrete standards that can be upheld in doubtful cases. A fair assessment should clarify what the issues are and judge them on the basis of these agreed-upon standards.

Some authorities suggest an extension of the probationary period for another two or three months when there are areas that resist clarification. This may be difficult to implement because of state and local civil service laws, but the idea has merit. Perhaps a policy of seeking a tentative decision two months prior to the end of the regular probationary period would serve to single out borderline cases that warrant increased observation during the final period of probation.

In the foregoing discussion of save-or-dismiss decisions, we have neglected to mention one primary guideline, and that is *the prime beneficiary of police services is the general public.* Therefore, any doubt about a police officer being able to function effectively should be examined in terms of possible consequences to the public.

In a study of employment opportunities in all police agencies in California,[12] the most common probationary period was found to be one year. Eighteen months was the next most popular length of probation, favored by forty agencies. Only twenty agencies reported a six-month probationary period, and at the other end of the spectrum, only nine required two years' service for tenure. An unknown variable in this survey was whether the probation period started at the time of graduation from basic training school or at the time of original appointment as a probationary employee. In the first instance, actual observation time would be six months, but in the second instance (discounting three to four months spent at the police academy), it would amount to a real-life probation of only two or three months.

Permanent Appointment—
Threshold Personnel Interview
The successful completion of basic training and the probationary period places the police recruit on the threshold of career development. (For an overview of the entire process, see Figure 6-2 on page 99.) He or she now becomes a permanent employee with some tenure rights. As soon as the personnel unit receives the necessary papers approving the retention of a probationary employee from a line commander, the employee should be scheduled for an interview with the personnel manager or a representative of the personnel unit.

The personnel unit may already have had some contacts with a new employee—perhaps via a background investigation by an assigned investigator or a personnel technician—but such problem-solving interviews are to be distinguished from the interview that takes place at the time of permanent employment.

The purpose of the threshold personnel interview is to formally welcome the recruit as a permanent employee and to form an initial impression of (1) the individual's interest in the role of police officer and (2) his or her potential for the many tasks and activities encompassed within the overall activities of the police agency. A related purpose is to "sell" the particular agency's career development plan. Thus, the interviewer makes it a point to spell out the routes of upward job mobility and what the agency can and will do to assist employees in developing progressively successful careers *within* the employing agency.

For most recruits, this interview represents their first direct contact with the police personnel unit, which so far has been a nebulous concept in comparison with the strong associations already formed about police academy faculty and line personnel. Because of the importance of first impressions—on

---

[12] *Employment Opportunities in California Law Enforcement—1975–76* (Sacramento, Calif.: California Commission on Peace Officer Standards and Training, 1977).

both interviewer and interviewee—the interviewer should structure the interview as an unhurried conversation between two individuals.

In preparation for each interview, the interviewer should examine a recruit's basic training record and a summary of the reports prepared by training officers and supervisors. Yet he or she should not allow the past to dominate the interview. Being aware of a recruit's strengths and weaknesses is primarily a tool the interviewer can use to direct the conversation toward realistic goals and objectives for a particular individual within the scope of police work.

Within the general structure of a threshold interview, the interviewer should note for the record what he or she perceives as the recruit's strong points and discuss them as warranted. Reference may be to the recruit's past work experience and educational achievements, and to any special talents or skills as these may relate to various career advancement or promotion patterns in the organization. These notes will undoubtedly provide a starting point for future interviews related to career development.

This threshold interview can be very beneficial to overall police management and the conservation of the human resources of an employing agency. The new employee is inexperienced, often insecure, and wants the advice and assurance of others in the new workplace. The personnel technician who conducts the interview may not be an authority figure, but the recruit's respect is probably assured because the interviewer's experience and knowledge is apparent. These are favorable circumstances for both participants in the interview.

Dismissal or Resignation— Exit Interview

Both the police agency and a recruit who fails the probationary period can benefit from an exit interview. The employee may have already been informed as to the reason(s) for dismissal, but an objective examination of the situation can help clarify in what areas the person needs to grow and can also help the agency see where it failed.

Interviewers should strive for information likely to reveal facts upon which remedial action can be based. Possibly the best posture for interviewers to assume is that the dismissal was justified, that the agency is now trying to find out how to guard against such events in the future, and that the former employee is the one who can provide the necessary data to prevent or reduce dismissals for cause.

A helpful technique is to open the interview with a general statement that one exit interview usually doesn't provide sufficient data for remedial action, but the facts obtained from a number of such interviews—upon analysis— may indicate a pattern amenable to remedial action. This is a true statement and is usually accepted by the interviewee.

When a new employee voluntarily terminates, the exit interview should probe the reasons for his or her decision. The interviewer should try to pin down the true facts leading to resignation. Particularly appropriate are questions as to the identity of other police employees tacitly encouraging the new employee to resign and what the person resigning believes their motives were for such encouragement. In summary, the essence of the interviewer's task in these interviews is to discover and record all the "dissatisfactions" leading up to the resignation.

The time spent on these interviews is only justified when the interviewer finds and records all of the circumstances leading up to the decision to resign. Again, it probably will require several interviews before a pattern is revealed that will suggest to the agency what corrective action it can undertake in the future to prevent or reduce resignations of new employees. Generalized summations such as "for the good of the service" are worthless, and the only pattern that can be developed is that the interviewer failed.

Chapter Review

Summary   Statewide training standards will promote minimum levels of skills and knowledge among police officers throughout a state, and full or partial funding by a state will reduce the cost of basic police training to local communities.

The objectives of basic police training should be decided upon jointly by line commanders and the police personnel manager. Curriculum content, quality control of instruction and faculty, and testing to determine whether recruits have achieved learning and performance objectives ensure that graduate recruits are adequately prepared for field training duty. Field training continues recruit instruction under the supervision of selected training officers, who instruct and evaluate recruits. Assignment to regular duty until the end of probation supplements field training and offers supervisors an opportunity to evaluate the job performance of recruits and prepare evaluations for the recruit's commanding officer.

Cost consciousness and the agency's genuine interest in its employees both warrant strong remedial action to upgrade recruits who are performing poorly at the police academy, in field training, or during the probationary period. A decision to dismiss a recruit must be based on facts that can be readily documented. Dismissed recruits, and those who resign, are interviewed to gather information useful to personnel management about the causes leading to termination. Retained recruits are designated permanent employ-

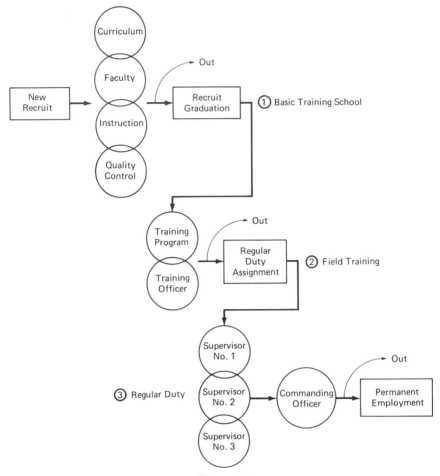

Figure 6-2
The Three Stages of Basic Training and Probation

ees, and interviewed by personnel technicians as an introduction to career development.

Critique   The combining of classroom and field training integrates learning and performance objectives with actual job performance; and the threefold evaluative process (school, field training, probation) assesses a recruit's ability to both learn and perform.

However, there are inherent shortcomings in this rather premature performance appraisal. Chief among these is the fact that the retention-dismissal decision is more concerned with screening out undesirable and unfit recruits then with seeking out excellent employees. The negativism of the selection process taken together with the finalityof the permanent employee classification, often locks in a borderline performance employee who profits from neither work experience nor in-service training, and to whom the phrase "career development" can in no way apply.

Questions for Discussion and Review

1. What is the value of statewide minimum training?

2. How are basic training learning and performance objectives established? By whom?

3. List and describe five instances of quality control of instruction in a basic training school.

4. Define and describe curriculum development in a basic training school; the delineation of instructional modules.

5. What are the advantages and disadvantages of a "stress" basic training school?

6. What are the qualifications for faculty in a basic training school?

7. Describe the concept of faculty renewal.

8. What is the value of field training to recruits? To their future associates? To the community?

9. Is evaluation while on regular duty before the end of the probationary period part of the learning process? Part of the selection process?

10. What is the most desirable period of probation? Why?

Workbook Project

Develop the outlines of a positive selection process to guide the retention versus dismissal at the end of a new employee's probationary period.

7

Personnel Information System

Chapter Objectives

- to explain the use of data about employees to guide personnel decisions
- to develop an inventory of employee skills, knowledge, and abilities as a basis for human resource planning by personnel managers

One of the major tasks of a police personnel unit is to acquire and record pertinent data about individual employees and to organize and correlate these data so that they can be retrieved easily whenever needed.

A personnel information system should provide an employer with a continuous inventory of employees' skills, abilities, and level of knowledge. With these data in hand, personnel managers and line commanders can make better decisions concerning transfers and assignments, advancements and promotions, and can better plan career development programs that will utilize all employees' skills and knowledge to the maximum.

A further objective of the personnel information system is to reveal through statistical analysis significant trends in the procurement, development, and utilization of employees. Personnel planners can then formulate long-range plans to meet the future human resources needs of their particular agency. This function of data gathering and assessment might be termed the "balancing" role of personnel management—matching personnel needs to the labor supply.

A well-designed police personnel records system should do all of the following:

1. Provide a data base of timely, selective, and accurate facts for planning decision making
2. Provide a common basis for the development and utilization of personnel

3. Utilize techniques to update information and correct errors

4. Optimize the activities of personnel

The *data base* of the personnel records system consists of an inventory of the skills and knowledge of employees from their time of entry into the agency until the present; in other words, it is a continuous inventory.

Personnel managers have a *common basis for personnel decisions* when similar data are collected and correlated for every employee with special attention to the accuracy of the stored information. Any review of one or more employees will be based on an evaluation of factual records regarding the employee's behavior and progress. It will examine personal data; education and training achievements; job history; skill, knowledge, and ability levels, and strengths and weaknesses.

Access to data stored in a personnel records system for the purpose of *updating and error correction* is a vital component of any information system. This capability preserves the basic accuracy (reliability and validity) of the data recorded and stored.

The utilization of personnel records for training and/or job reassignment can *optimize the activities of available personnel,* and thus avoid lateral hiring or the employment of a special employee as a consultant or on a contract basis.

A comprehensive personnel information system should include the following data elements (see Figure 7–1):

1. Personal information
2. Salary and benefits
3. Job history
4. Performance evaluation history
5. Commendations
6. Special skills
7. Training and education history
8. Disciplinary record
9. Medical history
10. Employee personnel requests

Personal
Information
Local and national authorities have set down specific recommendations for the personal information that should be included in the police employee's personnel file.[1]

1. Identification of employee
   a. Name, date of birth, residence, and social security number
   b. Physical description (height, weight, color of eyes and hair)

[1] Center for Police Management, *Law Enforcement Personnel Records Management* (Sacramento, Calif.: The California Commission on Peace Officer Standards and Training, 1974), p. 3; The National Advisory Commission on Criminal Justice Standards and Goals, *Report on Police* (Washington, D.C.: U.S. Government Printing Office, 1973), p. 440.

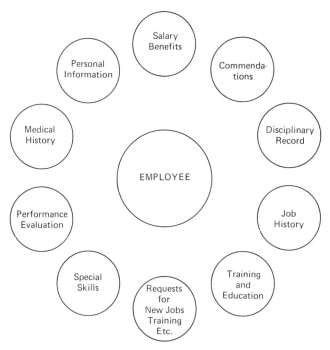

Figure 7-1
Personnel Information System

    c. Photograph

    d. Fingerprints

    e. Scars and marks

    f. Vehicle registration number(s)

2. Date employed

3. Assigned identification and/or badge number

4. Job assignment (current) and work location

5. Description and serial number of all handguns in possession of employee

6. Keys and other "issued" equipment

7. Marital status and number of children; address and telephone number of dependents if not living with employee

8. Designated next of kin for insurance purposes and retirement benefits

9. Other emergency contact—name, address, and telephone

10. Blood type

11. Known allergies

12. Family doctor

The quality of photographs of police personnel should be above average. At least one photograph should show the employee in civilian clothes, and photographs should be replaced at three- to five-year intervals. Release of photographs to the press should be restricted in the same manner as other material in personnel files; and any scanning of police photographs for the purpose of identification by complainants should be subject to the same rules of access as apply to the cumulative data in these personnel files.

Personal information is an element of the personnel information system that positively identifies an employee, establishes seniority, and provides data to meet the demands of various emergencies common to police work. The employee's job application can be included in this personnel history segment. If not, its location should be noted for reference.

Salary and Benefits   The official attendance and payroll records are usually maintained in a special unit (Financial, Payroll) of the police agency or public employer, with "time" records maintained by line commanders serving as the original documentation for payroll purposes. Data on salaries and benefits that should be part of the personnel information system include

1. Annual salary
2. Uniform (clothing) allowance
3. Overtime summary
4. Court overtime summary
5. On-call status and pay differential
6. Premium pay allowance
7. Deductions (tax, pension, charity, and so on)
8. Hospitalization/health insurance
9. Vacation and sick time credits
10. Attendance summary.

Taken together the data in this segment of the personnel information system will reveal the annual salary of an employee; salary supplements and their justification; deductions from salary for taxes, pension, and other authorized reasons—for example, employee group dues; hospitalization membership status; time credited for earned vacation and sick leave; time lost while sick or injured; time absent with leave and time on duty.

Job History   This segment of the personnel information system records each job assignment of an employee by date and job title. Under each such entry is noted the length of time in the job and all advancements and promotions, so that the resultant data give an occupational skills profile of the employee.

Any job that an employee has held for a considerable length of time should probably indicate to a personnel technician that the employee has the proper skills, knowledge, and abilities to perform such a job. For this reason, it is particularly important that the details of prior employment with a law enforcement agency be listed in this segment of the personnel information system. Past job assignments are a valid and reliable factor to use in deciding which employees are most likely to perform well in specific future job openings and which individuals are good candidates for job reassignment.

Performance Evaluation

Performance evaluation reports do more than evaluate an employee's skills, knowledge, or ability level—they link job requirements with the individual's qualifications as demonstrated in day-to-day job performance. In fact, performance appraisals usually indicate whether the individual evaluated met or exceeded the job requirements.

While the rating of a single performance evaluation may not be particularly reliable, a review of the performance appraisal history of an employee with several years seniority will generally have a high degree of validity and reliability, as it summarizes performance evaluations made by various supervisors and often in more than one job.

Commendations

Awards for heroism, letters of commendation, and other honors, from line commanders or citizens, offer recognition to employees for services "beyond the call of duty." While information in this segment of a personnel information system should not be quantified for advancement or promotion purposes, it can be utilized as a reflection of an employee's general aptitude for police work and, more importantly, his or her basic interests, values, and strengths. Such data are also excellent predictors of future job performance.

Special Skills

Data on special skills of employees should include the subject, the means by which the skills were achieved, and competency levels. A language skill would be identified by name, whether it was the result of study or exposure to the language at home or elsewhere, and whether the employee has a spoken and/or written fluency. A technical skill such as embalming or surveying would also be listed by name and sources, and competency would be indicated by whether the employee had been licensed or certified by the appropriate public agency.

A special effort should be made to list among special skills those in which competency has been acquired through avocational interest. For instance, many police officers are skilled in taking and/or developing photographs, but this information rarely appears on their personnel records.

Training and Education Information concerning the training and education history of an employee should be organized in three general categories as follows:

1. Training
   a. Basic
   b. In-service
   c. Prepromotion
   d. Specialized
   e. Optional
2. Education
   a. Undergraduate
   b. Graduate
3. Certification
   a. Agency
   b. Statewide

The training information is usually aligned with the job history of an employee, with in-service training related to seniority, prepromotion training as vestibule instruction just prior to assumption of the duties of a new supervisory or managerial rank, and specialized training as a necessary prerequisite to job assignments in other than the basic patrol unit. Optional training is not often available to employees, but in some agencies training in firearms such as SWAT (Special Weapons Attack Team) or a language identified with a local minority group may be offered on an optional basis. Of course, successful completion of such a course would be recorded.

The data on education should detail the course taken, date of successful completion, and degrees awarded. Although it is not usually found in these records, the grade point average (GPA) is a valid and reliable index of academic achievement on a scale from 4.0 (=A) to 1.0 (=D).

In addition, any special skills or honors achieved in training or education should be cross-referenced to the "Commendations" segment of the personnel information system.

Disciplinary Record Only "sustained" internal affairs investigation reports, and written reprimands or more serious action from line commanders, should be entered in this segment of the personnel information system. The substance of an internal affairs investigation upon which the complaint or allegation was sustained should be recorded along with the action taken (penalty). Written reprimands and more serious action by line commanders should be recorded in chronological order, along with the facts and penalty.

Medical History The personal health records of an employee should be part of any human resources data system. In some agencies health data are confined to sick leave, on-the-job injuries, and periodic physical examinations, and in many others, entries are made only when an employee requires medical aid because of injuries sustained on the job or seeks agency help of his own accord. Unfortunately, an employee can have a long history of sickness or ill health that remains undocumented except in the files of private physicians and hospitals. Of course, this is an area in which many employees wish to maintain a basic privacy, but it is also an area of valid concern for personnel managers. Most employers are motivated not only by self-interest—for example, to reduce time lost in sick days—but also by a sincere interest in helping employees solve problems that affect them personally and all those they come into contact with.

Employee Personnel Requests Employees should be afforded the opportunity to request transfer to another unit or to a new job assignment; and also to be included in special training or education programs. Action taken on such requests should be noted in personnel records along with the reasons for such action—or for denial or postponement of the request.

It is important to personnel managers to know the wants of employees as well as to be aware of how many of these requests were put into effect or denied, and the rationale for the action taken.

Background Investigation The employee's "Personal History Statement," and documents and reports collected in the course of a background investigation should *not* be retained in a personnel information system.

These data are normally dormant once the decision is made to employ an individual. Sometimes background data are useful when problems surface in the initial years of employment, but they should not be relied upon in any decisions as to career development, job assignment, advancement, or promotion.

In the few instances when such background data may prove useful, reference can be made to the basic file. Otherwise, this resource would not be used in any evaluation of the employee as a human resource.

Filing this material apart from an employee's personal records allows for administrative control of information secured by confidential inquiry, and assures employees that this information was collected for the sole purpose of determining their suitability for entrance employment. Of course, any event during the first few years of employment that indicates the employee may have falsified or concealed facts predating employment justifies a reexamination of these background data.

Access to and Security of Personnel Records

The personnel information system should be protected against unauthorized access. As a general rule, access should be limited to strictly official use by authorized personnel or to the subject employee for specific purposes, such as:

1. Employee concerned (review)
2. Error correction by employee concerned
3. Identification of employees with special skills
4. Career development—advancement and promotion
5. Statistical analysis of personnel resources
6. Official agencies

Access of an employee to data in his or her personnel file is human relations in action. The opportunity to know what is contained in these files is basic to employee morale, and the right of an employee to appeal for correction of materials therein is an additional morale booster as well as an assurance of the basic accuracy of these data.

A police personnel manager can provide both forms of access to the personnel information system by advising the police chief of the need for a directive which will give police employees

1. Access to their own employment records
2. The right to a copy of their own employment records upon request
3. The right to request a correction to or deletion from their records, or to be given the reason(s) in writing for the refusal to correct or delete as requested

It is clearly within the role of a police personnel manager to open up personnel files to employees and to put a stop to the secrecy surrounding what documents and papers are consulted prior to personnel decisions.

Access to personnel files is also warranted whenever an employer wishes to identify employees with special skills or to guide the career development of certain personnel. Statistical analysis of the human resources of an agency also warrants access at any time. Personnel planning for future recruiting and selection of employees as well as the development of career-oriented training programs, requires having these files at hand for comparison and completion of data.

Access to persons representing authorized agencies should be the subject of a written directive by the police chief. This directive should plainly identify those persons granted access, how the access is to be controlled, and any limitations on access. It is true that certain data may be open to public inspection, but it is equally true that a police chief can demand a court order prior to divulging a single piece of information from the agency's personnel records.

The concept that records having to do with the internal personnel matters of a police department are previleged has been supported by court decisions. In the 1968 decision of *Knott* v. *Perini* a U.S. District Court held that there were broad policy grounds for denying public access to confidential police records:

> The members of a police department must be able to rely upon their confidential records and notations being preserved for their internal use in *all* cases, for if it were otherwise, the knowldege that some of the confidential information recorded might be later exposed to outside parties would have a certain and chilling effect upon the internal use of such record making.[2]

Implementation of the Personnel Information System

The police chief should establish policy as to the responsibility of the personnel unit for gathering data for a personnel information system and allocate funds for establishing and maintaining such a system. In small departments a manual system can be employed, but larger police agencies should at least have access to a computer for some tasks. In any event, the personnel information system should interface with other management information systems in the agency.

In this policy directive, the chief should delegate authority to the personnel unit to design forms to be used in gathering and recording personnel data, and to assume responsibility for analyzing and utilizing all human resource information.[3]

These records should be updated quarterly or semi-annually, and computer or manual programs developed to compile available information into statistical reports that will graphically outline the total work force as to education, specific skills, language abilities, and scope of work experiences and/or professional specialty.[4]

Personnel Files and Internal Investigations

A special commission authorized to investigate corruption in the New York City Police Department, the Knapp Commission, was critical of that agency's administrators because this organization of close to 30,000 sworn personnel did not have a central

[2] Knott v. Perini, 283 F. Supp. 1 (1968), 2.

[3] See William P. Anthony, "Get to Know Your Employees—The Human Resource Information System," *Personnel Journal, 56, No. 4 (April 1977), 179–83.*

[4] See Wayne F. Cascio, *Police Personnel Management and Dade County Experience* (Washington, D.C.: The Police Foundation, 1977).

personnel file. In its report this commission recommended a central personnel information system:

> . . . This Commission was hampered in its investigations by the lack of an efficiently organized system of personnel records. There is no centrally located personnel file for each police officer. For example, his applicant record, his Academy record, his service record, his disciplinary record, his continuing education and training record, and his examination scores and promotion records are all maintained in different places. In order to check the record of an individual officer we found it necessary to go to as many as twelve different locations and search fourteen different files, since there was not even a central index to the various personnel files. It was not uncommon in these searches to discover all or part of a record missing or misfiled. Some records, maintained only at the precinct or unit headquarters level, are virtually inaccessible to investigators without alerting the subject of the investigation.
>
> The Department has had a stated intent for several years of creating a central personnel file for each member of the Department. A centralized index summarizing the dispersed records is in the initial stages of construction. Both steps are necessary. The system of personnel records centralization should provide for two sets of records. One set of confidential records should contain all facts and allegations concerning a police employee's career. It should be maintained by the Internal Affairs Division and located in their headquarters. Access to this confidential set of records should be rigidly controlled to maintain the integrity of the files, and the files should be so structured as to make the unauthorized removal of a record difficult and obvious. Their principal use would be in investigations. A second set of accessible personnel records duplicating the first should be located at Police Headquarters, but this set should omit unsubstantiated allegations. This second set could by maintained by the Chief Clerk's staff or the Personnel Bureau or any other unit which could provide response to legitimate inquiries.[5]

In regard to the recommendation of this commission that a duplicate set of personnel files be maintained in an Internal Affairs unit, it should be remembered that the main role of this commission was to investigate. It would certainly be a step backward to keep any kind of "unsubstantiated allegations" in the personnel file of any employee. In fact, the idea of keeping a set of "confidential" records as part of a personnel information system is repugnant to modern concepts of personnel management. It is also at odds with the belief that employees have a right of access to their personnel files and that personnel decisions should be based only on material in such files, unless written disclosure is made of other material along with the rationale for using this additional material.

[5] The Knapp Commission Report on Police Corruption (New York: George Braziller, Publisher, 1973), pp. 21–22.

Chapter Review

Summary A personnel information system provides up-to-date information about employees. Data such as job history, special skills, and training and education achievements are important to both line commanders and personnel managers who must decide whether to approve transfers and new job assignments and how to aid employees in career development planning. An analysis of the human resources available within an employing police agency will reveal shortages in specific skill or knowledge areas and thus point the way to new hiring or career development programs.

Internal personnel records are privileged. Public access should be granted only by court order or the written order of the police chief. However, employees have a basic right to review their own records and to request action to correct or delete material in such records.

Critique The lack of a personnel information system can seriously handicap personnel decisions and career development planning. Not knowing what skills, knowledge, and abilities are available within an organization means that such decisions and planning, as well as decisions about lateral hiring and civilianization, are no more than intuitive, or based on a calculated risk.

Questions for Discussion and Review

1. What personnel management needs are served by data in a personnel information system?
2. What is the relationship between the "Job History" and "Performance Evaluation History"? Between "Special Skills" and "Training and Education Achievements"?
3. Why is a "Medical History" element necessary? A "Disciplinary Record"?
4. Is public access to these records restricted? How?
5. What are the rights of employees as to their own records?
6. Discuss the relationship between the management of human resources and the concept of an "inventory" of employee skills, knowledge, and abilities.

7. Assume a personnel information system does *not* exist. Are personnel decisions such as transfers and assignments unfair to many employees? Explain.

Workbook Project   Design a printed form for recording and filing facts about employees in a personnel information system suitable for a law enforcement agency.

8 Employee Development Programs

Chapter Objectives

- to identify the job mobility needs and objectives of employer and employee
- to describe how an employee development program can meet these needs and help to achieve such objectives
- to show how to implement vertical mobility above the position of police officer
- to propose ways to avoid the "dead-end job" syndrome

The objectives of an employee development program are twofold. It is a staffing program to identify employees with skills, education, and experience who are likely to possess the competence and ability to become managers and executives, and it is also a program designed to diminish job dissatisfaction at the patrol officer level. It stands to reason, therefore, that such a program must reach down to operations level and that demands upon it will be heaviest when large numbers of employees will be affected.[1]

The objectives of an employee development program are easily stated: (1) to increase the staffing potential of the employee (actually an agency objective) and (2) to provide for on-the-job growth of employees.

The components of an employee development program, as diagrammed in Figure 8–1, are

1. Employees
2. Employing agency
3. Identification of needs and objectives

The Basic Staffing System As a staffing system for police agencies, employee development has two basic dimensions:

Los Angeles County Sheriff's Department, *Career Development for Law Enforcement* (Washington, D.C.: U.S. Department of Justice, Law Enforcement Assistance Administration, 1973), pp. 36–38.

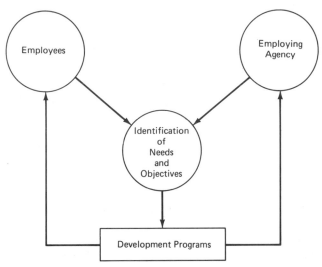

Figure 8-1
Employee Development Programs

1. A vertical process aimed at filling higher-level job openings from lower job levels
2. A horizontal process that permits hiring qualified individuals from outside the police agency for higher-level positions (lateral recruitment)

Police agencies have long favored vertical mobility in staffing decisions. As nontransient employees, police officers base hopes of job mobility upon positions above entry level being made available on a rank-ordered basis to regular employees of the agency. As a generalization, "skipping" is frowned upon by police employees, and lateral-entry hiring is totally disapproved.

"Skipping" is the process of opening up promotion procedures to those two or more levels below the rank specified. For instance, in screening for several executive-level jobs with the rank of captain, the job announcement would point out that experience at *any lesser supervisory-management level* (sergeant, lieutenant) would be acceptable. Although lieutenants may be the only protesters in this case, employee alienation is a phenomenon that can easily snowball upon repeated instances of perceived injustice. There is another equally valid reason to avoid skipping—it has a tendency to destroy the prestige of the job for which the screening is being conducted. In fact, incumbents in such jobs often speak out against this practice for just this reason.

From the viewpoint of nonpolice personnel consultants, lateral entry is a splendid technique for enriching the human resources of a police agency. They argue that in order to obtain the services of qualified individuals for positions above entry level, it is often expedient to recruit from other police agencies. Although applicants from outside agencies sacrifice some benefits (pension and seniority rights), they do so in the best traditions of professionalism: to work at their trade where the opportunity for career improvement is best for them. Outside consultants feel that such personnel would broaden the horizons of the employing agency by bringing to it attitudes and perspectives acquired in a different work environment. In addition, they argue, lateral hiring contributes to the overall professionalization of police employees by extending the concept of career development to the entire human resources of police agencies in a region, state, or the nation.

Despite such arguments, lateral recruiting remains an unpopular police personnel management technique:

> In those instances where qualified personnel are available within the agency but better qualified personnel are believed available outside it, the decision should be made in favor of agency personnel. To staff senior vacancies any other way would have a devastating effect on morale. Qualified in-house personnel would feel they were being denied what is rightfully theirs, and would feel resentment toward the organization. The police service has built its reputation as a career service. To disrupt the career aspects is to damage a reputation that does much to attract qualified and competent personnel to the police service in the first place.[2]

An interrelated horizontal intake and vertical promotion process may achieve the benefits of lateral hiring without meaningful alienation of individuals in an agency's internal labor pool. This is the "open" advancement or promotion process in which both in-house and outside police employees compete for existing and projected job openings on an equal basis. Such a policy is most likely to be acceptable when the personnel manager can document certain deficiencies in the internal labor pool.

Formal Employee
Development Activities

Every police agency should implement formal employee development programs designed to further the on-the-job growth of the employees, and to enhance the capacity of a meaningful number of employees to do better work in general as well as to successfully compete on a merit basis for jobs of greater responsibility and complexity.

While participation is voluntary, these programs should be open to all sworn personnel.

The National Advisory Commission on Criminal Justice Standards and Goals suggest a formal employee development program in which an employee is excused for forty hours annually with full pay to participate in one of the following activities:

1. Classroom training directed toward improved personal, vocational, conceptual, or managerial skills

[2] National Advisory Commission on Criminal Justice Standards and Goals, *Report on Police* (Washington, D.C.: U.S. Government Printing Office, 1973), p. 195.

2. Internship with another police, criminal justice, government, or private organization

3. Assumption of the position, responsibility, and authority of an immediate supervisor

4. Assignment to administrative and/or operational research and reporting

5. Service as a member of, or an advisor to, management committees and boards.[3]

Participation in any of the foregoing activities, particularly if rotated annually, will certainly contribute to an employee's ability to handle current and future assignments; it should also develop an employee's awareness and understanding of management philosophy and the decision-making process.

In lieu of any of the above activities, an employee can be given a leave of absence with pay to attend a college or university and pursue studies related to current or potential assignments.

Personnel rotation within an employing agency is another effective means of employee development. In smaller agencies, rotation may be limited to geographic areas of varying crime incidence and major functional assignments. In large agencies, rotation can also include assignment to specialized patrol and investigation units.

Although rotation is a positive technique that offers employees new and valuable perspectives on work and responsibility, personnel managers must exercise care to avoid any employee dissatisfaction. Rotation adversely affects employee devlopment when an employee is unhappy for any reason in a new job or assignment. Prior to any rotation, the concerned employee must indicate that she or he understands the reason for the transfer and acknowledge that the move is a necessary and desirable stage in her or his best career interests.

Lateral Transfer Lateral transfer of sworn police employees can contribute to the development of employees through specific work experience. The usual procedure for lateral transfers is to publicize the opportunities and screen the interested employees.

Involuntary lateral transfer may be administratively justified, but many employees consider such tactics authoritative management at its worst, despite loud protests by the personnel manager that such transfers are beneficial to employees and employer.

Fair notice of the lateral transfer opportunity should be coupled with an impartial—and defensible—selection process.

Lateral transfer does not involve any increase in pay or a job title conferring any significant increase in status. Therefore, the selection process does not require the formality of advancement or promotion, but it must have

National Advisory Commission, *Report on Police*, pp. 426–27.

a basic honesty and integrity with high visibility to negate any suspicions of favoritism.

Upward Job Mobility

There are three routes for moving upward in a police agency and securing increases in pay and status (title or rank) at each upward step:

1. Patrol generalist
2. Specialist (detective, youth, traffic, and so on)
3. Supervisor-manager

The first two routes are nonmanagerial, the third is the traditional managerial route. Nonmanagerial routes allow for career development without forcing employees to become first-level supervisors, middle-level managers, or executives. For many employees who prefer nonmanagerial work, this relatively new development means they are no longer dead-ended in their preferred jobs.

Eligibility for upward job mobility is a minimum period of experience (seniority, time in rank) and some demonstration of competence and ability.

Patrol Generalists

Pay increases and job title above the basic rank of patrol officer are being made available to those who wish to remain in the patrol division. It has always been difficult to impress upon patrol officers how important patrol work really is. As recruits they were placed in the patrol division and have since witnessed the exit of many of their fellow patrol officers to special assignments or promotion. It is, therefore, easy to denigrate the work of the patrol division. However, police agencies are funded to provide public safety services, and the ability of any police agency to fulfill this function is primarily dependent upon the capabilities of its patrol officers.[4]

Most important in this route to upward mobility is retaining qualified patrol officers long enough for them to develop special skills from experiences on the beat. Once this has been done, qualified personnel can be motivated to become generalists by offers of pay increases and new job titles. Once embarked on the generalist route, it should not be too difficult to persuade these personnel to seek advancement along this path.

The first salary step of patrol generalists should be approximately equal to the top salary of a senior police officer, and the last step should be equivalent to the pay of a middle manager or a top-level specialist. Steps would be allocated over a five- to ten-year period in the same manner as annual salary increments from junior to senior police officer. Local agencies may use the title

[4] See George W. O'Connor and Charles G. Vanderbosch, *The Patrol Operation* (Washington, D.C.: International Association of Chiefs of Police, 1967).

of "patrol generalist" or "patrol agent" to indicate an advance beyond the basic rank of patrol officer.

To motivate officers who enjoy working in patrol to remain and become qualified for other step salary increases, the attainment of the first step should be relatively easy. This could be a simple and eminently fair combination of seniority and satisfactory job performance. In actual observations of the generalist route, what appears to be developing is a screening out rather than an explicit selection process. In many agencies, generalists move steadily up the salary scale unless unsatisfactory work performance reports are filed by their supervisors and line commander. Even in this case, however, when work performance reports improve to satisfactory or higher levels the patrol officer is usually reinstated for salary increments. The whole issue of salary steps does present a bone of contention, however. Certainly the individual employee and an employee association would consider it unjust to drop an officer from whatever his or her salary was as a patrol generalist to the pay of a senior patrol officer. A far better plan would be to "toll" the salary level achieved pending satisfactory work performance reports.

In order to determine whether patrol generalists are earning these steadily increasing salary levels, it is not necessary to undertake overt testing and grading, but employees must understand that they will be asked to perform work of increasing responsibility, perhaps as training officers, or leaders (within the framework of team policing). Obviously, supervisors and line commanders will now evaluate these officers on the performance of their new duties as generalists.

***Advancement
of Specialists***
Advancement along the specialist route has traditionally meant transfer of patrol officers to detective duty in a Criminal Investigation Division. The initial transfer is usually an appointment to detective third-grade, with later advancements being to detective second- and first-grade. The salary steps are usually related to the pay of first-level supervisor and middle manager, for example,

1. Detective third-grade—salary less than that of sergeant but more than that of patrol officer
2. Detective second-grade—salary commensurate to that of sergeant
3. Detective first-grade—salary equal to salary of lieutenant

Upward job mobility along the specialist route has been extended to other police operational areas such as "juvenile specialist," "traffic specialist," and "technical specialist." Of course, these areas must be able to employ a significant number of employees before an advancement program similar to that for detective, with commensurate increases in salary and status, can be approved. Appropriate steps would be the same three grades as previously listed for detectives, with the same salary differential. However, to avoid any unintentional downgrading of the work of criminal investigation, this group of specialists should receive the title of "technician."

Just as patrol generalists receiving a salary above that of senior patrol officer are expected to serve as training officers or patrol team leaders, so specialists who receive the title of detective or technician are expected to perform work of increasing responsibility and complexity.

Selecting candidates for promotion to specialist may involve job-related tests and other job-related criteria, including written tests, oral interviews and an assessment of past job performance, participation in employee development programs, and demonstrated initiative in self-development.[5] Again, the honesty and integrity of the advancement process must be evident and easily defended against any claim of unfairness.

Job tenure in specialist positions continues to be a moot issue. Employees usually seek tenure for these positions, but police management has struggled for years to avoid "locking in" employees to positions such as detectives. The belief of police managers generally is that line commanders should hold the authority to terminate these assignments when they believe an employee is not "producing." Since the ultimate responsibility for the effectiveness of a line unit is the line commander's, this is a reasonable demand.

Promotion: Supervisor, Manager, Executive

The managerial career path in a police agency follows the same sequence as the agency's chain of command: (1) Supervisor, lowest level; (2) Mid-level manager; and, (3) Executive, highest level.

The term *supervisor* refers to the initial step along the managerial route, a position best described as overseer of police rank-and-file employees. *Mid-level management* positions are intermediary between the job of first-level supervisor and that of executive. The *executive-level* position may be equated with the role of administrator and is exemplified by such jobs as commanding officer of large groups of personnel or staff assistant to the top executive, the chief of police.

Selection for promotion is a more formal process than either of the other routes to advancement. Job-related written and/or oral tests determine the qualified candidates, and these must be administered scrupulously. No employee in the police agency should have any grounds for suspicion that one candidate is favored above others in any segment of the selection process.

Since tenure is an attribute of virtually all managerial positions, a short probationary period is not unusual. A six-month to one-year period of probation allows line commanders the opportunity to evaluate a newly promoted employee, and to take corrective action against unsatisfactory employees.

[5] National Advisory Commission, *Report on Police*, p. 433.

Promotion and the Assessment Center

An assessment center is a set of techniques for describing and measuring characteristics of applicants for various administrative positions. Assessment center procedures provide opportunities to observe the behavior of candidates in a wide variety of simulated work activities.

In assessment center processing, the assessors are examiners who have been specially selected and trained to evaluate job applicants for management positions. The ratio of assessors to candidates should not exceed 1:2 so that the techniques can be properly implemented.[6] The process itself is innovative in that the overall written and oral interview tests have been integrated into a single appraisal, which includes

1. An in-basket exercise and interview
2. Oral presentation and group discussion
3. Fact-finding "command" situation and interview
4. Decision making in an emergency situation and interview

The primary objective of the assessment center technique is to identify strengths and weaknesses of applicants and their potential for high-level managerial jobs.

The in-basket exercise presents job applicants with a set of memorandums and other reports similar to those they would confront daily in the position desired. Applicants are given an hour or more to familiarize themselves with the in-basket material and to write out a summary of their decisions for dealing with each of the issues. After assessors have time to examine these decisions, each applicant is interviewed to explore his or her reasoning, to determine whether the consequences of the various decisions were considered, and to get the applicant's reaction to alternative decisions.

The purpose of the oral presentation and interview is to evaluate the applicant's ability to communicate orally and to interrelate to others in a group (leadership, sensitivity, adaptability). A small group of applicants is assembled and each is asked to comment orally on how best to handle a stated problem with a common theme, for example, training or discipline. After the applicants have made their presentations, the group attempts to reach some agreement on concepts and the use of resources. Then assessors rate each applicant on their ability to get their point of view across, while being forceful yet not overbearing.

The fact-finding session calls for applicants to deal with a personnel problem requiring both investigation and action. Assessors meet with applicants and review what pertinent facts should be gathered and the range of dispositions possible.

---

[6] George P. Tielsch and Paul M. Whisenand, *The Assessment Center Approach in the Selection of Police Personnel* (Santa Cruz, Calif.: Davis Publishing Co., Inc., 1977), pp. 27–28.

The emergency session follows a similar format, with applicants being asked to make several on-the-spot decisions on a hypothetical emergency situation. Applicants are subsequently interviewed to determine their ability at both problem analysis and decision making.

After all applicants have completed the testing, the assessors meet and review the observed strengths and weaknesses of each applicant. Ratings on individual exercises and interviews and from one assessor to the next are averaged to obtain a final grade.

An assessment center evaluation is costly. It usually spans serveral days and involves as assessors a number of executives, line commanders and personnel technicians. However, since consequences of selecting the wrong employee for a top management position are tantamount to jeopardizing the police agency's operational effectiveness, the cost may well be warranted.

Despite the high cost of an assessment center, it is inadvisable to extend the life of an eligible list. The importance of the jobs and the need to fill them with qualified individuals suggests scheduling an assessment center approximately every two years, or sooner if unexpected vacancies crop up.

Civilian Employees

Upward job mobility for the civilian (nonsworn) employees of a police agency should be patterned on the foregoing program for sworn personnel. Of course, civilian specialists may be hired at the basic salary or at any of the higher levels (grades three, two, and one). Lateral entry presents no problems in civilian hiring.

Local agencies can decide whether they want to fill civilian supervisory and management positions by in-house promotions or by open hiring from outside the police agency—perhaps a combination of both methods. Personnel managers should keep in mind that it is as important to civilian employees as it is to sworn personnel that they have the freedom to develop their skills and talents to the fullest.

The "Fast Track" Program

An upward job mobility route favored by many large corporations is best described as a "fast track" route to top maagement positions. It identifies early in their career development those who will one day occupy key executive positions in the organization. These individuals are the outstanding achievers with a consistent history of exceptional accomplishment. They have an excellent academic record, demonstrated leadership ability, revealed flexibility in problem-solving actions, express themselves well, and exhibit a sustained and enthusiastic interest in their chosen field. During their first twelve to eighteen months of employment these individuals are identified as trainees. A contract usually assures these fast-track candidates that they will either be promoted to a management position or be released.

The usual prelude to fast-track programs is a special recruiting program focused on college and university campuses. Personnel technicians sent to conduct these interviews should seek out the top campus achievers, both in terms of grades and activities. If the recruits are the type of individual sought, they should view the success/fail job offer as a challenge and be willing to accept such terms—assuming they can view the police agency as having the integrity of the large corporations also utilizing a fast track program. A fast-track program has little chance of immediate adoption by police administrators, but personnel managers should keep in mind the proven advantages of this approach as demonstrated by large corporations, namely, that it is an excellent device to supplement in-house promotion to high-level management positions. In addition, the mixture of up-the-ranks executives with promising young "junior executives" should be mutually beneficial in developing agency leaderships highlighted by both stability and risk-taking.

One deterrent may well be the attitude of rank-and-file employees who will likely find any such trainee program repugnant to their closed career concept for staffing managerial jobs.

Chapter Review

Summary   Employee development programs are concerned with the job mobility needs of employees and employers. The concept of vertical mobility offers some degree of protection against dead-end jobs, but lateral entry and open testing of qualified applicants are more powerful tools in enriching an employer's human resources. A sampling of activities designed to promote career development includes paid leave to attend classroom training sessions or to participate in a special assignment pertinent to present or future job assignments. Another possibility is a leave of absence with pay to undertake job-related study in a college or university. Job rotation within an agency to enlarge an employee's perspectives on work and responsibility also comes within this category.

The two traditional routes to upward mobility—managerial and specialist—are now supplemented by a new route, patrol generalist. Advancement to generalist and specialist is based on job-related criteria for qualification and job-related tests for selection, but retention in these jobs usually demands continuing above-average performance. Promotion to supervisory and managerial positions is a more formal process, with tenure after a short probationary period. Assessment centers are a new procedure for evaluating candidates for promotion.

A "trainee" program to hire and rapidly advance those individuals who demonstrate exceptional merit has good potential but is in conflict with the concept of vertical mobility.

Critique   Staffing jobs above the entry level position in police agencies should no longer be confined within the straitjacket of vertical job mobility. Lateral transfers to specialist and generalist positions should be facilitated, and individuals of demonstrated competence as supervisors and managers should be hired. At the least, serious consideration should be given to opening up advancement and promotion opportunities to all qualified applicants, in and out of the employing agency.

Questions for Discussion and Review
1. Outline the scope of employee development activities.
2. What is the concept of vertical mobility? Why is it common in police agencies?
3. How does the advancement of specialists and generalists differ from promotion to supervisory and managerial positions?
4. What are the essential elements of assessment centers?
5. What are the advantages and disadvantages of "fast track" programs?
6. What circumstances are likely to aid a police personnel manager in convincing current employees of the need for open testing for positions above the entry level?
7. Are open testing and employee development programs mutually exclusive? Why or why not?

Workbook Project   List the advantages and disadvantaes of (1) open testing for positions above police officer and (2) vertical job mobility.

9

Professional Development

Chapter Objectives

- to examine all elements of employee education
- to discuss employee self-improvement programs and the concept of professional certification on the basis of training, experience, and academic achievements

When a police officer's academic goals are linked to job experience and in-service training, the result is almost certain to be professional growth.[1] Education is self-improvement. By this is meant that study and course work should complement work experience and in-service training. Such a productive use of leisure time contributes to the total growth of the individual.

To take advantage of educational opportunities, police personnel must not only make a decision to sacrifice a good portion of their leisure hours, they must also be willing to shoulder the costs of tuition, books, travel, and meals taken away from home. Reimbursement for educational expenses is possible in some jurisdictions, but it rarely equals out-of-pocket costs.

Employees with extensive educational backgrounds prior to entry level hiring are expected to take advanced study in a job-related area. These individuals and others who seek educational goals on their time off duty are usually individuals intent on qualifying for advancement and promotion. While the burden of proof as to whether education has upgraded an employee's level of skills-knowledge-ability is on the employee, personnel managers always consider the apparent impact of education upon employees.

Higher Education for Police

In the developmental years of criminal justice education, the two-year community colleges were strongly oriented to the perceived career needs of local police agencies. In fact, police agencies

[1] Graham W. Watt, "Professional Development Planning," *Public Management*, 58, No. 10 (October 1976), 15–18.

were commonly first in seeking the help of community college officials—as opposed to representatives of the corrections and courts areas of criminal justice. Agency support of the proposed education program was generally strong, target populations in the community college's service area were more than adequate, and police agency retirees and part-time instructors were available to inaugurate the new program. In 1968, the growth and direction of these law enforcement programs in community colleges were influenced by the publication of a suggested two-year curriculum: *Guidelines for Law Enforcement Education Programs in Community and Junior Colleges* (American Association of Community and Junior Colleges). These guidelines resulted from a series of regional seminars among leaders of police agencies and community colleges; the suggested curriculum was adopted by numerous institutions and is now recognized as a typical curriculum in the law enforcement area of criminal justice. In recent years, the instructional emphasis has changed to a "system" orientation (police, courts, corrections), and more courses have been added dealing with the behavioral approaches to criminal and delinquent behavior.[2]

In recent years, two developments have been supportive of this change: the increase in entrance and promotion standards throughout criminal justice agencies, and the staffing of community college programs with full-time qualified faculty. Associate degree (A.A.) programs now provide a theoretical orientation to the entire criminal justice system within a general liberal arts format focusing on the social sciences.

Four-year colleges or universities that offer a criminal justice program leading to a baccalaureate degree begin with a two-year program of sixty semester units similar to that offered in a community college. When these "lower division" studies are completed, the students go on to the final two years of "upper division" courses. Because the program is easily divisible into these two units, graduates of community colleges can pick up their studies at the junior-year level and eventually receive a baccalaureate (B.A.) degree.

There has long been a generalized concept in higher education that courses concerned with the administration of justice must be linked with the principles and ideal of democratic government and some understanding of social science in action. A liberal arts education is best suited to developing the kind of critical thinking that is required by decision makers at all levels of the criminal justice system.[3] The area of study concentration is criminal justice, but the various social sciences intersect this focal area to indicate a significant overlap of conceptual relationships (see Figure 9-1).

[2] James D. Stinchcomb, "The Two-Year Community College: An Assessment of Its Involvement in Law Enforcement from 1966 through 1976—With Future Projections," *The Police Chief*, August 1976, pp. 16–21.

[3] Larry T. Hoover, *Police Educational Characteristics and Curricula* (Washington, D.C.: U.S. Department of Justice, Law Enforcement Assistance Administration, 1975), pp. 34–39.

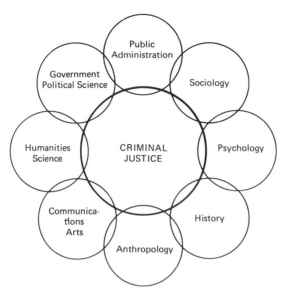

Figure 9-1
**Conceptual Relationship between Study Concentration in
Criminal Justice and Peripheral Areas of Liberal Arts and
Social Science**

In the past, such practical considerations as travel time virtually ruled out
for many police employees the possibility of obtaining a college degree. But
two developments have opened up educational opportunities in recent years:
An expanding number of community colleges has made the two-year program
highly accessible; second, "extended" campus or "external degree" programs
have brought the four-year college or university to many smaller cities. In
addition, the "cluster group" concept, as exemplified by Nova University in
Ft. Lauderdale, Florida, is bringing doctoral study opportunities to many
areas of the United States in which public employees have had difficulty
finding a welcome at nearby campuses.

Police employees starting out on a course of professional development
receive a broad liberal arts base with a generous sprinkling of professional
education.[4] Having completed their B.A. degree, graduate students can opt
either to continue in the major area of study or to specialize in one of the
peripheral areas. For example, a baccalaureate degree in criminal justice can
be developed into a master's degree, and doctoral study might then proceed in
public administration or political science. Adequate undergraduate preparation also permits students to move into the traditional social science areas of
psychology and sociology, or into the related area of business administration.

[4] Lawrence W. Sherman and Warren Bemis, "Higher Education for Police Officers: The Central
Issue," *The Police Chief*, 44, No. 8 (August 1977), 32–34.

In addition, many law schools now recognize criminal justice undergraduate degree programs as a prelaw field of study.

The overall impact of graduate education on the field of criminal justice can be gleaned from the following excerpt from one university's plans for its School of Criminal Justice.

The School of Criminal Justice

The State Legislature in 1968 authorized and directed Rutgers, The State University of New Jersey, to establish a School of Criminal Justice. The act stated:

> The legislature finds there is a need in New Jersey for academic contributions to the administration of criminal justice through teaching, research and leadership, including the training of administrators and those requiring scientific background in this field, by study and searching inquiries into crime causation, juvenile delinquency, law enforcement procedure, criminal rehabilitation and judicial doctrine relating to the trial of criminal cases, which dictate establishment of a school of criminal justice.

Thus, in authorizing the school, emphasis was given by the legislature to needs in three areas: instruction, research, and leadership. Similarly, the planning committee for the school, in its report to the President of the university, recommended equally weighted essential objectives of research, teaching, promotion, and outreach. The committee reported these objectives as both urgent and appropriate for an educational insitution to address:

1. Research into all aspects of the criminal justice system, both to increase our knowledge in general and to provide data on which to base institutional change.
2. Qualified teachers/scholars of criminal justice studies to staff training and educational programs created throughout the state to focus on criminal justice.
3. A pool of highly educated personnel available for planning, policy determination, and administrative positions within the criminal justice system.
4. The engaging of students through both academic studies and outreach programs in the criminal justice system.
5. An upgrading, educationally and professionally, of practitioners now working within the criminal justice system.
6. Opportunities for improved training and education of entry-level personnel.

In addressing instructional needs, the committee emphasized the education of qualified teachers/scholars in this field, as well as the education of personnel for planning, policy determination, and management of criminal justice. The committee recommended that the instructional staff of the school should concentrate on graduate education for practitioners within the criminal justice system, or for other individuals interested in focusing on criminal justice concerns, with such instruction leading toward graduate degrees.

They emphasized the need for a broad perspective on the interactions of the elements comprising the criminal justice system and stressed an integrative approach in the improvement of the functioning of the criminal justice system.

Goals of the School

The aims of the instructional program should be considered within the context of the proposed mission for the school as a whole. Consistent with the legislative mandate and planning committee recommendations noted above, a problem-focused, interdisciplinary program of research, education, and public service has been established. The program is described as problem-focused since the school addresses issues confronting the entire criminal justice system, from the nature of delinquency and crime to society's varied responses to it, including the organization and operation of each of the component criminal justice agencies such as the police, the judiciary, and corrections.

The school is interdisciplinary in structure, since no traditional discipline covers the wide spectrum of expertise required. It is a major center for scholarly research on all aspects of delinquency, crime and criminal justice administration, adding to knowledge, providing a basis for the educational programs, and meeting its public service obligations in part by addressing the major need of all criminal justice agencies for improved procedures of evaluation and planning. Within this setting, the school provides graduate programs of instruction and research to prepare students for positions in research, in teaching, and in criminal justice system management, and policy-making.

Program Resources Center

The Program Resources Center is an integral aspect of the School of Criminal Justice, and as such it has a central role to play in regard to the less didactic activities of the faculty and students of the school. The center provides a coordinating and "brokerage" function through which certain skills of the faculty and student are made available to those in the community who need such resources.

The basic objective of the center is to provide assistance in program development to the criminal justice system—especially those relevant agencies, institutions, and programs in New Jersey, and to provide field experience for students of the Rutgers School of Criminal Justice.

Specific functions of the Program Resource Center include:

1. Consultation on all aspects of the design and conduct of research and evaluation, program planning and development, and manpower development.

2. Design and conduct of innovative programs, including training programs and program evaluations.[5]

At present, the recommended base line for entry to the position of police officer is two years of education (sixty semester units or an associate degree) at an accredited college or university. However, this requirement is expected to be raised to a four-year minimum (120 semester units or a B.A.) within the foreseeable future.[6] In order to attract and retain better qualified personnel, most agencies provide a wide variety of educational incentives.

Because police personnel often work in shifts, and because of periodic changes in these shifts, colleges and universities have tried to develop schedules to minimize such job versus school conflicts. Of course, these educational "convenience" incentives are not always successful, but the many "extended campus" or "external degree" programs do reduce the travel time involved by presenting classes at convenient locations other than a main campus.

Another incentive is a salary increment to reflect the attainment of specified levels of academic achievement. Educational incentive pay is unrelated to any other salary incentive and should amount to at least 2.5 percent of the employee's current salary for each thirty semester units (roughly one year of college work) completed in pursuance of a job-related degree program. Employing agencies justify such incentives on the ground that job-related education will lead to improvements in the delivery of police services.[7]

Other educational incentives are

1. Payment of tuition
2. Reimbursement for purchase of books and materials
3. Educational leave with pay (job-related courses)

In a survey of 1,576 municipal police agencies conducted in 1976, a total of 865, or 54.9 percent, reported salary incentives for off-duty educational achievements above the high school level, and in cities in which the population ranged from 50,000 to 99,999 the percentage rose to 66.5 percent.[8]

[5] Catalog for 1977–78, School of Criminal Justice (New Brunswick, N.J.: Rutgers, The State University of New Jersey, 1977), pp. 10–12.

[6] National Advisory Commission on Criminal Justice Standards and Goals, *Report on Police* (Washington, D.C.: U.S. Government Printing Office, 1973), p. 369.

[7] National Advisory Commission, *Report on Police*, p. 372.

[8] James R. Mandish and Laurie S. Frankel, "Personnel Practices in the Municipal Police Service: 1976," *Urban Data Service Reports*, Vol. 8, No. 12 (Washington, D.C.: International City Managers Association, December 1976), pp. 2–14.

Planning
Self-Development

The burden of planning any self-development program is on the individual employee. However, police personnel managers can recommend and identify certain academic development programs and learning experiences—for example, a focused reading program of material in professional journals.

The first step is for the individual to do a self-appraisal of his or her strengths and weaknesses. This assessment should be in writing so that the person can more accurately judge whether certain programs will further develop an identified strength or help eliminate a weakness. The second step is to set out specific career goals: What future jobs, roles, or tasks does the person envision? One should avoid being too narrowly realistic or even pessimistic by concluding, for example, that the position of police executive is out of reach. Examples of shorter range goals might be to achieve competence in forensic science (criminalistics) or in labor-management relations. The third step is to decide on a viable option and to act on the academic training and experience opportunities that will help realize it.

These opportunities should be scanned for their relationships to the two major areas of development:

1. Self-development—opportunities relevant to any present or future job in the police service
2. Career development—opportunities that relate to one or more specific jobs in a career growth pattern

Professional
Certification

Statewide police training commissions, whose function is presently confined to certifying recruits who have completed basic training, should be empowered to convey advanced certification to those who have completed various educational objectives or have participated in a program of self-development.

The base of higher levels of professional certification should be (1) in-service training, (2) college and university education, and (3) work experience. These might be combined, for instance, to yield an "intermediate" certificate that would require (1) a specific number of in-service training hours; (2) an associate degree in criminal justice or a related discipline; and (3) several years experience at the entry level or above. An "advanced" certificate would require twice as much in-service training and police experience, plus a baccalaureate degree in criminal justice or a related discipline.

The certification program should be flexible enough for candidates to substitute educational achievements for in-service training and work experience at either level.

This substitution of educational achievements can be justified on the basis that men and women willing to devote time to self-development programs should be rewarded accordingly.

Chapter Review

Summary Job-related educational experiences, combined with on-the-job training are an ideal way to improve an employee's work performance. Curriculum development in two-year and four-year colleges and universities now offers police employees a criminal justice degree program oriented to the liberal arts and social sciences. Educational incentives include convenient scheduling of classes at a nearby "extended campus"; reimbursement for the cost of tuition and books; educational leave with pay, and additional salary. A self-development program should assess an employee's strengths and weaknesses and be both remedial and goal oriented. Professional certification by a statewide training agency can offer credentials that signify levels of training, education, and experience well above the basic training level.

Critique Justification for academic achievements rests upon a generalization that college-level courses of study are necessary to excel in any occupational-professional career. There is a great need for valid and reliable research findings indicating the net worth of college education to the professional development of police employees, and how much of it and what areas of study are most likely to aid police employees attain a progressively successful career pattern.

Questions for Discussion and Review

1. What is the contribution of community colleges to criminal justice education?

2. What educational incentives encourage police employees to attend college-level courses?

3. Is self-development necessary for police employees? Explain.

4. Why are community colleges important to self-development? What is the value of "extended campus" programs?

5. What is the main thrust of the Rutgers program?

6. Who is responsible for planning a self-development program? What should be its foundation and goals?
7. What is meant by "picking up the options"?
8. How would "intermediate" and "advanced" certification contribute to professional development?

Workbook Project Examine the Rutgers program and develop a 500-word theme about its possible contributions to the professional development of police employees.

IV

INTERNAL
JUSTICE
ADMINISTRATION

Internal Justice   A fair and effective system for internal
Administration   justice administration consists of subsystems, as illustrated in Figure IV–1:
performance appraisal, discipline, and grievances.
    Police personnel managers are not involved in the actual operations of

Figure IV-1
Internal Justice Administration in Police Agencies

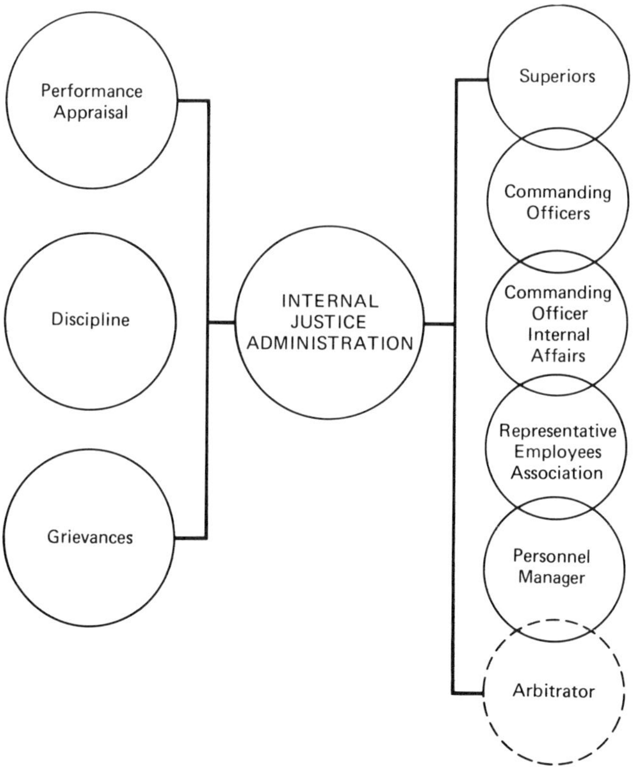

Performance Appraisal

Discipline

Grievances

INTERNAL JUSTICE ADMINISTRATION

Superiors

Commanding Officers

Commanding Officer Internal Affairs

Representative Employees Association

Personnel Manager

Arbitrator

these subsystems, which remain the responsibility of the following individuals:

1. Performance appraisal:	Line supervisors
	Line commanders
2. Discipline:	Line supervisors
	Line commanders
	Commander of Internal Affairs unit
3. Grievances:	Line supervisors
	Line commanders
	Representatives of the employees association

However, they do have a basic responsibility to see that each of these subsystems functions within the overall organization to ensure that all employees receive fair treatment in formal reviews of work or conduct and a fair hearing when they file grievances. In short, the personnel manager's role is not merely to react to malfunctions within the system, but rather to participate in planning and controlling operations to ensure the preservation of employees' basic rights within the employee-employer relationship.

Particularly in those actions alleging misconduct or in the presentation of grievances relating to working conditions, personnel policy must clearly delineate employees' rights. On the other hand, personnel managers must be apprised of the rights of management and of the public, and their expectations as to acceptable work performance and conduct.

Thus, although it may be easy to fall into the trap of thinking that he or she is the advocate of the employee, the personnel manager must hold fast to the primary role of intermediary. Police officers believe the burden of proof is on the supervisor making a performance appraisal, on the person making an allegation against them resulting in a disciplinary action, and on management in rectifying the situation that gives rise to a grievance. They may be correct in these beliefs, but personnel managers must seek ways to demonstrate how employees can act more responsibly toward their employers and the general public.

10 Performance Appraisal

Chapter Objectives

- to discuss the strengths and weaknesses of work performance appraisal by supervisors
- to examine supervisors as raters
- to develop the performance appraisal process as a communication of expectations from supervisor to worker

Performance appraisal is the evaluation of a worker's on-the-job performance of assigned duties by the direct supervisor. Performance appraisal reports are prepared periodically (quarterly, semi-annually, and annually), and become part of the worker's personnel record (file).

To achieve its stated objectives, a police agency must be able to depend upon satisfactory work performance from all its employees. Any employee whose work performance is substandard must be identified and so informed, and prompt remedial action taken. In order to perform the dual functions of identification and remediation, police agencies have instituted performance appraisal systems. Such systems facilitate communication of a supervisor's expectations to his or her work group and form a basis for corrective personnel action. Perhaps it may seem that the emphasis is on upgrading poorer workers, but performance appraisal rewards good workers by noting such effectiveness in personnel files.

Performance appraisal reports usually measure an employee's work performance on a broad scale such as one of the following:

1. Superior, satisfactory, weak
2. Outstanding, excellent, very good, good
3. Excellent, above average, average, needs improvement, unsatisfactory
4. Outstanding (absolutely no problem), very good (problems are rare), good (occasionally has a minor problem), average (often has minor problems), fair (occasionally has a serious problem)

In some agencies there may also be a rank ordering of employees by individual work group to reveal the effect of supervision style on work performance.

A core problem of performance evaluation has been the effects of alleged personal bias among raters. Unfortunately, there is no way to avoid the subjectivity a supervisor must use in making a judgment. Objective ratings such as counting arrests or the issuance of citations are inherently unfair, as all officers in a work group are not exposed to the same opportunities to make arrests or to serve citations. However, raters' performance can be upgraded, and overt favoritism can be prevented.

The role of personnel manager in performance appraisal is threefold: (1) to develop as foolproof a system as possible; (2) to assure all workers of fair treatment; and (3) to convince the majority of workers that the system opens up a mutually beneficial dialogue between worker and supervisor.

The Performance Appraisal System

Police personnel managers must work with line commanders and supervisors to set up and maintain a performance appraisal system that involves the worker in the evaluation process. To do less is an injustice to rank-and-file workers for poor performance appraisals can stunt a worker's career development, damage his or her self-image, and breed job dissatisfaction. Because even well-intentioned supervisors can be wrong, employees need a means of appealing supervisors' judgment without the need to institute formal grievance proceedings.

Among the characteristics of a performance evaluation system that encourages communication between workers and management are:

1. Communication of expectations
2. Evaluation based on job roles and tasks rather than on personal traits or characteristics
3. Report prepared by a supervisor who has had ample opportunity to observe the employee in a variety of on-the-job situations
4. Supervisors trained and monitored to enhance uniformity of ratings
5. Employee participation from self-measurement to appeal

The *communication of expectations* involves the establishment of work performance requirements, which are then relayed to the worker. In order to determine what would constitute adequate work performance, the supervisor may have to observe the worker's performance and then discuss with him or her the setting of equitable performance requirements. In some cases, adjustments may have to be made to the skills of individual workers. After this initial discussion, it is understood that work performance will be evaluated against these requirements.[1]

Performance appraisal based upon a job description that involves certain *assigned roles and tasks* makes the process more meaningful to evaluator and worker. Basically, supervisors can rate individuals on the performance of specific jobs instead of having to translate such behavior into a trait or characteristic dimension. For instance, in the traditional police area of quelling family quarrels (crisis intervention), a worker might be evaluated at unsatisfactory levels if he or she was known to escalate these disputes. On the other hand, an outstanding rating in this area would be given to a worker known to resolve these disturbances without assistance and to calm down both parties to prevent a recurrence of the quarrel.[2]

One of the complaints of patrol officers is that sergeants (direct, first-level supervisors) are not normally present to *observe on-the-job performance.* Usually, the officer answers the call, handles the situation, and makes a report; the sergeant's only knowledge of it is the officer's report and some possible monitoring of radio communications. As a result, officers are evaluated on report writing, not work performance at the scene of a crime or emergency. The basic validity of any evaluation is seriously threatened by supervisors who do not actually observe members of their work group in the performance of assigned tasks.

Performance appraisal through direct observation accords with the concept of appraisal by results, which is a diagnostic as well as an evaluative procedure. It begins with the supervisor's setting out certain objectives and communicating them to workers. Establishing objectives in an open manner permits supervisors to develop a dialogue with workers as to why the stated objectives were achieved or what prevented their fulfillment.[3] Figure 10–1 presents a graphic illustration of the performance appraisal process as dialogue.

Work performance appraisals are worthless unless periodic briefings by line commanders and the police personnel manager motivate supervisors to strive for reliability in measuring and reporting—that is, accuracy and consistency. Workshops designed to study the evaluative process in depth can help supervisors achieve more *accurate and consistent ratings.* In this exercise, a group of supervisors is given a printed description of a hypothetical worker's behavior under headings related to the agency's performance appraisal form. Each supervisor is then asked to rate this individual. When all participants

[1] Herbert J. Chruden and Arthur W. Sherman, Jr., *Personnel Management* (4th ed., Cincinnati, Ohio: South-Western Publishing Co., 1972), pp. 265–271.

[2] Sidney Epstein and Richard S. Laymon, *Guidelines for Police Personnel Appraisal, Promotion and Placement Procedures* (Washington, D.C.: U.S. Department of Justice, Law Enforcement Assistance Administration, 1973), pp. 6–8.

[3] See Fred Luthans, *Organizational Behavior* (2nd ed., New York: McGraw-Hill Book Company, 1977), pp. 488–489.

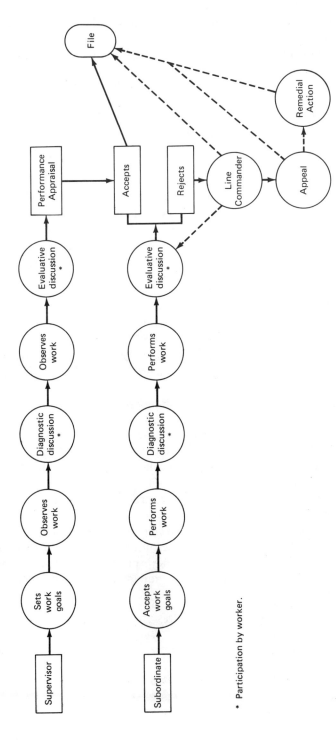

* Participation by worker.

Figure 10-1
Results-oriented Performance Appraisal Process

have completed their evaluations, the discussion leader can present ideas of a fair rating for each of the categories, and the supervisors can note how far their ratings deviated from this "norm" evaluation. In closing, the discussion leader will probably point out that any under- or over-rating should make supervisors seriously reflect on their evaluative standards.

To achieve more consistent evaluations among supervisors, personnel managers should schedule these workshops for small groups of supervisors a few weeks before the time performance appraisals are to be made. At each workshop the data on the hypothetical officer can be changed to cover new problem areas and to update the discussion.

The performance appraisal report is important to workers. Job satisfaction is usually linked to a worker's belief that he or she is doing a good job. When a performance appraisal challenges this belief, a worker usually reacts emotionally, not only because of the threat to self-image, but also because a negative appraisal jeopardizes salary upgrading, transfer requests, advancement as a specialist, promotion, and may possibly lead to termination.

For these reasons, the final item in our list of performance evaluation characteristics, *employee participation from self-measurement to appeal*, is not to be discounted. The first step in ensuring employee participation is to arrange for a meeting between supervisor and worker *before the report is finalized.* At the least, a worker should have an opportunity to present his or her own evaluation in rebuttal in the belief that this will have a serious effect on the final report. *Ex post facto* discussions may inform a worker of personal strengths and weaknesses and motivate him or her to do better work, but it does not allow for the necessary participation by the worker in the final product. On the other hand, a true dialogue between worker and supervisor can lead to a meeting of the minds, in which the supervisor understands the worker's disagreement and may even change a rating to give the employee benefit of doubt.

Second, when both participants feel the discussion is at an end, the employee should be asked to indicate agreement or disagreement with the evaluation by either signing the report or by noting his objections to it. Such disagreement should be an automatic and informal appeal to the line commander as reviewer. At this point, the disagreement is still resolvable through informal channels. Until the line commander has signed the report, there is still time for a review of the circumstances. It is usually profitable for the line commander to compare the involved supervisor's ratings with those of other superiors. This may indicate bias or inconsistent standards and be supportive of the worker's claim.

Last, when a worker is still convinced that the final evaluation is unjust, he or she must have an opportunity to appeal the performance appraisal. To avoid such appeals reaching the level of a formal grievance, a formal channel of appeal placing the performance appraisal before a nonpartisan committee (Board of Appeals) of workers from various ranks and units should be implemented. The worker challenging an adverse decision of such a board of appeals would still have the opportunity to file a grievance for an ultimate review of his or her challenge on its merits.

This procedure may appear unwieldy, but it safeguards employees from arbitrary and capricious action by a superior. Only by means of such safeguards can employers secure worker acceptance of the performance appraisal system as a personnel technique useful to both worker and management.

In a mass challenge to performance appraisals in the Mobile (Alabama) Police Department, the U.S. District Court in *Allen* v. *City of Mobile,* 331 F. Supp. 1134 (1971), suggested ratings by five persons as a means of ensuring truly objective performance evaluations prior to promotion ("potential promotability service rating"). This five-person rating might be useful when complaints of injustice reach a board of appeals. The five persons suggested by the court in *Allen* are the Chief of Police, the two most immediate current supervisors, and two others as requested by the worker from among the other supervisors he has had in the past.

Auditing Performance Appraisal

Auditing performance appraisals is difficult. The most that can be expected of such an audit is an indication that injustices exist in the system. The auditor should begin by seeking out instances of (1) extreme ratings and (2) contested appraisals.

A clustering of data at either end of the performance rating scale—that is, a disproportionate number of "unsatisfactory" or "outstanding" ratings—will indicate misuse of the performance rating scale. Supervisors are expected to have a certain number of workers who may be justly rated at these extremes. However, if the audit reveals supervisors are not using these extremes at all, or certain supervisors or units are making greater than average use of them, intervention by the personnel manager is warranted. The linking of extreme ratings to specific supervisors and units provides an early warning system for detecting problems in the performance appraisal system.

A performance rating scale can be converted to numerical grades and plotted to reveal a normal distribution (bell-shaped curve). Such a curve for 100 workers would show the following distribution:[4]

Performance Ratings Stated as Percentage	Number of Workers per 100 in Category
90–100	3
81–90	17
71–80	60
61–70	17
60 and less	3

Thus, if the auditor devises a normal distribution for each supervisory unit and compares the ideal figures with the actual distribution of ratings in

[4] Epstein and Laymon, *Guidelines,* pp. 22–23.

appraisal reports, supervisors can be helped to develop new and more realistic appraisal patterns.

Chapter Review

Summary

Supervision or the overseeing of work necessarily involves some sort of appraisal to communicate a supervisor's objectives for work performance. The process of performance appraisal must be fair to employees. For this reason, line commanders must make every effort to upgrade the rating ability of supervisors, using such techniques as rating workshops to help them avoid over- or under-rating errors. Workers should have an opportunity to discuss proposed ratings with their supervisor. Any disagreement is first referred to the line commander, who should duly note any major difference between current and past appraisals (particularly when made by different supervisors). However, even if a line commander corroborates an adverse rating, workers can appeal the decision. Another check on the performance appraisal system is the audit, which can alert commanders to possible injustices within a unit.

Critique

Performance appraisal is bound to result in dissatisfaction among some workers. Even well-intentioned supervisors are subliminally influenced by subjective factors such as race, appearance, and friendship. In instances such as these, discussions between supervisor and worker often become confrontations and contested appraisals may end up as vendettas between advocates of a "wronged" employee and a supervisor. As a result, the good will vital to the subordinate-supervisor relationship is ruined.

Questions for Discussion and Review

1. What is the role of the personnel manager in performance appraisal?
2. Outline the elements in a performance appraisal system likely to appeal to employees.
3. What is the format of a workshop in which the performance of a hypothetical worker is discussed by an assembly of supervisors? Why is this helpful to raters?
4. Why should supervisors discuss evaluation reports with employees before finalizing them?
5. Can performance appraisal reports be audited to detect injustices? How?

Workbook Project   Interview several members of the local or state police agency on performance appraisal practices and list whatever dissatisfactions they express.

11 Discipline

Chapter Objectives

- to review the role of discipline as the last, best chance of correcting employee misbehavior
- to describe the rights of police officers when confronted with possible disciplinary action
- to discuss what an equitable disciplinary process entails—from fair notice to the concept of substantial evidence and appropriate penalties

Discipline is an administrative process of organizations by which employers attempt to control employees' conduct in accordance with a set of written standards. We have already looked at some aspects of training and have seen that the encouragement of supervisors is a positive, or affirmative, method of controlling employee behavior. On the other hand, *discipline*, as generally used in police work, has a negative connotation; that is, disciplinary actions usually result in some punishment, from admonishment and warning to dismissal.

The rationale for instituting disciplinary procedures is that such action is a training technique of last resort, when other measures have failed to improve an employee's performance or to prevent misconduct. Of course, disciplinary action leading to dismissal of an employee foregoes any focus on training. On the one hand, it is an admission of failure of all other training efforts, but on the other, it acts as a deterrent or warning to other employees, especially when there is substantial evidence of wrongdoing. The impact depends upon the essential fairness of the dismissal.

The functions of a police personnel manager with respect to the disciplinary process of an internal justice system are threefold: (1) to develop a disciplinary action policy; (2) to cooperate with line supervisors, commanders, and the commanding officer of the internal affairs unit in its administration; and (3) to maintain the focus of discipline on the goal of improving employee performance.[1]

[1] Winston W. Crouch (ed.), *Local Government Personnel Administration* (Washington, D.C.: International City Management Association, 1976), p. 29.

Disciplinary Policy   In drafting and implementing disciplinary policy, management must seek to maintain an attitude of essential fairness toward all employees, toward the police agency itself, and above all toward the public. Rules of conduct for employees are a primary element of the basic policy as these rules communicate the employer's—and the public's—expectations as to employee conduct.

At the time of initial employment, each recruit should be issued a written statement of these rules. As amendments are made, employees should receive an addendum to be inserted into their booklets. Keeping employees up to date constitutes the "fair notice" provision of the police disciplinary code.

The National Advisory Commission on Criminal Justice Standards and Goals recommends that such written rules contain a general statement on what is traditionally known as "conduct unbecoming an officer"—in other words, conduct that would reflect unfavorably upon the employee or the agency.[2] However, many employee groups believe that such a generalized statement is purposely ambiguous. By not specifically prohibiting certain conduct, this segment of the traditional police code can be conveniently used in borderline cases to punish employees unjustly.

In *Bence* v. *Breier*, the Seventh Circuit of the U.S. Court of Appeals held that the Milwaukee (Wisconsin) Police Department rule proscribing "conduct unbecoming a member and detrimental to the service" was unconsitutionally vague.

The case had its origin in a letter sent by two police union officials of the Milwaukee Professional Policeman's Protective Association (MPPPA) to the city's chief labor negotiator alleging an abridgment of benefits under the current contract between the City of Milwaukee and the MPPPA (the recognized bargaining agent for all members of the Milwaukee Police Department of the rank of sergeant and below). The letter stated that some members of the MPPPA had been called back to duty on their day off because of a potential emergency, but had not been compensated at the contract rate of time and one-half. It asked the city's chief labor negotiator to investigate and direct payment be made to those police patrolmen and sergeants entitled to the additional pay. The two police union officials had copies of the letter posted on MPPPA bulletin boards in various precincts throughout the city.

Both police union officials, Bence and Hanneman, were subjects of an investigation as to the accuracy of the statements in the above-mentioned letter, and both were officially reprimanded as members of the Milwaukee Police Department for "conduct unbecoming an officer and detrimental to the service." They were advised that their reprimands would be made part of their personnel records, and were admonished for using poor judgment and for failing "to air grievances regarding conditions of employment" through departmental channels.

---

[2] National Advisory Commission on Criminal Justice Standards and Goals, *Report on Police* (Washington, D.C.: U.S. Government Printing Office, 1973), p. 474.

The two policemen sought legal redress in United States courts, and the case ended up in the U.S. Court of Appeals on the sole issue of whether the U.S. District Court correctly concluded that the phrase "conduct unbecoming an officer and detrimental to the service" is unconstitutionally vague.

In upholding the above conclusion of the lower court, the appeals tribunal noted:

> In determining whether the rule "conduct unbecoming a member and detrimental to the service" conforms with the constitutionally-mandated "rough idea of fairness," it is necessary to examine whether the rule creates a standard of conduct which is capable of objective interpretation by those policemen who must abide by it, by those Departmental officials who must enforce it, and by any administrative or judicial tribunal which might review any disciplinary proceeding. *Bence* v. *Breier,* 357 F.Supp. 231 (E.D. Wis. 1973). On its face, the rule proscribes only conduct which is both "unbecoming" and "detrimental to the service." It is obvious, however, that any apparent limitation on the prohibited conduct through the use of these qualifying terms is illusory, for "unbecoming" and "detrimental to the service" have no inherent, objective content from which ascertainable standards defining the proscribed conduct could be fashioned. Like beauty, their content exists only in the eye of the beholder. The subjectivity implicit in the language of the rule permits police officials to enforce the rule with unfettered discretion, and it is precisely this potential for arbitrary enforcement which is abhorrent to the Due Process Clause. Further, where, as here, a rule contains no ascertainable standards for enforcement, administrative and judicial review can be only a meaningless gesture. There is simply no benchmark against which the validity of the application of the rule in any particular disciplinary action can be tested. The language of the rule additionally offers no guidance to those conscientious members of the Department who seek to avoid the rule's proscription. Assuming that the Department (A) formulated the rule to apply to specific acts which it might constitutionally regulate, while (B) choosing not to regulate or to regulate in the remaining thirty prohibitions other acts which it might also constitutionally regulate, given the language of the rule, whether any particular act could be classified as (A) or (B) would be purely a matter of guesswork for policemen seeking to abide by the Department's rules.[3]

In the concluding paragraphs of this opinion the U.S. Court of Appeals questioned the essential fairness of reprimanding these two police officers for their conduct as officials of a recognized police employee group:

> Even if the rule at issue in this case were not unconstitutionally vague on its face, its application in these circumstances would be constitutionally impermissible. Bence and Hanneman, as officers of the policemen's collective bargaining unit, merely sent a letter to the city's labor negotiator outlining a proposed bargaining demand for the next round of negotiations, explaining the incident which provided the basis for the demand, and requesting that if

[3] Bence v. Breier, 501 F. 2d 1185 (1974).

the facts relative to the incident were found to be true, the appropriate compensatory measures be taken. To inform the MPPPA membership of action taken by their officers, copies of the letter were posted on various MPPPA bulletin boards. First, even if the rule respecting prior intradepartmental consultation on employment conditions could be constitutionally applied to Milwaukee policemen in general (an issue we need not reach), that rule could hardly be intended to stifle or filter communications between duly elected representatives of the officially recognized collective bargaining unit of the Milwaukee Police Department and the city's chief labor negotiator. Moreover, in permitting the erection of MPPPA bulletin boards at police stations and bureaus, the Milwaukee Police Department obviously realized that the boards would be used to display matters pertaining to conditions of employment and implicitly recognized that the dissemination of such matters through the use of the bulletin boards would not constitute unbecoming conduct.[4]

Investigative Responsibility

Internal affairs units have come into being in response to the need for independent investigation of serious charges of police misconduct made by superiors or civilians outside the agency. Before these units were initiated, such charges could be investigated by any agency personnel except the employee's direct supervisor or line commander. The investigation could be assigned to another supervisor of the same unit or to a commander of another unit. Allegations of "whitewashing" and "buddy-buddy" investigations led to a demand for review by a board of civilians, and this in turn led to the development of the internal affairs unit concept. These units are charged with the responsibility of conducting investigations of serious police misbehavior reported by any source, either within or outside the police agency, as well as the complaints made against police officers by civilians for police brutality, abuse of authority, and similar misbehavior.

The raison d'être of the internal affairs unit is to conduct investigations in such a manner as to bring all evidence to light while simultaneously preserving the dignity of everyone involved and maintaining the confidential nature of the investigation.[5]

Investigative responsibility for minor misbehavior related to work performance still remains the responsibility of the employee's direct supervisor and failing settlement, the appropriate line commander. Usually, cases of minor infringement of rules do not require any in-depth investigation, as the complainant and supervisor are one and the same person. However, in serious cases of misbehavior known to an officer's direct supervisor, that person has a responsibility to report the matter to those directly above him or her in the

[4] Bence v. Breier, 501 F. 2d 1185 (1974).

[5] National Advisory Commission, *Report on Police*, p. 483.

chain of command. Once the matter comes to the attention of the internal affairs unit, neither supervisor nor line commander must play the role of investigator.

Administering the Disciplinary Process

Administering the disciplinary process is part of the role of police personnel manager. Specific responsibility should be assigned to personnel working in this area.

The disciplinary process involves the following steps:

1. Receipt of complaint
2. Assignment of investigative responsibility
3. Notice to employee
4. Adjudication hearing
5. Verdict and disposition
6. Appeal

All *complaints* alleging police misconduct should be permanently recorded in a specially designated central file according to date of receipt. Civilian complaints may be recorded in a form different from those made by internal personnel, but each complaint recorded should contain subsequent notations of what has been done about it until and including final disposition.

Assignment of investigative responsibility depends upon the nature of the complaint and its source. Minor complaints made by direct supervisors are assumed to need no investigation, but line commanders routinely verify the facts to prevent internal conflicts from developing within the agency. Citizen complaints and charges of serious misconduct are assigned to an internal affairs unit or investigator.

Employees should be promptly *notified* of complaints unless the nature of the complaint warrants investigation prior to notice. However, notice should be given an employee in advance of any adjudicatory hearing. As in civilian proceedings, the accused police employee is entitled to sufficient time to prepare an adequate defense and—depending upon the seriousness of charges—legal representation and support in securing the attendance of witnesses.

Only sustained complaints are scheduled for an *adjudication hearing*. In the case of allegations involving criminal behavior, the local prosecutor is informed and asked to take independent and appropriate action.

The purpose of the adjudication hearing is to probe into the merits of the complaint. The defendant should have every opportunity to confront and cross-examine adverse witnesses and present evidence in his or her own behalf. As in civil proceedings, the burden of proof is on the complainant or the employer, as the case may be.

The direction and control of an adjudication hearing may be assigned to a single qualified person or to a board of three or more individuals. At least one member of such board should either represent the employee organization or be selected by the defendant. The finder(s) of fact shall examine all of the evidence presented at the hearing and base a *verdict* upon such evidence. If the verdict is that the defendant is responsible ("guilty"), the trier(s) of fact should set the penalty.

In the past, the trier(s) of fact in a disciplinary hearing recommended an appropriate penalty to the chief of police, and the chief decided on the penalty.[6] However, no matter how well-intentioned a chief executive of a police agency might be, he or she is unlikely to be as well-acquainted with the facts of the case as the trier(s) of fact.

The details of each hearing, along with the subsequent verdict and *disposition*, should be recorded; and in cases involving serious charges verbatim transcripts are warranted.

In the interest of fairness, it is desirable to treat all defendants found responsible of a specific breach of conduct equally. Penalties in case of major misconduct, or where aggravating factors are involved—such as a recent history of other sustained complaints—are usually more severe. On the other hand, mitigating factors are often taken into account; these include a previously blameless record, a lengthy period (three years or more) since prior sustained charges, and the fact that the action was obviously a mistake. (See Figure 11-1 for a diagram of the uniformity of penalties concept.)

Figure 11-1
Uniformity of Disciplinary Penalties

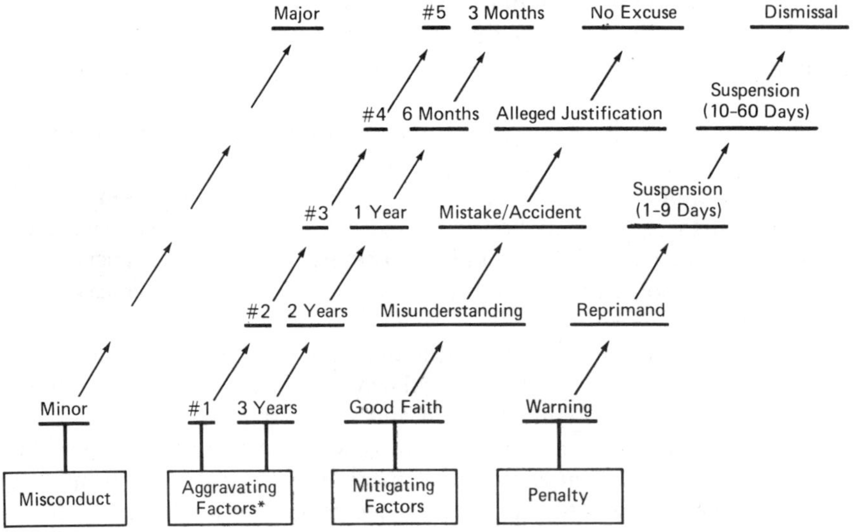

Frequency of charges;
time since last adverse
action

[6] National Advisory Commission, *Report on Police*, p. 487.

In recent years the trend has been toward less severe penalties. Concomitant with this, has been the move toward securing the defendant's agreement to a penalty prior to imposition.

Appeals should be available to defendants who believe the hearing was unfair, the verdict was not based on the evidence produced, or the penalty unjustified. Appeals should be reviewed by individuals not involved in the adjudication hearing and should be considered on their own merits.

Audit of
Disciplinary Actions

An audit of disciplinary actions in a police agency need not contain the names of officers involved, but data should be collected monthly under the following headings:

1. Date
2. Charges
3. Disposition
   a. unsubstantiated or substantiated
   b. penalty
   c. date

Periodic analysis of collected data will provide the police personnel manager with information as to the nature and trends of police misconduct, charges dropped and charges brought to formal action stages, and the various penalties assessed. On the basis of such facts, personnel managers can develop a basis for improving the personnel practice known generally as "discipline."

Rights of
Police Officers

The rights of police officers under investigation have been expanded. Court decisions in recent years have had a nationwide impact; legislation in several states has established statewide provisions; and "police officers' bills of rights" have been included in collective bargaining agreements at city, county, or state levels.[7]

While the route of implementation may differ, the common core of these police officers' rights are

1. Notice of the nature of the investigation, and the name of complainant(s), if known
2. Time and place of interrogation and/or hearing
3. Right to have legal counsel present at interrogation and/or hearing
4. The recording of interrogation and/or hearing
5. Due process and other constitutional rights during interrogation and/or hearing

[7] See Chapter 16 for details of the "Police Officer's Bill of Rights" in the Tulsa (Oklahoma) contract.

6. Use of polygraph (lie detector)
7. Written notification of determination and disposition, and reasons therefor

On occasion, police employees' constitutional rights as citizens come into conflict with their role as law enforcement officials—that is, representatives of a governmental agency. In the case of *Biehunik* v. *Felicetta,* 441 F. 2d 228 (1971), the U.S. Court of Appeals for the Second Circuit identified the area of conflict as "the substantial public interest in ensuring the appearance and actuality of police integrity."

In *Biehunik* the following series of actions occurred: There was a riotous situation involving a sniper attack on police and ten to twenty-five police officers entered a building to search for and apprehend the sniper. The police chief later received civilian complaints charging that several police officers burst unannounced into occupied apartments of the building being searched, and without justification beat the occupants severely. Thereupon, the commissioner ordered an investigation, and when other attempts at identification of the accused officers failed, he ordered sixty-two policemen to report to the police academy in their usual duty dress for a lineup. The policemen promptly instituted a civil rights action, alleging the proposed lineup would deprive them of various constitutional rights, and in support of their contention, the U.S. District Court issued an *ex parte* temporary restraining order enjoining the lineup. After hearing evidence, the District Court issued a permanent injunctive order forbidding the lineup, which the police commissioner then appealed.

The Court of Appeals, however, rejected the police officers' argument that the compulsory lineup of sixty-two officers constituted a seizure of their persons, unsupported by an arrest warrant or probable cause to arrest. The injunctive order of the lower court was reversed. The concluding segments of the court's opinion in *Biehunik* (footnotes omitted) reveal the judicial balancing of public and individual interests:

> . . . We do not believe that the public must tolerate failure by responsible officials to seek out, identify, and appropriately discipline policemen responsible for brutal or unlawful behavior in the line of duty, merely because measures appropriate to those ends would be improper if they were directed solely toward the objective of criminal prosecution. A trustworthy police force is a precondition of minimal social stability in our imperfect society, a fact repeatedly dramatized by tragic incidents of violent conflict between police and some groups of civilians that continue to break out periodically in so many of our cities. Moreover, it is a correlative of the public's right to minimize the chance of police misconduct that policemen, who voluntarily accept the unique status of watchman of the social order, may not reasonably expect the same freedom from governmental restraints which are designed to ensure his fitness for office as from similar governmental actions not so designed. The policeman's employment relationship by its

nature implies that in certain aspects of his affairs, he does not have the full privacy and liberty from police officials that he would otherwise enjoy. So long as the actions of a policeman's superior remain within reasonable bounds, there can hardly be that affront to expectations of personal autonomy which marks the state's coercive power in the typical arrest case.

Thus that plaintiffs are not only citizens protected by the Constitution but also policemen is relevant in two respects. Their status both heightens the public interest served by the planned lineup and lessens the adverse impact of the investigation on the plaintiffs' legitimate interest in personal autonomy.

We should not, of course, be understood as suggesting that policemen will be required to tolerate invasions of their freedoms which are not reasonably related to the special considerations arising from their relationship of employment. Policemen do not abandon their constitutional rights upon induction into the department. The facts before us on this appeal, however, do not require that we precisely delineate the outer bounds of reasonableness in investigations of suspected police misconduct, for this is not a doubtful case.

The lineup was ordered by that official of the police department charged with running an efficient and law-abiding organization—the Police Commissioner—and was clearly and highly relevant to the legitimate end of assuring his employees' trustworthy performance of their assigned tasks. Commissioner Felicetta's reference in his order directing the lineup to a possible criminal prosecution did not dilute the potential usefulness of the lineup in administering disciplinary measures. We therefore need not consider at this time the propriety of enjoining a similar lineup conducted exclusively with criminal prosecution in mind. Finally, the lineup was to be conducted at a time and place that were well within the usual demands of a policeman's job.

Under these circumstances, to forbid defendants to proceed with the lineup would unduly hamper police officials in their difficult task of supervising and maintaining a dependable and trusted police force, with little compensating gain to plaintiffs' individual rights.[8]

Chapter Review

Summary In police agencies, the term *discipline* has the negative connotation of punitive action of some sort, from verbal warnings to dismissal. Clearly written rules of employee conduct are the basis of any fair and equitable dis-

---

[8] Biehunik v. Felicetta, 441 F. 2d 228 (1971).

ciplinary policy, just as strict adherence to legal principles is necessary to preserve the essential fairness of any disciplinary action. Supervisors have original jurisdiction to investigate police misconduct, but the police internal affairs unit has an overriding responsibility to investigate any serious reports of police misconduct or complaints lodged by civilians. An audit of current disciplinary actions gives line commanders and police personnel managers data on the nature of police misconduct and leads to possible preventive action through amendment of training and/or supervisory procedures.

Rights of police officers under investigation for alleged misconduct have come under the scope of legal precedent, legislation, and collective bargaining. The courts have also recognized that police officials must be granted some latitude in supervising and maintaining a dependable and trustworthy police force.

Critique
Unless negative discipline is exercised only under a set of carefully stated rules and regulations, it can result in widespread employee dissatisfaction. Supervisors preferring charges are likely to incur the wrath of punished subordinates, who become embittered and hostile. Semi-military uniforms and rank names taken from the military tend to maintain the stereotypical image of "discipline" in police agencies. In organizations without these military overtones, on the other hand, negative discipline is the exception, and affirmative—or nonpunitive—action to correct misbehavior is the rule.

Questions for Discussion and Review

1. Why should a disciplinary policy have an essential fairness?
2. Why are clearly written rules necessary to the smooth functioning of a police unit?
3. What does "conduct unbecoming an officer" mean?
4. What is the direct supervisor's responsibility for appropriate and timely disciplinary action?
5. Why are civilian complaints of police misconduct specially investigated by internal affairs personnel?
6. Who investigates allegations of serious police misconduct?
7. Outline the core of a police officer's "Bill of Rights."
8. Is the decision in *Biehunik* in line with the concept of fairness to the concerned employee?

Workbook Project
List in order of importance what you believe should be the rights of police employees accused of serious misconduct.

12 Grievances

Chapter Objectives

- to define the term grievances
- to describe an essentially fair grievance system for the prompt handling of grievances
- to outline the role of personnel manager in this area of internal justice administration

---

A grievance is a complaint alleging an employee has been treated unjustly by another employee, usually a direct supervisor or line commander, or that an existing situation in the agency is working unjustly to the complaining employee's disadvantage. Misunderstandings, gaps in communications, disagreements, and real or imagined inequities or dissatisfactions are the usual origin of grievances.

Many grievances are interpersonal in nature, but others arise from contractual disputes that pit the police agency (city, county, or state) employer against the police employees' group. Contract-related grievances are generally related to interpretation or implementation of contract provisions, often with respect to working conditions.[1]

Police personnel managers have a responsibility to administer the agency's grievance system as a subsystem of its internal justice system. This responsibility extends to

1. Assisting in developing a grievance system
2. Aiding line commanders in reducing grievances
3. Conducting periodic audits of grievances and developing among line commanders a better understanding of causes involved in past grievances

In a survey of police agencies throughout the country, 94 percent of the 461 responding agencies stated they had formal grievance procedures in use

[1] Charles W. Maddox, *Collective Bargaining in Law Enforcement* (Springfield, Ill.: Charles C Thomas, 1975), p. 106.

157

for sworn employees. In 99 percent of these agencies, the procedure called for a hearing, and in 89 percent (410 agencies) the complaining employee had a right to a "representative" at the hearing.[2]

The Grievances System

A grievance system should seek to settle disputes as *fairly* and *expeditiously* as possible.

The first stages of a grievance proceeding registers the employee's complaint with his or her direct supervisor. If the dispute is not resolved at this level, it comes to the attention of the commanding officer and finally the police chief. When workers are unionized, the labor-management contract invariably spells out the stages of the grievance procedure and usually calls for the services of an outside mediator or arbitrator to intervene in unsettled disputes (see Figure 12–1).

Figure 12-1
A Four-stage Grievance System with Binding Arbitration as the Last Resort

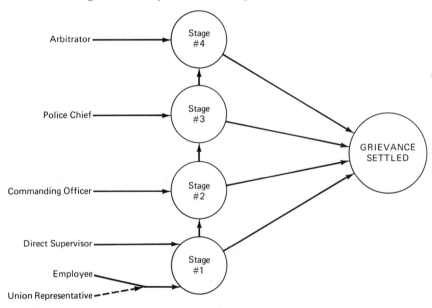

Direct supervisors usually try to settle oral complaints before they become formal grievances. However, when the supervisor cannot settle the grievance to the employee's satisfaction, the employee is instructed to present a written grievance to the supervisor. In a union setting the employee may first contact the union representative in his or her work group; then the employee

[2] Terry Eisenberg, Deborah Ann Kent, and Charles R. Wall, *Police Personnel Practices in State and Local Government* (Washington, D.C.: Police Foundation, 1972), pp. 30–31.

or the union representative, or both, present the grievance orally to the employee's supervisor.

The next stage is presentation of the written grievance to the line commander. In some large police agencies, the line commander may have established a "shop committee" patterned after private industry, in which a group of three to five fellow employees reviews the grievance and makes a recommendation as to appropriate action to the line commander.

If the grievance is not settled to the worker's satisfaction at this level, the employee can again appeal the decision—this time to the top executive level, the chief of police. As at the lower level, the chief may seek the help of a shop committee.

In both nonunion and union settings, the next stage would be to submit the grievance to an impartial third party. Prior agreement by both parties to this action is one of the primary elements of a grievance system that ensures its essential fairness.

A few line commanders and police chiefs establish an open-door policy that encourages employees to bring their complaints directly to them for discussion and possible settlement. However, this bypassing of line commanders and/or supervisors weakens the authority of lower-level supervisors and managers, blocks their sources of information, and destroys their morale.[3]

At each stage of the grievance procedure a reasonable time limit is established. Ten to thirty days is a common limit at each level. Of course, the tighter the time limit, the greater the likelihood of expeditious processing.

Sometimes a grievance is filed because an employee believes he or she has been unfairly disciplined. In such cases the grievance is based upon the employee's assertion that "just cause" for the disciplinary action did not exist. In a union setting this claim of unjust disciplinary action may be developed under the terms of the contract and may offer the employee a better opportunity for essential fairness than a civil service appeal. This is particularly true when an employee is working under the provisions of a contract calling for arbitration at the last stage of the grievance system.

In 1977 Florida's state legislature enacted legislation that mandates the drafting of grievance procedures by public employers and employee groups. It is part of an act relating to collective bargaining for public employees.

Grievance Procedures   Each public employer and bargaining agent shall negotiate a grievance procedure to be used for the settlement of disputes between employer and employee, or group of employees, involving the interpretation or application of a collective bargaining agreement. Such grievance procedure shall have as its terminal step a final and binding disposition by an impartial

---

[3] Paul Pigors and Charles E. Myers, *Personnel Administration: A Point of View and a Method,* 8th ed. (New York: McGraw-Hill Book Company, 1977), pp. 218-220.

neutral, mutually selected by the parties. However, an arbiter or other neutral shall not have the power to add to, subtract from, modify, or alter the terms of a collective bargaining agreement. If an employee organization is certified as the bargaining agent of a unit, the grievance procedure then in existence may be the subject of collective bargaining, and any agreement which is reached shall supersede the previously existing procedure. All public employees shall have the right to a fair and equitable grievance procedure, administered without regard to membership or nonmembership in any organization, except that certified employee organizations shall not be required to process grievances for employees who are not members of the organization. A career service employee shall have the option of utilizing the civil service appeal procedure or a grievance procedure established under this section, but such employee cannot use both a civil service appeal and a grievance procedure.[4]

So-called voluntary or advisory arbitration is worthless to employees as failure to agree merely returns decision-making power to the chief of police. By contrast, the Florida statute calls for binding arbitration within the legal terms of the contract; that is, it does not allow the neutral person selected as arbiter to modify the contract in any way.

Reducing Grievances   Supervisors have a basic responsibility to help subordinates articulate their grievances. Employees are sometimes resentful about relatively minor job-related issues but fail to communicate this resentment to the proper person. Unless a supervisor can get the employee to speak out promptly, the employee's work may be adversely affected and the minor unhappiness grow into a full-fledged grievance.

Supervisors have a collateral responsibility to take a problem-solving approach to the task of settling any grievance. It is at this level of management that grievances can be settled informally with no more than an entry in the supervisor's records.

The supervisor's first job is to aid the employee in identifying the issue involved, then to ascertain what the employee considers to be a fair settlement of the issue. When it is within the supervisor's means to resolve the problem at this level, he or she must decide on appropriate action and take it. No executive expects a supervisor to settle all grievances; on the other hand, supervisors are expected to shoulder their responsibilities, not just to refer complaints to the next higher level for settlement.

Police personnel managers can work with line commanders to develop supervisors' skills at settling complaints before they reach the stage of formal written grievances. Personnel managers can also foster an attitude of responsibility among line managers for settling disputes at their level and thus reducing the costliness of grievance proceedings.

[4] Florida Statutes, Section 447.401.

Ideally, from a personnel viewpoint, only grievances related to agency policy should reach the third or fourth stage of the grievance system. If all participants adhere to the concept of essential fairness, the complaining employee is not likely to appeal a reasonable decision.

Auditing of Grievances

The purpose of auditing a grievance system is to develop feedback that is likely to pinpoint problems affecting employees, management, or various units of the agency. Continuous auditing of grievances will, of course, provide no automatic solutions, but it will indicate areas in which corrective action is necessary.

In an audit of grievances only the formal, written grievances are evaluated. Complaints resolved at the first stage of the grievance system are unlikely to indicate real problem areas. Data should be collected under the following headings:

1. Date grievance filed
2. Nature of grievance (categorization)
3. Settlement
4. Stage and date of disposition

Taken together, items 1 and 4 will reveal whether the grievance system is functioning expeditiously and whether supervisors and line commanders are reducing the upward progress of grievances by achieving settlement at lower levels.

Data that categorize grievances should help the auditor identify recurring patterns of grievances that may implicate a particular supervisor or a unit of the agency, or a specific working condition involving an agency rule, standard, procedure, or policy.

A study of the nature of employee complaints will immediately reveal several major categories of complaints, for example "very frequent," and "quite frequent" and so on, to typological categories such as,

1. Things—complaints about equipment, supplies, and so on
2. Working conditions—subjective reactions to work setting
3. Fears—dissatisfactions linked to threats to job security, health and safety, and so on[5]

Data on settlements will indicate what was done to solve the problem and highlight possible corrective action if a pattern of grievances develops. Overall summaries and trends can indicate employer-employee relations over a time period, and give valuable feedback as to the efficacy of various corrective action strategies.

[5] Pigors and Myers, *Personnel Administration*, pp. 214–216.

Mass Grievances   A new development in police labor-management relations has been the filing of a grievance by two or more employees. When employee organizations exist and the complainants are members of the local association, they may seek union support.

Of course, a mass grievance need not become part of a police agency's grievance procedure. On occasion class action suits are filed on behalf of certain police officers who are seeking injunctive relief against alleged denial of specified rights. For example, in *Allen* v. *Mobile*, 331 F. Supp. 1134 (1971), a group of black police officers sought legal redress in a class-action claim that they were being denied equal protection of the laws. While many of their demands were rejected, the court's decision was a landmark in that it established many safeguards to protect black police officers against racial discrimination in the future.

Chapter Review

Summary   Grievances are work-related complaints presented by employees who feel that they have been unfairly treated or unjustly disadvantaged by an existing situation on the job. Police personnel managers are responsible for administering a grievance system, and are jointly responsible with line commanders and supervisors for reducing grievances as much as possible. An essentially fair four-stage grievance system calls for sequential attempts to settle grievances by the direct supervisor, the line officer next in command, and the police chief, prior to requesting the services of an arbitrator; it also sets maximum time limits for each stage of the process. The right of employees to a fair and equitable settlement of grievances is now recognized in law, and grievance proceedings are often the subject of agreement between legally recognized employee groups and public employers. An audit of the subject matter of contemporary grievances and the nature of settlements will identify all developing patterns and alert the personnel manager to problem areas requiring correction.

Mass grievances and class actions seeking legal remedies on behalf of a group of police employees indicate the existence of widespread dissatisfaction not amenable to normal grievance procedures.

Critique   Supervisors and managers contribute in no small measure to situations in which grievances originate, then they often stonewall any settlement favoring workers. Police personnel managers should be more responsive to employee reactions that may indicate unfair or prejudicial treatment—or unfavorable working conditions—and encourage management to change behavior contributing to the origin of grievances.

<table>
<tr><td>Questions for Discussion
and Review</td><td>1. Define a grievance.
2. What are the essential characteristics of a grievance system?</td></tr>
</table>

3. Do the stages of a grievance system in a police agency follow the chain of command? What is expected of various participants in the system?
4. What are "mass grievances"? What are their implications for personnel managers?
5. Can grievances be reduced? Audited? Explain.

<table>
<tr><td>Workbook Project</td><td>List the advantages and disadvantages of compulsory and binding arbitration</td></tr>
</table>

of unsettled grievances between employee groups and public employers.

V

EMPLOYEE SUPPORT AND RETENTION

When we speak about employee retention, we must begin with the recruitment process. If the employing agency
has selected its new officers from the best possible sources—including
minority persons, women, and college graduates—and has done so by means
of job-related and racially neutral tests, then it has taken the first step toward
retaining qualified and well-motivated employees.

The second step calls for the employer to develop programs for employee
growth and also to encourage self-development along professional lines. A
career development system to enhance all employees' skill and knowledge
levels is an excellent combatant against "dead-end" thinking. Of course,
employers must not only make workers aware of the possibilities for self-
development, they must also communicate a sense of concern for each individual's growth and well-being.

A job classification plan for upward job mobility on merit and with
salaries upgraded to match jobs of increasing dificulty and responsibility is the
third step in retaining employees. This step is oriented to holding employees
who are ambitious and have responded meaningfully to career development
opportunities.

Labor-management relations, either in a union or nonunion setting
constitutes a fourth factor in employee retention. Personnel managers serve a
vital function as mediators in securing adequate or better terms of
employment and working conditions for employees, and counterbalancing
these efforts, in reinforcing the employer's claim of fair and equal treatment
for all employees. Of course, both parties to a conflict may occasionally need
to be reminded of the greater good of the public whom they serve, and this
reminder should also be forthcoming from personnel. The four factors and
their mutual influence on employee retention are graphically illustrated in
Figure V–1.

The influence of the various factors working for or against employee
retention is reflected in the employee turnover rate. When this is high, it is indicative of failure in the retention process. As the final step in the retention
process, personnel managers should attempt to identify the reasons for

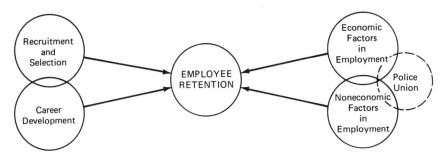

Figure V-1
Factors Influencing Employee Retention
Police unions contribute when employers fail to upgrade economic and
noneconomic factors in employment.

employee turnover. Because of the significant investment that each employee represents in terms of training and on-the-job experience, personnel managers will attempt to deter employees considering resigning and to terminate only those who fail to respond to all corrective measures.

13

Job Structure
and
Salary Planning

Chapter Objectives

- to develop the relationship between jobs and salaries
- to discuss the classification of jobs

Job structure depends primarily upon the size of an employing agency. Thus decisions on departmentation result from serious consideration of what jobs can be grouped within a reasonable span of control at the supervisory, managerial, and executive levels. This division of work by major groups identifies the basic organization and leads to a job classification plan.

Salary plans reflect changing economic conditions and local pay rates for public employees. A sound salary schedule should do all of the following: (1) set salaries at levels that will attract and retain satisfactory employees; (2) motivate employees to work for advancement and promotion; (3) reduce demands for nonbudgeted salary increases by employee groups; and (4) provide a limiting framework for the agency's largest single budget item—salaries.[1]

In a growing number of civil service systems, collective bargaining has put an end to management's unilaterally establishing salaries and benefits. Salary determination has now become a bilateral process between "management" and police rank-and-file with numerous built-in agreements on salary increases at each level and related fringe benefits.

Job evaluation establishes the relationships between jobs and salaries. It is a means of guiding management's decisions on how much one job should pay as opposed to another job.

A salary plan in public employment is not based on a salary-profits relationship as in the private sector. Entrepreneurs are limited in what they can

---

George Strauss and Leonard Sayles, *Personnel: The Human Problems of Management,* 3rd ed. (Englewood Cliffs, N.J.: Prentice-Hall, Inc., 1972), pp. 553-590.

pay workers by the terms of the profit equation. Police agencies' budgets are limited, on the other hand, by how much the city budget allows for their services. As has already been noted, salaries constitute the largest part of a police agency's budget. This is as it should be, for here, even more than in industry, securing and retaining above-average employees is a matter of prime concern. As a general maximum, then, salaries should be set at levels which will provide workers with a living standard equal to the social and occupational status of the work performed.

In terms of the practical limits on an individual's time, it is well-nigh impossible to reconcile serious efforts at professional self-development with working at a second job to gain a reasonable standard of living. This was the major bone of contention between former New York City police commissioner Stephen P. Kennedy and the city's chief executive. Up from the ranks, Kennedy used his leisure time for self-development, first completing high school, then college, and finally law school by the time he was promoted to captain. As commissioner, he battled for salaries that would allow police officers to stop "moonlighting" and spend some of their off-duty time in self-development. He considered it demeaning for police officers to spend their off-duty time driving trucks and working on the docks to supplement their salaries. Unable to convince the city government of the merit of these claims, he resigned.

Salary Plan

A salary plan is basically a listing of pay schedules that correlate with the various job performances listed in the employer's job classification plan. The National Advisory Committee on Criminal Justice Standards and Goals (NACCJSG) has set out a number of guidelines that not only provide a broad framework for determining police salaries but also suggest specific methods for arriving at various items of the salary plan:

1. *Entry-level salary* should be no less than the minimum set by the state based on: (a) required police qualifications, (b) state and local economic conditions, and (c) recommendations of representatives of local criminal justice agencies.
2. *Entry-level salary* should exceed statewide minimum when: (a) required police qualifications exceed state requirements, (b) economy of the jurisdiction is high, (c) limited local labor market, and (d) the specific police functions of the employing agency.
3. *Maximum salary* in the basic occupational classification (police officer) should be well above entrance-level salary in order to provide for significant salary advancement without promotion beyond the basic rank.
4. *Salary separation* between job classifications to provide advancement and promotion incentives and to retain career personnel.

5. *Police chief's salary* should be equivalent to the salaries of local judiciary and chief executives of other governmental agencies.

6. *Merit salary increases* should be established to reward demonstrated excellence in job performance.

7. *Police salary plan* to be separate and distinct from the salary structure of other local governmental agencies. (No longer linked to the salaries of fire personnel.)

8. *Annual salary review* should adjust police salaries to meet increases in the cost of living, the local prevailing wage pattern, competition from other employers, and other factors affecting take-home pay levels.[2]

A 1978 nationwide survey of the International City Managers Association scanned the salaries of police officers in 647 cities of over 10,000 population. The average salaries in 1972 and 1977, and the percentage increase between the two years, were reported as[3]

	1972	1977	Percent increase
Entrance salary	8,029	11,072	37.9
Maximum salary	9,477	13,484	42.3

Arbitration awards appear to set salary schedules well above the foregoing averages. In Boston, an arbitrator favored the Boston Police Patrolmen's Association demand for a pay raise of 7 percent, setting the 1978 salary for police officers at a base pay of $14,800. Another arbitral decision favored the demand of the Yonkers (New York) Police Benevolent Association for pay raises setting the following scale:

Entrance salary: $11,900
Salary after one year of employment: $15,900
Salary after three years of employment: $17,400

In police agencies, a salary plan is linked to ranks in the chain of command. Entry-level police officers receive the minimum base pay and can look forward to annual increases that will eventually raise their salaries to a maximum base pay level *at the patrol officer level*. Once the maximum base pay is achieved, a police officer must be advanced or promoted on merit to earn a higher salary. *Advancement* means assignment based on a required proficiency such as patrol generalist or specialist in one of the recognized areas; *promotion* is upward job mobility along the supervisory-managerial route.

[2] National Advisory Commission on Criminal Justice Standards and Goals, *Report on Police* (Washington, D.C.: U.S. Government Printing Office, 1973), pp. 354–355. Reprinted by permission.

[3] *Municipal Year Book: 1978* (Washington, D.C.: International City Managers Association, 1978), pp. 94–96.

The term *table of organization* is used to identify the distribution of rank in a police agency. Starting with the chief of police, the table identifies each lower rank by name and number of incumbents per rank.

Compliance with a table of organization ensures a salary plan in which no more than a specified number of employees are to be advanced or promoted to each rank. These limits simultaneously set the broad dimensions of a salary plan. Of course, an agency can save money in salaries by not filling vacancies as they occur, but this would jeopardize the concept of employee development and significantly lower employee morale.

Salaries for various jobs in police agencies are generally linked to the military ranks and chain of command that have been traditional in America's police establishment. These ranks and ascendence in the chain of command are

1. Patrol officer
2. Sergeant
3. Lieutenant
4. Captain
5. Inspector/commander
6. Deputy chief
7. Chief

Police personnel managers do not initiate an entirely new salary plan without encountering some major problems in implementation and administration. They are confronted with an existing plan in which current differentials are zealously defended by job incumbents in the various ranks. Unless a new plan offers some tangible advantages to a particular group of employees, they will be extremely reluctant to accept any adverse effect on their salary ratio. To minimize friction that could develop between various groups of police employees, changes in a salary plan should be phased in over a period of years.

A salary schedule for advancement of patrol generalists would be linked to the ranks of sergeant and lieutenant. NACCJSG recommendations on police salaries and job classifications hold that advancement along the non-managerial career path of patrol generalist and specialist should lead to a maximum salary level at least equal to that of a sergeant's maximum salary, and possibly peaking at the minimum level of lieutenant.[4]

Among the other considerations that a well-thought-out salary plan should take into account are the effect of any "cost of living" increases. In some jurisdictions these increases are one-time, across-the-board allotments that do no more than hold salaries at selected living standard levels. Since such increases will affect the pay differential between ranks, police personnel man-

[4] *Report on Police*, pp. 362–363.

agers should work to replace the across-the-board concept with percentage salary increases.

Another inequity that should be eliminated from salary plans is the outdated concept of longevity pay. Step increases are earned not with the mere passage of time, but as time in rank indicates improved performance.

Because the opportunities for promotion diminish as a worker moves upward in an organization, the time in rank to achieve the maximum salary step is shortened. A suggested diminishing of the "min/max" steps sets time periods as follows:

Rank	Time interval from minimum to maximum salary steps
Patrol officer	5 years; annual increases
Sergeant	4 years; annual increases
Lieutenant	3 years; 9–month increases
Captain	2 years; 8–month increases
Inspector/Commander	18 month; 6–month increases
Deputy chief and Chief	1 year; quarterly increases

Special Considerations of the Salary Plan

Any premium or "hazard" pay for work in a bomb squad, on motorcycle duty, or on a night watch is added to the base salary of individuals assigned to such work and, of course, applies only to the duration of the employee's assignment. On-call pay, which accrues to designated employees for being available for overtime work whenever needed, is subject to the same stipulations.

Overtime pay for on-the-job duty or court attendance is awarded at the standard overtime rate to employees who put in these extra hours. This is usually at an hourly rate one and one-half times the officer's current base pay. Compensatory time off (CTO) for overtime is rapidly becoming a relic of the past. Employees asked to work beyond a normal tour of duty expect premium pay for overtime work.

At some point in the chain of command the base work week of forty hours ceases to apply. When we talk about executive-level jobs, we are referring to a professional level at which public service and responsibility can no longer be compensated at an hourly rate. It would probably be difficult to justify overtime pay for the chief of police or his or her deputy chiefs.

Salary Adjustments and Parity

Most salary demands by police employee groups are based on the increasing cost of living (Consumer Price Index). Employers often claim they cannot adjust salaries upward because such pay raises would require funds in excess of existing appropriations. Employees of police agencies make the counter-claim that wages in private industry and other public employment *have* been adjusted upward to meet the rising cost of living.

At one time, parity between the salaries of police officers and fire personnel was traditional. Despite the fact that distinctly different abilities, skills, and knowledge are demanded of police and fire personnel, police in the United States have only recently broken this parity concept and achieved higher salary levels than fire personnel.

The parity principle as it now applies to police salaries states that comparable duties and responsibilities shall be rewarded equivalently. This concept links local police salaries with salaries in other police agencies of similar size, located in areas in which the consumer price index is also similar or equal. Of course, prevailing salaries for comparable services in private employment must also be taken into consideration, but in general police employees are concerned with norms within their own profession.

Total Equivalent Compensation: Salary and Benefits

So-called "fringe" benefits have come over the years to have substantial value. Total Equivalent Compensation (TEC) is a term used to describe salaries plus all benefits that apply at each level.[5]

The extent of the following benefits should be considered when evaluating the TEC of employees:

1. Amount of pension deduction
2. Amount of overtime (rate and hours allowed)
3. Uniform allowance
4. Payment of hospitalization (and other) insurance premium
5. Number of paid holidays allowed
6. Sick leave policy
7. Vacations
8. Premium pay
9. Shift (watch) differential pay

Job Evaluation and Classification Plan

A job evaluation and classification plan in a police agency should:

1. Group jobs into classes (ranks, grades) sufficiently similar to justify the same descriptive title
2. Be based on merit selection and retention, advancement, and promotion

[5] Winston S. Crouch (ed.), *Local Government Personnel Administration*, (Washington, D.C.: International City Management Association, 1976), pp. 209–210.

3. Offer multiple salary levels (steps) in each job classification
4. Provide career incentives and opportunities for patrol generalists and nonmanagerial specialists

Each of these characteristics of a job evaluation and classification plan finds expression in the NACCJSG's Report on Police.[6]

In order to evaluate a particular job, personnel technicians must first collect all the information they need to develop a job-related title and description. Such data are usually obtained through "task analysis," a process that selects from all the tasks that comprise a job those which can be termed important, difficult, and frequent.

Task statements are the basic units of job analysis. A task statement will include the following information:

1. What a worker does
2. To whom or to what he does it
3. For what purpose
4. On instructions from whom
5. When and where
6. With what materials and equipment

A task statement can be made more understandable by presenting collected data in the above 1–6 sequence. In order to achieve simplicity and clarity, all technical or little known terms, including occupational jargon, should be defined either at the outset or in conspicuous footnotes.

Once definitive task statements have outlined the work requirements for each job, personnel technicians can proceed to group jobs with similar requirements into classes (levels) and set an appropriate minimum/maximum salary for each class. This completes the process of job evaluation.

The following factors are useful in devising the basic job classification:

1. Supervision or guidance received
2. Supervision executed over others
3. Knowledge and abilities required
4. Responsibility for decisions (consequence of error)
5. Analytical requirement
6. Public contact
7. Working conditions

Personnel technicians assigned to job classification should develop a point system that will weigh the relative complexity of each job on the basis of the tasks and responsibilities involved and award salary "points" accordingly.

[6] See National Advisory Commission, *Report on Police*, pp. 363–364.

Since job "classes" in a police agency are usually linked to rank, the job classification should specify the job titles and descriptions for each of the traditional ranks of a police agency: patrol officer or deputy sheriff, sergeant, lieutenant, captain, and chief. These rank designations may have slightly different names, but the progression upward is usually the same.

Because personnel managers usually inherit a ready-made job classification plan, a good approach is to tackle job evaluations piecemeal, using whatever data-gathering techniques are best suited to task identification. Because of the greater allowance for individual differences, face-to-face methods such as interviews and so-called desk audits are to be preferred over questionnaire sampling. Participant observation by personnel technicians of various tasks and group discussions with the workers involved should help personnel technicians to relate better to fellow-employees and to understand better the police agency's goals.

Chapter Review

Summary

Police salaries are generally responsive to local economic conditions, but they should keep pace with rising costs in order to ensure employees an adequate standard of living. Inadequate salaries force police employees to seek second jobs. Entry-level salaries should be no less than the state-established minimum and the range to maximum salary should be sufficient to satisfy senior employees who remain at the basic rank. Salary differentials between job classes should provide incentive for upward job mobility and retention, and the chief's salary should be on a par with the salaries of local judges and heads of government agencies. Merit salary increases should be available to reward work excellence, and premium and overtime pay should be accorded to those who have rendered such service. Police salaries should not be dependent on the pay of other public employees, and annual salary reviews should revise police salaries to meet cost-of-living increases and to achieve parity with other police agencies in similar jurisdictions.

A job evaluation and classification plan groups jobs into classes on the basis of tasks identified as important, difficult, and frequent. Once a job has received a title and a description it can be evaluated in terms of a salary level appropriate to the work requirements. Salary differentials exist between all job classes, from the entry level position to that of police chief.

Critique

Demands of police employees to participate in establishing salary plans, and their struggle for parity with employees of other agencies or in other occupations, handicap police personnel technicians in projecting salary costs from year to year. Various vested-interest groups among police employees are opposed to salary separations based on job analysis and evaluation. Despite the fact that adequacy of salaries is an important element of personnel management, personnel managers should be responsive to the public demand to reduce the costs of government. New and intermediate job classes may achieve the goal of lowered costs without seriously modifying an existing salary plan, but this may require a break with the traditional ranking system.

Questions for Discussion and Review

1. What are the elements of a salary plan?
2. Should police salaries be linked to the cost-of-living index? Why?
3. What factors should determine the salary of a chief of police?
4. What is the recommended range between minimum and maximum salary for the basic job of police officer?
5. What salary separations are likely to provide incentive for upward job mobility?
6. What is the meaning of "parity" in relation to police salaries?
7. What are the goals of a job classification plan?
8. Define job analysis; task statements; job evaluation.
9. What factors are useful in setting salaries for various job classes?

Workbook Project

Research available material on the local or state police agency, and develop the ongoing salary schedule and job classification plan by (1) job title and description, and (2) salary.

14

Labor Relations

Chapter Objectives

- to enumerate employees' major concerns about the terms and conditions of employment
- to review the concept that a police chief must have certain "managerial rights"
- to develop a personnel policy that can be used in either a nonunion or a union setting to prevent work stoppages and job actions

Police employees today are better educated and more concerned about their careers than in the past. The rigors of the contemporary selection process, both at the entrance level and at various advancement stages and promotional steps, impart a basic professionalism to police work. Police officers are concerned about their public image, the impact of inflation on existing salaries and benefits, job security, and improved working conditions. To achieve these legitimate wants, police employees have found that collective action is necessary in order to multiply the latent power of each individual.

The collective power of police employees has been slow to develop. The specter of anarchy and the vulnerability of communities to criminal activity during police work stoppages has resulted in a generalized public rejection of strikes by police employees. Many police officers share this public rejection of any police work stoppage. The need to keep the peace during numerous labor disputes over many years has subliminally aligned many police workers with management; the role of police in these disputes has always been to control strikers and protect the employer's property, as well as the rights of nonstriking employees. In addition, many police employees harbor a certain cynicism about employee groups and have little faith in group action. Perhaps there are also a few who feel that group action is self-defeating as it will incur the animosity of the police chief and others in positions of power locally.

Despite these reservations, police employee groups are growing. Significantly, this growth is not the outcome of any recruitment program conducted by a national labor union to organize police employees into

179

"locals" affiliated with a nationwide union. The growth of police unions, as any police employee's group may be termed regardless of its name or general orientation, has occurred at local levels. The increasing percentage of employees joining these local groups is affirmative evidence that police employees believe in and are willing to support their local organization.

Police officers usually join, or form, a police employee group for a number of reasons. Some of these include

1. To combat public hostility to police
2. To awaken legislators unresponsive to needs expressed by police
3. To make public officials more responsive to police needs
4. To protect job security
5. To protect and improve the police image
6. To secure salary increases and more fringe benefits
7. To better working conditions
8. To protect individual and consitutional rights
9. To train and select spokespersons who can represent the group in negotiations with management
10. To secure a variety of other services available only in an employee organization[1]

The stated objectives of police employee groups are usually simple: improving the public image of police officers, protecting the constitutional rights of officers, and establishing a line of communication between police management and its members.[2] However, there is little doubt that among the overall aims of any police union is the goal of seeking a broader share in the governance of the agency.

Terms and Conditions of Employment   Wages, hours, and other terms and conditions of employment are divided into two general classifications—economic and noneconomic conditions.

Economic factors in police employment are

1. Salary
2. Overtime pay
3. Court overtime pay
4. Premium pay for special assignments (motorcycle duty, bomb squad, pilot, and so on)

[1] See Charles W. Maddox, *Collective Bargaining in Law Enforcement* (Springfield, Ill.: Charles C Thomas, 1975); "Police Unions," *Management Information Service Report,* 8, No. 3, (March, 1976), 1-19; and Ralph Showalter and Richard F. Dart, *A Guide for Police Administrators and Police Union Leaders* (Hartford, Conn.: Social Development Corp., 1976).

[2] Allan Edward Bent, *The Politics of Law Enforcement: Conflict and Power in Urban Communities* (Lexington, Mass.: D.C. Heath & Co., 1974), p. 145.

5. Night differential pay (night or special shift)
6. On-call pay (standby duty during normal off-duty hours)
7. Uniform allowance
8. Health insurance (hospitalization, life)
9. Meal allowance (during overtime or when on special assignment)
10. Paid holidays
11. Vacations
12. Paid sick days
13. Pay for roll-call "briefing" time (about 30 minutes prior to daily tour of duty)
14. Employee pension contribution
15. Disability (for example, a heart disability makes an employee eligible for a disability pension)
16. Reimbursement of tuition (attendance at work-related college courses during off-duty hours)
17. Longevity pay (annual bonus for years served; or years served after reaching pension eligibility)
18. Expansion of off-duty employment opportunities for second jobs
19. Pay upon termination of employee for accumulated "compensatory time off," accrued vacation leave, and unused sick days
20. Time off for blood donations (one or two days for each donation)
21. Paid lunch time (during tour of duty)
22. "Acting" rank pay (compensation for temporary service in a higher rank)

Noneconomic factors are also of major concern to union leadership, despite the claim by police management that most of these noneconomic factors are prerogatives of the chief of police. The following subjects have been specified as areas in which police union leaders believe management should share governance with rank-and-file employees:

1. Recruiting and selecting new hires (determining applicant qualifications; testing and screening procedures)
2. Patrol shift assignments (number of hours, time of shift)
3. Assignment to patrol cars
4. Transfers ("Fair Transfer Policy")
5. Disciplinary procedures
6. Promotions
7. Selection and advancement of specialists
8. One-officer versus two-officer cars
9. Home pickup (of officer going on or off duty)
10. Physical fitness
11. Payment of "service fee" by nonunion police officers
12. Residence requirement
13. Use of department bulletin boards for union notices

14. Use of police reserves (reduction of use in place of salaried police officers)
15. Use of civilians to replace sworn police personnel
16. Layoffs (necessity, conditions of, and assurance of reemployment)
17. Rights of police officers when under investigation
18. Use of firearms (departmental policy, review procedures)
19. Selection of weapons
20. Productivity (prevent "speed-up," work force reduction, and any undesirable working conditions under a "productivity" program)

Noneconomic factors have in many cases replaced economic issues as the primary target of police labor-management negotiations. Unions claim that any term or condition of employment should be open to labor-management negotiations. For personnel managers, the thrust of this development is that they must concern themselves with these noneconomic factors that can at times cause considerable employee unhappiness and dissatisfaction. More specifically, police personnel managers should work to keep communications open between individual employees (or the employee group) and management; secondly, they should stem any efforts by the police chief and line commanders to take any action that would represent an arbitrary, unreasonable, capricious, or prejudiced change in the terms and conditions of employment.

Shared Governance   The leaders of police unions seek a voice in police management to improve the total work environment of their membership. The base philosophy of union leaders is that by sharing in the governance of the police agency they will be able to raise issues impinging on the terms and conditions of employment. They no longer want to limit negotiations to wages, hours, and fringe benefits; instead they want to bring to the negotiation table for discussion any procedures they believe to be unjust, unfair, or unnecessary. The concept of shared governance is illustrated in Figure 14-1.

On the other hand, police management claims that certain decisions are the prerogative of management, and thus not negotiable. Further, any erosion of these rights will impair a police chief's ability to manage effectively.

Court decisions and the provisions of current police contracts offer guidelines as to which terms and conditions of employment are *not* "bargainable issues" and should be reserved as management rights. However, it is more than likely that an issue is "bargainable" when police union leaders present affirmative evidence revealing that (1) the disputed procedure has caused employee dissatisfaction; threatened employee safety; is basically unfair, unjust, or unnecessary; or (2) negotiations leading to a possible change in procedures will not impair the ability of the police chief to manage the police agency effectively.

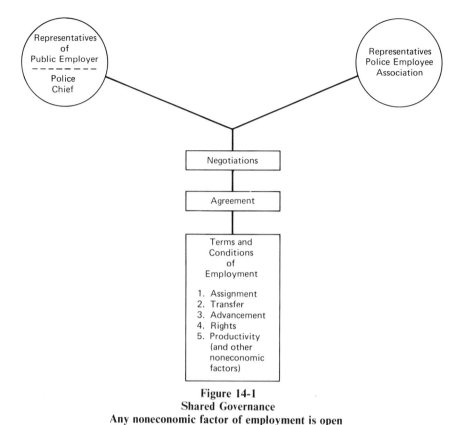

Figure 14-1
Shared Governance
**Any noneconomic factor of employment is open
to labor-management negotiations.**

Three factors continue to limit the extent of shared governance:

1. The paramilitary atmosphere prevalent in police agencies
2. The police chief's belief in "sovereignty"
3. The possible cost of labor-initiated changes

To expand briefly on these three influences, we first note that while police executives have accepted the concept of participative managment in theory, it has had only limited application down the police line of command.

Some police chiefs subscribe to the belief that a police agency assigns a certain sovereignty to its chief. In this role, the chief is reluctant to share any direction or control over certain terms and conditions of employment.[3]

Negotiations that result in changes in work procedures, let us say, may not have a dollars-and-cents price tag of direct expenditures, yet still affect police budgets in some measure. Here the well-known phrase, "time is money," is particularly apt. A few years ago New York City underwent a fiscal

[3] Maddox, *Collective Bargaining,* p. 18.

crisis that has been blamed in part upon the gains made by organizations of workers during collective bargaining. In the case of New York's Patrolmen's Benevolent Association, these noneconomic gains meant less on-duty hours and less "production" for the resources expended.[4]

**Personnel Policy—
Labor Relations**

Police personnel managers should establish a personnel policy in labor relations that is designed specifical- cifically to achieve the employing agency's objectives:

1. Concern for the welfare and performance of all employees
2. Interest in developing the full potential of all employees as individuals
3. Intent to help all employees achieve greatest satisfaction from their jobs
4. Decision to provide the most effective and responsive police services to the public[5]

Labor relations in police agencies are usually based on one of three models: nonunion, civil service, or union.

In a nonunion setting the personnel manager would draft personnel policies for labor relations from guidelines established by other nonunion governmental agencies or business organizations.

For those agencies operating under civil service regulations, personnel policy is determined in large measure by merit system laws dealing with labor relations.

In a union setting—where an employee group has been selected as bargaining agent for all employees and a contract has been agreed upon— labor relations proceed on the principle of a management/union adversary relationship (collective bargaining).[6]

Most police agencies operate under a dual model: civil service combined with either nonunion or union. When employees are not organized, the civil service model dominates the labor relations sector of personnel policy. When employees are organized, specific provisions of the contract may override certain civil service regulations.

**Politics and
Police Unions**

Police employee organizations have quasi-political power as a group of workers, a labor organization. There is power inherent in the recognition of a labor organization as a bargaining agent, in collective negotiations, and in the threat of work stoppages or other job action believed necessary to gain the organization's demands. Police un-

---

[4] Ken Auletta, "More for Less—A Reporter At Large," *The New Yorker,* August 1, 1977, pp. 28–48.

[5] "This is Where We Stand On Labor Relations," *Public Management,* 59, No. 6 (June 1977), 7.

[6] "This is Where We Stand," p. 5.

ions also have true political power in their ability to endorse political parties and candidates they believe sympathetic to the goals of the union and its membership and to reject those they feel are hostile.[7]

Appeals to local and state legislators is a bypass route around collective negotiations. The political power of a local police union is multiplied many times when a state organization such as the Peace Officers Research Association of California (PORAC) comes out in favor of a certain policy. Even when a statewide group has only an informal organization, legislators no doubt recognize the strength in such unity of action and react accordingly.

An example of the bypass at the state level is New Jersey's law establishing procedures for binding arbitration if an impasse develops during police contract negotiations.[8] Despite the fact that the new law specifically requires the arbitration panel to consider the public employer's "ability to pay," it is doubtful that most public officials in New Jersey are happy with legislative action that forces them to move the disputed issue to binding arbitration.

From the above, we see that legislation which requires compulsory or binding arbitration to avoid a strike has the disadvantage of forcing managment to submit to collective bargaining economic issues it feels would be better settled through continued negotiation. What usually happens in the case of salary disputes is that the arbitrator is not allowed compromise (that is, split the difference) between what management has offered and what the police union will accept. Thus, if the arbitrator determines that the wage figure sought by the police union is the one that should be adopted, management may feel that it is headed toward a fiscal liability it cannot afford. Alternatively, if the figure is in favor of management, the police union may decide to strike even though a strike is expressly prohibited by law. Some unions do not hesitate to strike because leaders hold out the possibility of an amnesty provision.

It becomes apparent from the foregoing that there needs to be some mutually accepted means of impasse resolution that is more than mediation and fact finding but less than compulsory arbitration. State governments that have legislated compulsory arbitration have typically received the tacit support of police associations. Other jurisdictions across the country, however, are struggling for some middle road that will resolve labor disputes without the finality of binding arbitration.

The legal provision of disability benefits for police employees suffering from heart disease was also secured through statewide lobbying by leaders of police unions. By assuming that any heart disease is job-related, it offers many police employees a new route to disability pensions. To secure this type of benefit during collective negotiations at local levels might be difficult or impossible. However, political pressure has made local action unnecessary, since any contested case of heart disease would be settled under state law.

[7] Alan Edward Bent, *The Politics of Law Enforcement: Conflict and Power in Urban Communities* (Lexington, Mass.: Lexington Books, D.C. Heath and Company, 1974), pp. 76–79.

[8] *Police Labor Review,* No. 34 (April 1977), pp. 10–11.

There is little disagreement with the argument that binding arbitration for police, as law, will block police strikes; nor with the argument that the stress of police work affects the health of police employees and commonly causes various forms of heart trouble. On the other hand, such legislative action forecloses certain areas usually the subject of collective bargaining and forces the employer—that is, the public—to foot the bill for the costs that develop from such laws.

Work Stoppages and Job Actions

The National Advisory Commission on Criminal Justice Standards and Goals is of the opinion that any concerted work stoppage or job action by police employees should be prohibited by state or local law, and forbidden by formal written policy of police agencies. Police executives are advised by the Commission's section, "Work Stoppages and Job Actions," to

1. Develop a plan to maintain emergency police services in the event of a concerted employee work stoppage; and
2. Consider the initiation of internal disciplinary action, including dismissal, against police employees who participate in a concerted work stoppage or job action[9]

The Commission suggests that the definition of a police strike should include the concerted failure to report for work, the willful absence of an employee from his or her job, or the abstinence in whole or in part from the full, faithful, and proper performance of the duties of employment, for the purpose of influencing or coercing a change in the terms or conditions of employment.[10]

Work stoppages and job actions take on a number of forms:

1. Strikes
2. Call in sick ("blue flu")
3. Work slowdown
4. Work speedup (increase in traffic citations, minor crime arrests)

Concerted work stoppages or job actions may have the full support of the membership of a police union. Usually the planned action is discussed at a formal meeting and a vote taken of the membership. If the vote for the planned action exceeds the percentage required by the union's constitution and by-laws (perhaps a simple majority, two-thirds, or three-quarters), the union as a group is committed to act. "Wildcat" work stoppages or job action are those in which a small segment of the union's membership takes unilateral action.

[9] National Advisory Commission, *Report on Police,* p. 465. Reprinted by permission.

Since the 1919 strike of Boston police officers, public sentiment has strongly opposed the use of this labor technique at any time. The judicial branch is generally supportive of this stance and, upon application of public officials, will issue an injunction to stop the strike and impose penalties if court orders are violated. It is true that striking police officers are frequently granted amnesty upon settlement of the dispute, but the consequences of public anger at the strike—and possibly at the terms of settlement—can harm the police union and destroy its future bargaining effectiveness. Without an amnesty provision, employees who participated in the strike may be penalized through internal disciplinary procedures if investigation reveals willing and voluntary participation. Court action may also be taken to secure some sanctions against the union or its membership, particularly those employees who encouraged, instigated, or led the strike.

In addition to these deterrents to initiating a strike, police employee groups are coming to realize that local governments *can* survive a police strike. The record shows that many police strikes are short-lived and are concluded without meeting the union's demands.[11]

The value of post-strike punitive action against strikers and their leaders is questionable. This is the reason negotiators for the public employer often agree to an amnesty provision to settle a strike. There is a definite value in a return to normal managment-labor relations as soon as possible, with adversary roles forgotten and all working toward achieving the employer's stated objectives and providing police service to the community.

This is also true of work stoppages and job actions less than a strike. It is often difficult for a police chief and line commanders to overlook a work stoppage or job action that threatens their command and authority. However, the value of a return to normal without the exacerbation of punitive action should also be considered. Possibly some face-saving action will suffice, but even this action should be ended as quickly as possible and only directed against employees when the charges can be easily substantiated.

A police union's vote of "no confidence" in a police chief is an action short of a work stoppage; it is a technique—relatively new—to communicate to the public the membership's lack of confidence in the chief's leadership.[12]

Contingency Plans

Despite newspaper accounts of "crime waves," criminal activity does not generally increase during a police strike; in fact, the public usually makes a fair adjustment to diminished police services. Often nonstriking police and superior officers, or superior officers who are not members of the same police

[10] National Advisory Commission, *Report on Police,* p. 466.

[11] "Police Unions," Management *Information Service Report,* 8, No. 3 (March 1976), pp. 14–15.

[12] David Marc Kleinman, "Zinging It To The Chief," *Police Magazine,* Vol. 2, No. 3, May, 1979, pp. 39–44.

employee union, provide sufficient personnel to provide basic emergency services. In some municipalities, the sheriff appoints deputies for this emergency duty, and in some states the governor orders state police or highway patrol—or even the National Guard—to supplement nonstriking personnel. This has led to claims of strike-breaking by union leadership, but police protection is too sensitive an area for such claims to negate the use of other police or of guardsmen to provide police protection to a community when its police strike.

An effective contingency plan should be prepared before a strike or serious work stoppage is threatened. Emergency duty charts (leaves cancelled; tours of duty extended to twelve hours) can be utilized to make better use of nonstriking personnel, with the additional hours worked compensated as overtime. Tentative arrangements can be made with outside police agencies (sheriff, state police) for help if emergencies develop during a future strike.

The contingency plan must establish the amount of service that will be provided during a strike, listing priorities for lesser emergency services and for any patrol service. It is very difficult, prior to any strike, to accurately estimate the number of police employees who will respond to a strike call by an employees' group. Priorities can be established for emergency and other services which will permit field commanders to adjust the delivery of police services to the available personnel.

Chapter Review

Summary   As responsible professionals, police employees have long been concerned with taking a greater role in determining the conditions of their employment. A stronger voice in police management would allow employee groups to improve the economic and noneconomic working conditions of their membership. Police chiefs have traditionally claimed they have certain "management rights" and that any erosion of these rights threatens their ability to manage effectively. By contrast, leaders of police employee groups believe such unilateral "rights" as transfers and assignments are negotiable elements of a labor-management agreement.

The political power inherent in police employee groups is bound to affect labor-management relations even more strongly in the future. To date, lobbying by police union officials has brought about two legislative trends. In some states it has resulted in compulsory arbitration laws, and in others legal recognition of heart disease as a job-related illness has meant special pension benefits for a number of police officers.

Concerted work stoppages, from slowdowns to strikes, are problem areas in labor-management relations, but police management must be prepared with contingency plans that will allow them to deliver services despite major work stoppages by police employees.

A "no confidence" vote by the membership of a police union is a public complaint indicating dissatisfaction with the chief of police.

Critique

The concept of participative management has been too conservative for many of today's police union leaders; by contrast, most police chiefs have found it too radical. Clearly, shared governance is a step forward in that it builds in legal safeguards to prevent management from taking arbitrary and unreasonable action against employees. However, despite the fact that it opens up the terms and conditions of employment to negotiation, shared governance cannot be realized until paramilitary concepts of management and the traditional sovereignty of police chiefs are discarded.

Questions for Discussion and Review

1. Why do police employees form and join employee associations?

2. Upon what basis can police employee groups be said to have political power?

3. Define and describe the concept of shared governance. Does it favor employees? The police chief?

4. List five economic factors of police employment; five noneconomic factors.

5. What are the essential elements of an effective police personnel policy?

6. Do police personnel have a right to strike? To engage in other concerted work stoppages?

7. Is compulsory and binding arbitration of disputes a desirable means of avoiding police strikes and other work stoppages?

8. Can the implementation of a contingency plan by a police chief in the event of a concerted work stoppage properly be termed "strike-breaking"? Explain.

Workbook Project

Interview three or more members of the local or state police agency and develop a list of noneconomic demands they believe should be negotiable in labor-management relations.

15

Collective
Bargaining

Chapter Objectives

- to describe and discuss collective bargaining between public employees and public employers
- to probe the dimensions of collective bargaining in the police workplace

---

Collective bargaining quite naturally entails an adversary relationship between the two parties involved (see Figure 15-1). The bargaining agent for police employees (police union) initiates the bargaining by presenting to representatives of the public employer (management) certain specific demands. The public employer reacts by opposing the union's demands. The union then offers evidence to support its demands, and the public employer explains its opposition. Subsequent bargaining sessions attempt to reach a compromise that will satisfy the most pressing demands of each group. As in the adversary system in America's courts, each "side" is expected to bolster its own position and demolish its opponent's claims.

Police unions are usually represented by union officials including the president, vice-president, and selected other officials, along with their legal counsel. As spokesmen for their membership, union officials gather data on employee demands and on the priority assigned to each demand, but it is often the responsibility of the union's legal counsel, or a specialist in labor relations, to develop a negotiating strategy. The president of the union may be the chief negotiator, but only if he or she can demonstrate a competence equal to that of the chief negotiator for the public employer.[1]

The public employer is represented by the mayor or city manager, by an elected county official, or by the governor (or their designated representatives). The titles of the individuals comprising the public employer's

---

[1] Charles W. Maddox, *Collective Bargaining in Law Enforcement* (Springfield, Ill.: Charles C Thomas, 1975), pp. 48-50.

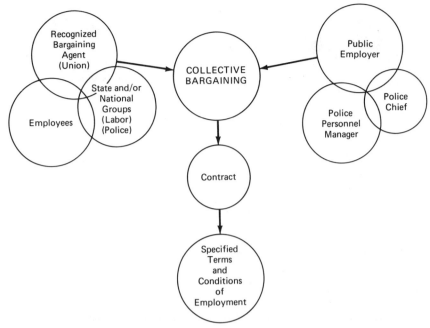

Figure 15-1
Collective Bargaining Process

"team" depends on the level of government involved: municipal, county, state. Many of these units of government now have "chief labor negotiators" who represent management as chief negotiator during bargaining with various employee groups. Additional negotiators for the public employer are the personnel manager, a labor specialist, an attorney, a finance expert, and a representative of the police chief.[2]

The police chief should not become directly involved as part of management's "team" during bargaining sessions. Of course, a chief would be viewed by members of the management bargaining team as an advisor and resource person; yet he or she should remain on the fringe of an adversary relationship for the following reasons:

1. He or she may jeopardize work relationships with rank-and-file police, either as subordinates or former co-workers (many chiefs moved up from the ranks of "sworn" personnel)

2. An active role in bargaining may impair the chief's capability to implement future contract provisions impartially

3. As a supporter of management's position, the chief may become a scapegoat if bargaining does not achieve union's demands[3]

[2] "Police Unions," *Management Information Service Report,* 8, No. 3 (March 1976), pp. 6-8.

[3] "Police Unions," *Management Information Service,* p. 6.

Collective Bargaining:
Public Employees

Over two-thirds of the states have enacted legislation that prescribes collective bargaining procedures in the public sector, and most of these statutes also encompass police agencies and their employees. An examination of such legislation enacted since 1970 by six states (California, New York, Massachusetts, Minnesota, Florida, and Iowa) indicates an emerging commonality. Words and organization differ, but the essential elements are remarkably similar. The legislation is in the public interest; the rights of both public employer and public employee are established; and an impasse procedure is spelled out for use when negotiations are deadlocked.

The following extracts from the "Public Employment Relations Act" of Iowa illustrate the major segments of this type of legislation:

Public Policy

The general assembly declares that it is the public policy of the state to promote harmonious and cooperative relationships between government and its employees by permitting public employees to organize and bargain collectively; to protect the citizens of this state by assuring effective and orderly operations of government in providing for their health, safety, and welfare; to prohibit and prevent all strikes by public employees; and to protect the rights of public employees to join or refuse to join, and to participate in or refuse to participate in, employee organizations. (Section 20.1, Iowa Code)

Public Employer
Rights

Public employers shall have, in addition to all powers, duties, and rights established by constitutional provision, statute, ordinance, charter, or special act, the exclusive power, duty, and the right to:

1. Direct the work of its public employees.
2. Hire, promote, demote, transfer, assign and retain public employees in positions within the public agency.
3. Suspend or discharge public employees for proper cause.
4. Maintain the efficiency of governmental operations.
5. Relieve public employees from duties because of lack of work or for other legitimate reasons.
6. Determine and implement methods, means, assignments and personnel by which the public employer's operations are to be conducted.
7. Take such actions as may be necessary to carry out the mission of the public employer.
8. Initiate, prepare, certify and administer its budget.
9. Exercise all powers and duties granted to the public employer by law (Section 20.7, Iowa Code)

Public Employee Rights

Public employees shall have the right to:

1. Organize, or form, join, or assist any employee organization.
2. Negotiate collectively through representatives of their own choosing.
3. Engage in other concerted activities for the purpose of collective bargaining or other mutual aid or protection insofar as any such activity is not prohibited by this chapter or any other law of the state.
4. Refuse to join or participate in the activities of employee organizations, including the payment of any dues, fees or assessments or service fees of any type. (Section 20.8, Iowa Code)

Scope of Negotiations

The public employer and the employee organization shall meet at reasonable times, including meetings reasonably in advance of the public employer's budget-making process, to negotiate in good faith with respect to wages, hours, vacations, insurance, holidays, leaves of absence, shift differentials, overtime compensation, supplemental pay, seniority, transfer procedures, job classifications, health and safety matters, evaluation procedures, procedures for staff reduction, in-service training and other matters mutually agreed upon. Negotiations shall also include terms authorizing dues checkoff for members of the employee organization and grievance procedures for resolving any questions arising under the agreement, which shall be embodied in a written agreement and signed by the parties. If an agreement provides for dues checkoff, a member's dues may be checked off only upon the member's written request and the member may terminate the dues checkoff at any time by giving thirty days' written notice. Such obligation to negotiate in good faith does not compel either party to agree to a proposal or make a concession.

Nothing in this section shall diminish the authority and power of the merit employment department, board of regents' merit system, educational radio and television facility board's merit system, or any civil service commission established by constitutional provision, statute, charter or special act to recruit employees, prepare, conduct and grade examinations, rate candidates in order of their relative scores for certification, reclassification or appeal rights in the classified service of the public employer served.

All retirement systems shall be excluded from the scope of negotiations. (Section 20.9, Iowa Code)

Prohibited Practices

1. It shall be a prohibited practice for any public employer, public employee or employee organization to willfully refuse to negotiate in good faith with respect to the scope of negotiations as defined in Section 20.9.
2. It shall be a prohibited practice for a public employer or his designated representative willfully to:
   a. Interfere with, restrain or coerce public employees in the exercise of rights granted by this chapter.

b. Dominate or interfere in the administration of any employee organization.

c. Encourage or discourage membership in any employee organization, committee or association by discrimination in hiring, tenure, or other terms or conditions of employment.

d. Discharge or discriminate against a public employee because he has filed an affidavit, petition or complaint or given any information or testimony under this chapter, or because he has formed, joined or chosen to be represented by an employee organization.

e. Refuse to negotiate collectively with representatives of certified employee organizations as required in this chapter.

f. Deny the rights accompanying certification or exclusive recognition granted in this chapter.

g. Refuse to participate in good faith in any agreed upon impasse procedures or those set forth in this chapter.

h. Engage in a lockout.

3. It shall be a prohibited practice for public employees or an employee organization or for any person, union or organization or their agents willfully to:

a. Interfere with, restrain, coerce or harass any public employee with respect to any of his rights under this chapter or in order to prevent or discourage his exercise of any such right, including, without limitation, all rights under Section 20.8.

b. Interfere, restrain, or coerce a public employer with respect to rights granted in this chapter or with respect to selecting a representative for the purposes of negotiating collectively on the adjustment of grievances.

c. Refuse to bargain collectively with a public employer as required in this chapter.

d. Refuse to participate in good faith in any agreed upon impasse procedures or those set forth in this chapter.

e. Violate Section 20.12 [Strikes prohibited.]

f. Violate the provisions of Section 736B.1 to 736B.3, which are hereby made applicable to public employers, public employees and public employee organizations. [Section 736B.1 prohibits any sympathy boycott or strike, and Section 736B.3 forbids any jurisdictional strike or slowdown (dispute between unions).]

g. Picket in a manner which interferes with ingress and egress to the facilities of the public employer.

h. Engage in, intiate, sponsor or support any picketing that is performed in support of a strike, work stoppage, boycott or slowdown against a public employer.

i. Picket for any unlawful purpose.

4. The expressing of any views, argument or opinion, or the dissemination thereof, whether in written, printed, graphic, or visual form, shall not constitute or be evidence of any unfair labor practice under any of the provisions of this chapter, if such expression contains no threat of reprisal or force or promise of benefit. (Section 20.10, Iowa Code)

**Impasse Procedures—
Agreement of Parties**   As the first step in the performance of their duty to bargain, the public employer and the employee organization shall endeavor to agree upon impasse procedures. Such agreement shall provide for implementation of these impasse procedures not later than one hundred twenty days prior to the certified budget submission date of the public employer. If the parties fail to agree upon impasse procedures under the provisions of this section, the impasse provided in Sections 20.20 to 20.22 shall apply. (Section 20.19, Iowa Code)

Mediation   In the absence of an impasse agreement between the parties or the failure of either party to utilize its procedures, one hundred twenty days prior to the certified budget submission date, the board shall, upon the request of either party, appoint an impartial and disinterested person to act as mediator. It shall be the function of the mediator to bring the parties together to effectuate a settlement of the dispute, but the mediator may not compel the parties to agree. (Section 20.20, Iowa Code)

Fact-finding   If the impasse persists ten days after the mediator has been appointed, the board shall appoint a fact-finder representative of the public, from a list of qualified persons maintained by the board. The fact-finder shall conduct a hearing, may administer oaths, and may request the board to issue subpoenas. The fact-finder shall make written findings of facts and recommendations for resolution of the dispute and, not later than fifteen days from the day of appointment shall serve such findings on the public employer and the certified employee organization.

The public employer and the certified employee organization shall immediately accept the fact-finder's recommendation or shall within five days submit the fact-finder's recommendations to the governing body and members of the certified employee organization for acceptance or rejection. If the dispute continues ten days after the report is submitted, the report shall be made public by the board. (Section 20.21, Iowa Code)

Binding Arbitration   1. If an impasse persists after the findings of fact and recommendations are made public by the fact-finder, the parties may continue to negotiate or, the board shall have the power, upon request of either party, to arrange for arbitration, which shall be binding. The request for arbitration shall be in writing and a copy of the request shall be served upon the other party.

2. Each party shall submit to the board within four days of request a final offer on the impasse items with proof or service of a copy upon the other party. Each party shall also submit a copy of a draft of the proposed collective bargaining agreement to the extent to which agreement has been

reached and the name of its selected arbitrator. The parties may continue to negotiate all offers until an agreement is reached or a decision rendered by the panel of arbitrators.

As an alternative procedure, the two parties may agree to submit the dispute to a single arbitrator. If the parties cannot agree on the arbitrator within four days, the selection shall be made pursuant to subsection 5. The full courts of arbitration under this provision shall be shared equally by the parties to the dispute.

3. The submission of the impasse items to the arbitrators shall be limited to those issues that had been considered by the fact-finder and upon which the parties have not reached agreement. With respect to each such item, the arbitration board award shall be restricted to the final offers on each impasse item submitted by the parties to the arbitration board or to the recommendation of the fact-finder on each impasse item.

4. The panel of arbitrators shall consist of three members appointed in the following manner:

   a. One member shall be appointed by the public employer.

   b. One member shall be appointed by the employee organization.

   c. One member shall be appointed mutually by the members appointed by the public employer and the employee organization. The last member appointed shall be the chairman of the panel of arbitrators. No member appointed shall be an employee of the parties.

   d. The public employer and employee organization shall each pay the fees and expenses incurred by the arbitrator each selected. The fee and expenses of the chairman of the panel and all other costs of arbitration shall be shared equally.

5. If the third member has not been selected within four days of notification as provided in subsection 2, a list of three arbitrators shall be submitted to the parties by the board. The two arbitrators selected by the public employer and the employee organization shall determine by lot which arbitrator shall remove the first name from the list submitted by the board. The arbitrator having the right to remove the first name shall do so within two days and the second arbitrator shall have one additional day to remove one of the two remaining names. The person whose name remains shall become the chairman of the panel of arbitrators and shall call a meeting within ten days at a location designated by him.

6. If a vacancy should occur on the panel of arbitrators, the selection for replacement of such member shall be in the same manner and within the same time limits as the original member was chosen. No final selection under subsection 9 shall be made by the board until the vacancy has been filled.

7. The panel of arbitrators shall at no time engage in an effort to mediate or otherwise settle the dispute in any manner other than that prescribed in this section.

8. From the time of appointment until such time as the panel of arbitrators makes its final determination, there shall be no discussion concerning recommendations for settlement of the dispute by the members of the panel of arbitrators with parties other than those who are direct parties

to the dispute. The panel of arbitrators may conduct formal or informal hearings to discuss offers submitted by both parties.

9. The panel of arbitrators shall consider, in addition to any other relevant factors, the following factors:

a. Past collective bargaining contracts between the parties including the bargaining that led up to such contracts.

b. Comparison of wages, hours and conditions of employment of the involved public employees with those of other public employees doing comparable work, giving consideration to factors peculiar to the area and the classifications involved.

c. The interests and welfare of the public, the ability of the public employer to finance economic adjustments and the effect of such adjustments on the normal standard of services.

d. The power of the public employer to levy taxes and appropriate funds for the conduct of its operations.

10. The chairman of the panel of arbitrators may hold hearings and administer oaths, examine witnesses and documents, take testimony and receive evidence, issue subpoenas to compel the attendance of witnesses and the production of records, and delegate such powers to other members of the panel of arbitrators. The chairman of the panel of arbitrators may petition the district court at the seat of government or of the county in which any hearing is held to enforce the order of the chairman compelling the attendance of witnesses and the production of records.

11. A majority of the panel of arbitrators shall select within fifteen days after its first meeting the most reasonable offer, in its judgment, of the final offers on each impasse item submitted by the parties, or the recommendations of the fact-finder on each impasse item.

12. The selections by the panel of arbitrators and items agreed upon by the public employer and the employee organization, shall be deemed to be the collective bargaining agreement between the parties.

13. The determination of the panel of arbitrators shall be by majority vote and shall be final and binding subject to the provisions of Section 20.17, subsection 6. The panel of arbitrators shall give written explanation for its selection and inform the parties of its decision. (Section 20.22. Iowa Code)

The section of Iowa's Public Employment Relations Act prohibiting strikes by public employees is strongly and positively worded, and contains legal remedies for the employer and severe penalties for strikers:

Strikes Prohibited 1. It shall be unlawful for any public employee or any employee organization, directly or indirectly, to induce, instigate, encourage. authorize, ratify or participate in a strike against any public employer.

2. It shall be unlawful for any public employer to authorize, consent to, or condone a strike; or to pay or agree to pay any public employee for any day in which the employee participates in a strike; or to pay or agree to pay any increase in compensation or benefits to any public employee in response to or as a result of any strike or any act which violates subsection 1. It shall be unlawful for any official, director, or representative of any public employer to authorize, ratify or participate in any violation of this subsection. Nothing in this subsection shall prevent new or renewed bargaining and agreement within the scope of negotiations as defined by this chapter, at any time after such violation of subsection 1 has ceased; but it shall be unlawful for any public employer or employee organization to bargain at any time regarding suspension or modification of any penalty provided in this section or regarding any request by the public employer to a court for such suspension of modification.

3. In the event of any violation or imminently threatened violation of subsection 1 or 2, any citizen domiciled within the jurisdictional boundaries of the public employer may petition the district court for the county in which the violation occurs or the district court for Polk county for an injunction restraining such violation or imminently threatened violation. Rules of civil procedure 320 to 350 regarding injunctions shall apply. However, the court shall grant a temporary injunction if it appears to the court that a violation has occurred or is imminently threatened; the plaintiff need not show that the violation or threatened violation would greatly or irreparably injure him; and no bond shall be required of the plaintiff unless the court determines that a bond is necessary in the public interest. Failure to comply with any temporary or permanent injunction granted pursuant to this section shall constitute a contempt punishable pursuant to chapter 665. The punishment shall not exceed five hundred dollars for an individual, or ten thousand dollars for an employee organization or public employer, for each day during which the failure to comply continues, or imprisonment in a county jail not exceeding six months, or both such fine and imprisonment. An individual or an employee organization which makes an active good faith effort to comply fully with the injunction shall not be deemed to be in contempt.

4. If a public employee is held to be in contempt of court for failure to comply with an injunction pursuant to this section, or is convicted of violating this section, he shall be ineligible for any employment by the same public employer for a period of twelve months. His public employer shall immediately discharge him, but upon his request the court shall stay his discharge to permit further judicial proceedings.

5. If an employee organization or any of its officers is held to be in contempt of court for failure to comply with an injunction pursuant to this section, or is convicted of violating this section, the employee organization shall be immediately decertified, shall cease to represent the bargaining unit, shall cease to receive any dues by checkoff, and may again be certified only after twelve months have elapsed from the effective date of decertification and only after a new compliance with section 20.14 [Bargaining re-

presentative determination.] The penalties provided in this section may be suspended or modified by the court, but only upon request of the public employer and only if the court determines the suspension or modification is in the public interest.

6. Each of the remedies and penalties provided by this section is separate and several, and is in addition to any other legal or equitable remedy or penalty. (Section 20.12, Iowa Code)

Collective Bargaining: The first step in organizing a union
Police Employees authorized to bargain collectively is for
the employee group to be legally recognized as the exclusive bargaining representative of a "bargaining unit."

A petition for such recognition is usually directed to the appropriate state labor board. It should allege that the employee group represents a designated group of public employees and that it wishes to bargain collectively with the public employer concerned; and it should present evidence supporting its claim to majority representation or, failing that, the preponderant share among competing groups.

The state board or commission then authorizes an election in which the ballot questions are: (1) Do employees desire to have an employee group represent them as exclusive bargaining agent? and (2) Which employee group do they desire? (Groups that have filed petitions are listed.) A majority vote determines the exclusive bargaining agent or establishes the fact that employees do not want one designated.

These voting procedures are, of course, restricted to employees within a designated bargaining unit. Each such unit is identified on the basis of a mutuality of job interests. The term *unit determination* refers to the allocation of employees to units for the purpose of collective bargaining.

The nature of police work and the policy of hiring primarily at the entrance level assure rank-and-file employees that they will be members of a single bargaining unit. In some jurisdictions supervisory personnel are grouped with rank-and-file officers in unit determination on the ground that they have a basic community of interest. The trend, however, is toward forming discrete bargaining units for superior officers (managers and supervisors), a tendency that has also surfaced in regard to "confidential" employees— those who assume special roles of trust in management.

Leaders of police unions are quick to recognize a divide-and-conquer theme in this tight categorization of employees into bargaining units. Any concerted action by members of a rank-and-file bargaining unit is less of a threat to police management when sergeants and other supervisors are not involved. Even threats of work stoppages are of less concern to management when they can count on supervisors to work emergency duty charts and provide minimal patrol services to keep the department functioning at a nominal level.

Collective bargaining can and does break down into two major issues: substantive matters of an economic or noneconomic nature and emotional questions of which side has the greater power. Representatives of a union can refuse to amend their demand for a wage increase, and management can refuse to budge from an inability-to-pay position. An apparently minor demand to negotiate a specific condition of employment, perhaps promotions or transfers, can lead to a deadlock when management refuses to bring this working condition to the bargaining table.

When collective bargaining breaks down, the two adversaries must have a prior agreement to use mediation or arbitration to break the deadlock. Such an agreement should specify the form of impasse resolution and the circumstances which warrant its use. Impasse resolution may call for mediation, fact finding, or arbitration of disputed issues.

Mediation calls for the appointment of a neutral third party to bring the parties together to effect a settlement. The role of mediator demands persuasive tactics and diplomacy.

Fact finding is an attempt to get to the nub of a dispute. A person or a board of several persons, agreeable to both parties, has the task of determining truths and delineating the issues involved. Fact finding requires the fact finder(s) to prepare a report of findings and a statement of recommendations, usually within a specified time period.

Arbitration may be voluntary or compulsory, advisory or binding. The least effective is voluntary and advisory arbitration, as both adversaries must agree to submit the disputed issue for arbitration, and neither adversary is bound by the arbitrator's decision. Compulsory and binding arbitration is most effective, since a disputed issue must go to arbitration and the arbitrator's decision is binding on both adversaries. It also has the greatest potential for preventing work stoppages.

Compulsory and binding arbitration decisions can be appealed through legal action. Either participant in collective bargaining may seek legal redress for what they believe to be an unjust or unfair decision. Attorneys for the party refusing to accept the arbitrator's decision can plead various grounds for the refusal and secure a judicial review of all the circumstances leading to the decision.

Last-best offer arbitration is an innovative concept in impasse resolution. By restricting arbitration efforts to the last best offer of each adversary, much time and effort is conserved, and the arbitrator (or arbitration panel) is made aware of each adversary's true position.

These so-called "final offers" may also be placed on the ballot. A special election could also be a public forum for the determination of a disputed issue. A public referendum on final offers is a form of arbitration in which the voters make the final and binding decision.

Summary   Collective bargaining is a two-sided process for negotiating terms and conditions of employment. In the police workplace, representatives of the police employee group selected as exclusive bargaining agent are opposed to representatives of the public employer. The police chief assumes a low-profile role on the fringe of negotiations.

Most states now have legislation regulating collective bargaining for public employees. Extracts from Iowa's Public Employment Relations Act reveal that this legislation resulted from general concern about labor relations in the public sector. Such statutes address themselves to employer-employee rights, scope of negotiations, impasse resolution, and prohibited practices (including strikes).

To afford themselves of collective bargaining rights, police employees must select a single employee group as exclusive bargaining agent. Since all police employees have a mutuality of job interests, the designated bargaining unit will contain all police officers, men and women, and may include superiors.

Critique   In the absence of explicit legislation, statutes governing labor relations apply only to private industry, not to the public sector and its political subdivisions. Legislators aware that police management as well as the general public fears and rejects police strikes may enact laws limiting or restricting the right of police employees to bargain collectively.

Questions for Discussion and Review

1. Discuss the adversary relationship in the collective bargaining process. Is it essential?
2. What is the role of the police chief in collective bargaining?
3. Why has legislation been enacted to allow collective bargaining between public employers and public employees?
4. What are the major elements of public employee collective bargaining legislation?
5. List and explain the common steps in impasse resolution.
6. How is collective bargaining in the police workplace initiated?
7. Describe compulsory and binding arbitration; last-best offer arbitration.

Workbook Project   Review the extracts in this chapter from Iowa's Public Employment Relations Act and develop two lists—one of changes you believe to be necessary, the other of changes that would be desirable.

16

Police Union
Contracts

Chapter Objectives

- to promote an understanding of the scope and nature of contracts resulting from collective bargaining
- to use the provisions of contracts to reveal trends in police labor-management relations

---

The written and signed agreement resulting from collective bargaining is a contract between the public employer and representatives of the police union. It is frequently referred to as a "memorandum of understanding," but this does not lessen the contractural responsibilities of the parties to this memorandum.

Under the terms of these contracts city officials and police chiefs, police union leaders and police employees must all deal with reality: (1) there is a contract, (2) the contract covers specific areas of employer-employee relations, and (3) both parties to the contract are legally and morally obligated to abide by contract provisions.

To understand the scope of police union contracts is now a necessity in police personnel management. What are the areas of employee-employer relations commonly covered in these contracts? Are unusual provisions indicative of a regional or national trend, or are they only responsive to local problems? To fully develop the police personnel management role, personnel managers must collect data on police union contracts. In this way, they serve all concerned, whether they are working in a union setting under a contract or in a nonunion setting with no threat of employee organization.

At the time of collective bargaining both adversaries are usually well informed of the content of existing police union contracts in nearby cities or cities of similar size and composition elsewhere.

Public employers get their data from various public administration sources, particularly the activities and publications of the International City

Management Association. The police chief and his representative have a special resource in the many publications of the International Association of Chiefs of Police.

Neither are police union representatives lacking in resources. California's Peace Officers Research (PORAC), an organization of rank-and-file police officers, is representative of statewide groups. National groups such as the Fraternal Order of Police (FOP), the International Conference of Police Associations (ICPA), and the American Federation of State, County, and Municipal Employees (AFSCME) provide an even wider perspective. The Fraternal Order of Police boasts over one thousand lodges in communities throughout the country. Originally the greater part of its membership was in the Southern states, but the success of the organization in bettering police working conditions has resulted in its spreading to both the north and west. The AFSCME is part of the national labor movement, the American Federation of Labor and Congress of Industrial Organizations (AFL-CIO).

Among the contracts currently in force are agreements between public employers and police unions with links to one of the foregoing state or national police groups. Selected for examination are four of these contemporary contracts:

1. Tulsa, Oklahoma
2. Memphis, Tennessee
3. West Haven, Connecticut
4. Concord, California

Tulsa is a city in the Southwest with a population approaching 400,000. The contract is between the City of Tulsa and the Fraternal Order of Police, Lodge No. 93.

Memphis is a major metropolis in the South with a population of over 600,000. The parties to this agreement are the City of Memphis and the Memphis Police Association (MPA). The MPA was formed in early 1973, a few months later the membership voted unanimously to affiliate with the International Congress of Police Associations (IAPA).[1]

The New England city of West Haven, Connecticut, has a population between 50,000 and 60,000. This agreement is between the Board of Police Commissioners and West Haven Police Local 895, Council 15, American Federation of State, County and Municipal Employees, AFL-CIO.

Concord, California, is a Pacific Coast city with a population of close to 100,000. It is located on the fringe of San Francisco's metropolitan area. This contract is between the City of Concord and the Concord Police Association (CPA). Since police unions in California are generally supportive of the Peace Officers Research Association of Calfornia (PORAC), it can be assumed that

Alan Edward Bent, *The Politics of Law Enforcement: Conflict and Power in Urban Communities* (Lexington, Mass.: Lexington Books, D.C. Heath and Company, 1974), pp. 144–147.

PORAC had some influence on the CPA during the meet-and-confer sessions leading to this agreement.

The following review of the major provisions of these four contracts reveals many common areas and a few areas unique to each contract.

Purpose and Intent

The *Tulsa* contract states the purpose and intent of this agreement:

The general purpose of this Agreement is to set forth terms and conditions of employment and to promote orderly, peaceful labor relations for the mutual interest of the City of Tulsa in its capacity as an Employer, the Employees, the Lodge and the people of the City of Tulsa.

The parties recognize that the interest of the community and the job security of the Employees depend upon the Employer's success in establishing proper and efficient services to the community.

To these ends the Employer and the Fraternal Order of Police encourage to the fullest degree friendly and cooperative relations between their representatives at all levels and among all Employees.

The *Memphis* agreement is similar, stating that the purpose of this contract is to "assure harmonious relations between the City and the Union." The *West Haven* document notes that it establishes an "equitable and peaceful procedure" for the resolution of disputes and differences. The *Concord* contract states that it is the result of meeting and conferring in good faith between representatives of the city and union.

Recognition of the Bargaining Unit

All four agreements recognize that the police union party to the contract is the exclusive bargaining agent for specified police employees. Union membership varies in each contract. The *Tulsa* contract specifies by exclusion:

The Employer recognizes Lodge No. 93, Fraternal Order of Police, hereinafter referred to as Lodge, as the exclusive bargaining agent for all employees of the Tulsa Police Department except:

A. Employees in the classifications of Lieutenant and above

B. Probationary policemen

C. Civilian employees

The *Memphis* agreement states that the bargaining unit shall include all "commissioned officers of the Memphis Police Department of the rank of sergeant and below," but excludes probationary employees and what are now being termed confidential employees. Commissioned officers are described as those officers who have successfully completed the Memphis Police Academy.

Officers assigned to the Internal Affairs Bureau, Personnel Bureau, and Fiscal Affairs Bureau are excluded from the bargaining unit.

The *West Haven* contract recognizes the union as sole and exclusive bargaining agent for "all full-time regular and permanent investigatory and uniform members of the Police Department, with authority to exercise police powers up to and including the rank of Deputy Inspector." Full-time employees are those who are regularly scheduled to work at least twenty hours per week. Other segments of this contract indicate that the rank of Deputy Inspector is above the rank of lieutenant.

In the *Concord* agreement, the Concord Police Association is recognized as the "Certified Employee Organization for the Peace Officer Representation Unit" (PORU). In its section on salaries, the job classifications within the PORU are identified as police officer, policewoman, identification technician, and police sergeant.

A summary of employee representation under these four contracts is as follows:

	Tulsa	Memphis	West Haven	Concord
Rank and file (patrol officers; detectives)	Yes	Yes	Yes	Yes
Sergeants	Yes	Yes	Yes	Yes
Lieutenants	No	No	Yes	No
Deputy Inspector (above lieutenant)	No	No	Yes	No

No-Strike Clause

The no-strike clause of the *Memphis* contract is a clear and simple waiver of the possible use of this labor tactic[2] and acknowledges the union's link to the International Conference of Police Associations:

> It is acknowledged by the full membership of the Union that the protection of the public health, safety, and welfare demands that the members of the Police Division not be accorded the right to strike or engage in any work stoppage, slow-down, or any and all similar activities. This necessary prohibition does not, however, require the denial to such employees of other well recognized rights, such as the right to organize, be represented by an employee organization of their choice and the right to meet and confer in accordance with the provisions of the Labor Policy of The City of Memphis.

However, the Memphis Union and its full membership acknowledges that there have in fact been strikes in other cities by Police Unions that are now members of the International Conference of Police Associations. Accordingly, a clear and unequivocal no strike commitment is a definite

---

[2] In 1978 rank-and-file members of the Memphis Police Association voted to strike, despite this no-strike agreement and the expressed disagreement of their union leaders. National Guard troops policed the city until this "wildcat" strike was settled. The issue in dispute was salaries; the settlement included a pay rise for police.

necessity to the City of Memphis as a demonstration of good faith on the part of the Union and its membership.

The membership of the Union recognizes, therefore, that participating in a strike as defined herein shall subject the member or members to immediate and permanent dismissal, together with the loss of all employee benefits, including, but not limited to pension benefits.

Disciplinary action, the Union and the individual members agree, shall be available to the City not only against the individual employee engaged in the strike but against any other employee who is guilty of honoring, aiding or assisting in a strike as defined herein, as well as against the Union, both local and International.

The term "strike" as used herein means the failure with others to report for duty, the willful absence from position, the stoppage of work, any individual or concerted slow-down, sit-down, sick-out, refusal to work, work interruption, work stoppage, call-in, failure to respond to official dispatch or order to render public service or assistance, or failure in whole or part to carry out the full, faithful and proper performance of the duties of employment, and without the lawful approval of the Superior, or in any manner interfering with the operation of the Police Division of the City for the purpose of inducing, influencing, or coercing the recognition of any employee organization or a change in the conditions or compensations or the rights, privileges or obligations of employment or in sympathy with others or for any other purpose. All orders will be obeyed.

During the term of any Agreement between the Union and the City or prior to any such Agreement, or after the expiration thereof, the Union and its membership agree that it will not engage in, encourage, or approve any strikes as defined hereinabove growing out of any dispute relating to the terms of the Agreement or for any other reason. The City agrees it will not lock out employees during the term of any agreement or prior thereto. The Union will take such lawful steps as may be necessary to prevent any interruption of work prior to or after any agreement comes into existence, recognizing with the City that all matters of controversy concerning employment shall be settled by applicable law and City Personnel Policies or, after any Agreement, by established grievance procedure not in conflict with the applicable law.

Further, in the event of a strike as defined herein, the Union and individual members agree that all dues being withheld from the wages of the members of the Union and which have not theretofore been paid over to the Union shall be retained by the City and applied to the cost and/or personnel.

It is understood and agreed that the Union and the International Conference of Police Associations as well as its members individually, who participate in the violation of the provisions herein, shall hold the City of Memphis harmless from any and all liability or claims which it may incur or sustain as a result of any violation of the provisions embodied herein.

It is further understood and agreed that the provisions embodied herein shall inure to the benefit of any individual, company, corporation, or other legal entity who shall sustain damage as a result of a violation of the provisions herein.

Nothing in this Agreement is construed to limit relief under the common law or any applicable statute that the City may have for injunctive relief or for damages suffered against the individual members, the Union, or the International Conference of Police Associations.

The *Tulsa* contract has substantially similar provisions prohibiting strikes and the same provision that the employer will not lock out employees because of a labor dispute during the term of the agreement. In addition, the *Tulsa* agreement calls upon the union to cooperate in ending any "wildcat" (unauthorized) strike:

> Upon notification confirmed in writing by Employer to Lodge No. 93 that certain of its members are engaging in a wildcat strike, Lodge No. 93 shall immediately, in writing, order such members to return to work at once and provide Employer with a copy of such an order, and a responsible official of Lodge No. 93 shall publicly order them to return to work. Such characterization of the srike by Employer shall not establish the nature of the strike. Such notification by Lodge No. 93 shall not constitute an admission by it that a wildcat strike is in progress or has taken place or that any particular member is or has engaged in a wildcat strike. The notification shall be made solely on the representations of Employer. In the event that a wildcat strike occurs, Lodge No. 93 agrees to take all reasonable effective and affirmative action to secure the members return to work as promptly as possible.

West Haven's contract provision prohibiting strikes is short and to the point:

> . . . During the course of this agreement there shall be no strike, slowdown, suspension or stoppage of work in any part of the City's operation authorized by the Union, nor shall there be any lockout by the City in any part of the City's operation.

Concord's contract does not have a no-strike clause. However, the nature of the agreement implies that any matter not covered in the contract but within the scope of union representation would not be open to discussion until the existing contract had expired or unless such discussion were mutually agreeable to both parties.

Economic Factors Salaries and fringe benefits differ slightly in all four contracts. The scope of the coverage of these agreements is shown in the accompanying table.

The *Concord* contract is the only agreement in which salaries are linked to the cost of living. Otherwise, salary schedules do no more than list the wages

	Tulsa	Memphis	West Haven	Concord
1. Salaries	Yes	Yes	Yes	Yes
2. Overtime	Yes	Yes	Yes	Yes
3. Uniform (clothing) allowance	Yes	Yes	Yes	Yes
4. Meal allowance	Yes	No	No	No
5. Educational pay	Yes	Yes	Yes	No
6. Hospitalization insurance	Yes	Yes	Yes	Yes
7. Premium pay	K-9 Officers*	No	No	No
8. Satisfactory performance increase	Yes	No	No	No
9. Out-of-rank pay	No	Yes	No	No
10. Shift differential	No	Yes	Yes	No
11. Longevity pay	No	Yes	Yes	No
12. Life insurance	No	Yes	Yes	No
13. Tuition refund	No	Yes	No	Yes
14. Court overtime	No	No	No	Yes
15. Dental plan	No	No	Yes	Yes
16. Pension plan deduction	Not specified	Not specified	Not specified	8%

* Dog squad.

agreed upon as part of the agreement. The consumer price adjustment of the *Concord* contract states:

> Beginning at the start of the first pay period in July 1978 (July 10, 1978), the pay ranges for all classifications within the Peace Officer Representation Unit shall be adjusted as provided below:
>
> 1. The Consumer Price Index for all items for the San Francisco-Oakland area (1967 = 100) as reported by the Bureau of Labor Statistics, U.S. Department of Labor, for March 1978 shall be compared with the equivalent index reported for March 1977 and the change in Index Points shall be calculated as a percentage of change from the March 1977 Index, and
>
> 2. The percentage change in the Consumer Price Index as identified in (1) above shall be multiplied by eighty-five percent (85%), and
>
> 3. The product found by the multiplication in (2) above shall then be multiplied by two (2) and rounded to the nearest whole number. This process identifies the number of one-half percent (1/2%) increments on the "Schedule of Monthly Pay Ranges" (Table II) which shall be used in adjusting the salary range for each class within the Peace Officer Representation Unit. The hourly rates for each class will be derived in a similar fashion as applied to the "Schedule of Hourly Pay Rates" (Table III). [Tables II and III are attachments to the contract.]

The *Memphis* contract recognizes the overtime traditionally required before—and sometimes after—roll call. Claims to compensation for roll call have often been ridiculed by management as "counting minutes," but many rank-and-file police officers have long felt they should be paid for this time on duty. The *Memphis* segment on early roll call compensation is complex, involving overtime pay when this roll call time exceeds a maximum limit, and a conversion of sick time to compensatory time off immediately prior to retirement to make up for accumulated uncompensated early roll call time:

> Officers may be required to report up to seventeen (17) minutes prior to the start of the shift or may be detained up to seventeen (17) minutes following the end of the shift for purposes of roll call, equipment check-in or check-out or other administrative processes without same being considered for overtime premium pay as provided in Article XIX. When an officer is required to report more than seventeen (17) minutes early or is directed to remain more than seventeen (17) minutes following the end of the shift, then the total time before or after when in excess of seventeen (17) minutes shall be paid at the overtime rate.
>
> In recognition of the above time required of police officers before and after the start and finish of their shift without compensation, it is agreed that 13 percent of unused sick leave in excess of 65 days may be converted to compensatory time to be used by the officer in the final year prior to his retirement date. The amount of sick leave available for conversion is to be calculated by subtracting 65 days from the amount accumulated by the officer as set forth in Article XXXIV, Sick Leave. Such compensatory time must be utilized by the officer as time off during the final year of employment prior to effective date of retirement. No officer may claim compensation in lieu of unused compensatory time credited under this Article.
>
> To calculate this provision, determine the total number of unused sick days, not to exceed a maximum of 450 days accumulation pursuant to Article XXXIV—Sick Leave; subtract 65 days pursuant to Article XXXIV—Sick Leave; multiply the resultant figure by 13% to calculate entitlement under this provision. For example, an employee with the maximum of 450 accumulated sick days should subtract 65 days, leaving 385 days. Thirteen percent (13%) of 385 days is fifty (50) working days or ten (10) week entitlement.

The *Memphis* contract also has a provision for out-of-rank pay:

> Employees who are designated to perform supervisory responsibilities over other employees of equal rank or below shall be compensated as follows:
> 1. The employee shall receive 5% of the base rate for the top pay of his classification except as noted in item 2 and 3.
> 2. No officer supervising other patrolmen or warrant officers shall receive more than the top base rate for sergeant.
> 3. No officer supervising other sergeants shall receive more than the top base rate for lieutenants.

Such pay for work out of rank shall be made only when the officer is assigned to a supervisory responsibility and is so designated by his commanding officer who is required to record that action on the roll call sheet. For purposes of this Agreement, it shall apply only to officers below the rank of sergeant who are assigned to supervise other employees of equal rank or below, and for sergeants who supervise other sergeants. Warrant officers who are assigned supervisory responsibilities over other warrant officers or patrolmen shall be compensated at sergeant's rate.

It is agreed by both parties that no pay shall be made until such temporary assignments exceed three hours, but then the pay for work out of rank shall be retroactive to the first hour served.

It is further agreed by both parties that the provisions of this paragraph shall not apply to training officers, senior officers in a car, or senior officers in a detail, but is designed to apply only to those situations where officers of the same rank are designated as temporary supervisors for other officers at the same or lower ranks.

The *West Haven* contract has an unusual provision regarding the minimum staffing levels for each watch. It has implications for overtime, as management must staff outgoing watches (shifts) at the specified levels, and it also tacitly recognizes that the delivery of police services at specified times requires that a certain number of personnel be available. This segment of the contract states:

A full complement of men shall be ten (10) patrol beats 4 P.M. to Midnight and Midnight to 8 A.M. shifts and 3 P.M. to 11 P.M. and 11 P.M. to 7 A.M. on the 4 P.M. to Midnight (3 P.M. to 11 P.M.) and Midnight to 8 A.M. (11 P.M. to 7 A.M. shift), and nine (9) men on the 8 A.M. to 4 P.M. (7 A.M. to 3 P.M. shift).

There will be a minimum of three (3) Detectives and one (1) Detective Sergeant or Detective Lieutenant working the Detective Bureau on the 4:00 P.M. to Midnight shift.

One (1) uniformed desk Sergeant and one (1) uniformed Street Sergeant will work per shift at all times.

There will be minimum of one (1) Shift Commander working per shift at all times. A Shift Commander could be a Lieutenant or a Deputy Inspector.

In the event any additional beats are created, the full complement of men as herein stated shall be increased accordingly.

**Hours of Work
and Time Off**

While the hours of work and time off for vacation, holidays, and other excused absences are not usually considered economic factors, they do bear a direct relationship to productivity. The total number of hours worked annually for a specific salary is the true measure of service received by an employer. As time off with pay increases, employers receive less in exchange, and may even have to consider hiring additional employees to field an adequate number of officers each day.

All four contracts stipulate a basic work week of forty hours. Since none of the four agreements mentions ten-hour days or flex time, we can assume that these departments work a five-day week, with the typical eight-hour tour of duty. Therefore, each day off for vacation, holiday, or other excusability is presumed to be a day during which the employee would otherwise have worked an eight-hour tour of duty.

Vacation The *Memphis* contract awards annual paid vacations to employees based on the length of continuous service. For the first five years, the vacation time is ten days. Vacation time is thereafter increased at the rate of one day for each year of service up to a maximum of twenty-five days. Officers may split their vacations, setting aside no more than five days to be taken at the discretion of the officer with the prior approval of the commanding officer.

In the *Concord* agreement, vacations are available after six months of employment and earned at the following rates for each bi-weekly pay period worked:

Year	Vacation Hours Per Pay Period
First	3.077
Second	3.692
Third to twelfth	4.615
Thirteenth to fourteenth	5.538

In the *West Haven* contract, annual vacation leaves are specified in accordance with the employee's length of service as follows:

Six months to one year	one week
After one year	two weeks
Five to ten years	three weeks
Ten to fifteen years	four weeks
Fifteen years to retirement	five weeks

The *Tulsa* contract has an unusually extensive and informative provision on vacation leave:

Section 1. Vacation leave with pay shall be granted to employees in accordance with the following provisions:

A. An employee must be on regular employment status and have been employed by the City continuously for twelve (12) months before being eligible to expend vacation leave.

B. Vacation leave shall normally be requested and granted during the twelve (12) month period following the employee's vacation accrual year.

C. Vacation leave shall not exceed the total amount credited to an employee at the time of the proposed departure.

D. Employees shall not be permitted to use either accrued vacation leave or accrued compensatory time during a period of suspension.

Section 2. Vacation leave shall be accrued to each regular employee as follows:

A. Ten twelfths (10/12) of a working day for each full calendar month of service.

B. Upon completion of four (4) years of service an employee will accrue one (1) day of vacation for each full calendar month of service thereafter.

C. Upon completion of seven (7) years of service an employee will accrue one and one-fourth (1 1/4) days of vacation for each full calendar month of service thereafter.

D. Upon completion of sixteen (16) years of service an employee will accrue one and two-thirds (1 2/3) days of vacation for each full calendar month of service.

Section 3. The maximum amount of vacation leave that may be accrued by an employee shall be twice the amount for which the employee is eligible to accrue in one calendar year. No additional vacation leave shall be credited nor expended by an employee who has reached the maximum amount.

Section 4. The recording of the expenditure of vacation leave shall be as follows:

A. Holidays or other nonscheduled workdays shall not be included in computing vacation leave.

B. Vacation leave normally shall be taken in five (5) consecutive day increments.

Section 5. Any vacation leave accrued to an employee at the time of transfer from one department to another shall be recorded on the Personnel Action form and shall be transferred to the new department.

Section 6. Upon separation, an employee shall be paid for the unused portion of his accrued vacation leave provided he has completed twelve (12) continuous, consecutive months of employment with the City.

Section 7. An employee who is dismissed from the service of the City for embezzlement of City funds, theft of City property, shall be ineligible for payment of accrued vacation leave.

Section 8. Accrual of vacation leave shall not be retroactive prior to the effective date of this Agreement.

Section 9. An employee shall not receive pay for accrued vacation leave in lieu of time off except as provided in Section 6 of this Article.

Holidays

Each of the four contracts allows for a specific number of holidays. The number of holidays under each contract are

Memphis	9
Tulsa	10
West Haven	11
Concord	not specified but in accordance with citywide policy

Both the *Tulsa* and *West Haven* agreements specify one of the holidays as the employee's birthday; the others are major holidays.

Sick Leave

The *Memphis* contract states a clear and simple sick leave policy that includes a thoughtful section providing rewards of "bonus days" for unused sick leave:

> Members of this bargaining unit shall be covered by the City's sick leave policy as of the effective date of this Agreement. The effective date of this Agreement shall be that time which is used in determining future eligibility for bonus days and for the provision governing compensation for unused sick leave at time of retirement. Bonus day provisions and retirement benefits shall not apply prior to the effective date.
>
> It is agreed, however, that for purposes of determining accumulated days of sick leave, that the employee's seniority on July 1, 1969, shall be used in the initial calculation with accumulation rates since July 1, 1969, to be in accordance with city policy. Any employee with more than ten (10) years of seniority as of July 1, 1969, shall be credited with 120 days sick leave on that date and employees with less than ten (10) years shall be credited with an accumulated rate equal to the actual number of months of city service. Accumulation rates since July 1, 1969 to July 1, 1972, were as follows:
>
> 1. One (1) day for each month of service during the first five years (5) years of service.
> 2. One and one-half (1 ½) days for each month of service from the sixth (6th) year through the tenth (10th) year of service.
> 3. Two (2) days for each month of service from the eleventh (11th) year and thereafter.
>
> Accumulation rates from 1972 for the term of the Agreement shall be in accordance with the schedule provided below:
>
> Upon completion of three (3) months of consecutive service after official employment, all regular employees shall be eligible to receive pay while absent from work due to sickness to be charged against accumulated sick leave time.
>
> Sick leave shall be accumulated beginning with the first day of employment in accordance with the following schedule, not to exceed a maximum of 450 days accumulation:

1. One (1) day for each month of service during the first five (5) years of service.
2. One and one-half (1 ½) days for each month of service for the sixth (6th) year through ninth (9th) year of service.
3. Two (2) days for each month of service from the tenth (10th) through the fourteenth (14th) year of service.
4. Two and one-half (2 ½) days for each month of service from the fifteenth (15th) year and thereafter.

Sick leave will not accumulate while an employee is absent on sick leave fifteen (15) days or longer, during unauthorized absence, or during other leaves of absence, except military leave, and/or officially granted educational leave.

Pay for holidays that occur while an employee is on sick leave shall not be charged as sick leave.

Employees shall be compensated in cash for accumulated unused sick leave when they retire, not to exceed sixty-five (65) days beginning July 1, 1974, or at the applicable rate by city policy. The amount of payment for unused sick leave is to be calculated at the employee's rate of pay in effect on the pay day immediately preceding the employee's retirement. Such payment shall not be counted as compensation for the purpose of computing retirement benefits.

After completion of three (3) monthis of service, an employee who works three (3) consecutive months without sick leave, or any unauthorized absence, will be eligible for one (1) bonus day leave with pay, to be taken off within twelve (12) months from the day it is earned. Bonus days will be earned in a like manner for subsequent three (3) month periods so that an employee may earn up to four (4) bonus days a year.

The *Tulsa* agreement's sick leave provisions are substantially the same as the above. Sick leave is earned at the rate of one day for each full calendar month of service; a maximum of one hundred and fifty (150) days may be accrued; and when this limit is reached any excess can be converted to annual leave at a ratio of one vacation day for each three days of sick leave.

The *West Haven* contract defines sick leave as absence from duty without loss of pay because of a nonservice connected illness or injury, and includes medical or dental office visits which cannot be scheduled during nonworking hours. The provisions as to accumulating sick leave are

Employees covered by this agreement shall be entitled to one and one-quarter (1 ¼ days of sick leave for each full month of service, computed from date of hire.

Unused sick leave as accrued may be accumulated up to one hundred twenty days (120) and credited toward earlier retirement, or the employee shall receive one day of pay for each day of accumulated sick leave up to a maximum of one hundred twenty days (120).

Upon service connected death of an employee, the amount of sick leave due to such employee shall be payable to his designated beneficiary at his going rate of pay.

This contract also includes an unusual provision allowing employees to "borrow" sick leave:

> An employee who has exhausted his sick leave in any one year may request, in writing, an advance of future sick weeks. Such employee shall be allowed to borrow subject to the approval of the Board of Police Commissioners an additional fifteen (15) days' sick leave time. Such approved time shall be charged to the following year's sick leave. Upon his return to active duty, all earned sick leave credit shall be applied to his borrowed leave until repaid. Should for any reason an employee be terminated before the borrowed time is repaid, the days owed will be deducted from any monies owed to said individual upon his termination of employment.

The *Concord* agreement is nonspecific on sick leave. However, it contains an unusual section not appearing in the the other contracts. This provision is titled "Job Injury With Pay for Police Officers" and reads:

> There shall be provided a category of leave known as "Job Injury Leave With Pay for Police Officers." Such leave shall be administered according to the following provisions:
>
> a) *Eligibility*: Any full-time, sworn police officer occupying a regular position, regardless of such employee's period of service with the City, who may be disabled arising out of and in the course of work with the City of Concord shall be eligible for such leave with pay.
>
> b) *Clothing Allowance*: No clothing allowance shall be paid an officer while on this leave. However, upon return to work as a peace officer, the officer may be credited with a proportionate amount of the periodic clothing allowance payment in relation to the amount of time actually worked in the time period for which payment is made.
>
> c) *Disability Determination*: The determination of temporary, total or partial disability shall be made by the City's appointed medical examiner. In the event of a dispute, the finding, and order, of the Worker's Compensation Appeals Board (WCAB) regarding an application filed in connection with the injury, or disease, claimed to have arisen out of or in the course of employment, shall be binding upon both the City and the police officer with respect to: (1) disability, and (2) whether the disability is job incurred, and (3) whether the disability is total, temporary, partial, or permanent and stationary.
>
> d) *Duration of Leave*: The eligible police officer shall be entitled to this leave without loss of base salary in lieu of worker's compensation temporary disability indemnity benefits for the period of the disability not to exceed one year cumulatively from the date of the job incurred disability.
>
> If when on this leave, the appointing authority finds that the disability is permanent and stationary and the employee will be unable to return to work in his/her classification and so notifies the employee and within ten days thereof the employee advises the City in writing that he/she

does not consider the condition permanent and stationary to the extent that the employee is unable to return to work in that classification, the matter shall be resolved by the Worker's Compensation Appeals Board under the provisions of Labor Code Section 6144.

The decision of the Worker's Compensation Appeals Board upon this issue may be appealed by either party to the Superior Court providing this appeal is filed within twenty days from the date the arbitration award is issued by the Worker's Compensation Appeals Board or the court in the event an appeal is taken from the decision of the Worker's Compensation Appeals Board. While such appeals are pending, the employee shall be removed from full-pay benefits hereunder and shall apply for Long-Term Disability benefits under the City's insurance policy.

Pending the accrual of benefits under the Long-Term Disability Insurance policy, or benefits under the Concord Retirement System, there shall be paid to the employee by the City a sum equivalent to that which the employee would ordinarily receive under the City's Long-Term Disability Insurance policy or Retirement Benefits, whichever program the employee elects to proceed under. In the event the Worker's Compensation Appeals Board finds that the employee's disability is not permanent and stationary, and that the employee's condition is such that he/she cannot at that time be considered permanently unable to return to work, there shall be paid to the employee retroactively to the date the employee's payments were reduced, a sum sufficient to pay the employee's full salary for the period not to exceed one year. In the event the Worker's Compensation Appeals Board or the court upholds the position of the City, the payments as made by the City above shall be acknowledged as received under the provisions of this paragraph when an employee's disability is considered permanent and stationary and the employee is unable to return to work in the classification from which disabled.

e) *Life Insurance*: The amount of life insurance then in effect and provided by the City at the time of the police officer's job incurred disability shall remain in force and continue to be provided at the City's expense throughout the duration of this leave.

f) *Medical Plan*: While on this leave, the City will continue to pay on behalf of the disabled police officer, and the officer's eligible dependents, coverage under the City's group plan with either Blue Cross or the Kaiser Foundation Health Plan.

g) *Other Disability Income*: Benefits paid the disabled police officer by private plans paid for by that employee and without participation by the City shall be in addition to income provided by this leave.

h) *Probationary Appointments*: If the police officer was serving a Probationary Appointment when disabled on the job and the officer is subsequently reinstated from this leave to a position in the class occupied at the time of disability, the probation appointment period shall be extended by the duration of this leave.

i) *Retirement System*: Employee contributions are to be continued by the police officer while on this leave and this period of time shall be included as years of service under the Concord Retirement System.

j) *Return to Work*: If the disabled police officer recovers and is released for full-time employment and duty status in the officer's own classification, all benefits under this leave program shall cease and the employee shall immediately return to work upon medical release. This reinstatement from leave shall be made even though it requires the use of the City's layoff procedure. Medical release for return to work shall be determined and provided by the City's appointed medical examiner.

k) *Salary*: The salary to which the police officer is entitled while on this leave shall be the base salary step then in effect on the date of the job incurred disability.

l) *Seniority*: The police officer's seniority shall continue to accrue during the duration of this leave and may be used for whatever purpose seniority is used by the Police Department according to their regulations.

m) *Sick Leave*: While on this leave, the disabled police officer's sick leave accrued will be frozen as of the date of the disability and made available for use only upon return to full-time employment and active duty status with the City. There shall be no accrual of sick leave credits to the police officer during the duration of this leave.

n) *Social Security*: As a condition of receiving this Job Injury Leave With Pay, the disabled police officer shall apply, when eligible, for disability benefits from Social Security. Benefits paid to the police officer or the officer's dependents during this leave shall be made payable to the City by the disabled police officer. Failure of the employee to make application for Social Security benefits shall not prevent the City from making a deduction from the amount owing the employee consisting of the Social Security benefits to which the employee may have been entitled.

o) *Step Increases*: The interval between any step increase for which the police officer would otherwise be considered shall be extended by the duration of this leave and a new anniversary date shall be established as the effective date of any step increase granted following the reinstatement of the police officer from this leave.

p) *Vacation*: There shall be no accrual of vacation credited to the police officer during the duration of this leave.

q) *Worker's Compensation*: As a consideration of receiving this Leave With Pay, all temporary disability indemnity payments received as a Worker's Compensation benefit covering all or any part of the duration of this leave, shall be made payable to the City by the disabled police officer.

The *Memphis* contract also has an "On-the-Job-Injury" provision similar to Concord's but not quite as extensive.

Other Leaves   Each of the four agreements provides for other allowable leaves of absence with pay. The *Concord* contract is not specific, but the others are:

Memphis   Death in immediate family, 3 days
              Death in family, 2 days
              Military leave, 15 days
Tulsa   Educational leave, job related course(s)
              Maternity leave
              Leave for serious personal matters
              Leave to be married or to attend wedding of employee, brother, sister, son
                or daughter, when employee has no accrued vacation or compensatory time off
West Haven Death in family, 3 days
              Death of non-family member of employee's household, 2 days
              Military leave

The *Concord* agreement stands alone in a provision formalizing traditional "breaks" while on duty:

1. A Policy & Procedure Statement will be developed which shall provide one fifteen-minute relief break within each four-hour work period with no travel time permitted to go to some other site for that break. Relief break time may not be accumulated and, if not taken, shall be lost.
2. The Chief of Police shall administer such a program which will provide police officers no greater benefit than indicated above.

Management's Rights—   The *Memphis* contract contains a
Memphis   general statement reserving traditional rights to management, but specifically excludes from employer's prerogatives those working conditions and terms of employment covered elsewhere in the agreement:

It is understood that the management and the direction of the working force is vested exclusively in the City as the Employer except as specified in the other Articles of this Agreement. It is the City's right to hire, demote, suspend or discharge for just cause, retire, lay off, promote, assign or transfer employees to any job or any work, any time or anywhere, to increase or decrease the working force, to determine the number and size of the work shifts, to determine the number of employees assigned to any work or any job, to determine the hours of work per day or week, to make reasonable work rules for the purpose of efficiency, safe practices and discipline, to determine the equipment to be used, to make technological changes, to determine the number and location of its offices, to move, close, or liquidate its offices in whole or in part, to separate or reassign its employees in connection with said moving, closing or liquidating; the right to transfer or subcontract work, to establish new jobs and the wage rates for them, to determine the duties and production standards, to combine jobs, to eliminate classifications of work, to require overtime work, and to select employees for overtime.

The rights and powers of management mentioned in this Memorandum do not list or limit all such powers, and the rights listed together with all other rights, powers and prerogatives of the City, not specifically ceded in this Agreement remain vested exclusively in the City.

The exercise by the City of, or its waiver of, or its failure to exercise its full right of management or decision on any matter or occasion, shall not be a precedent or be binding on the City, nor the subject or basis of any grievance, nor admissible in any arbitration proceeding. The City's right of management shall not be amended or limited by any claimed or unwritten custom, past practice or informal agreement, nor by any claim the City has claimed or condoned or tolerated any practice or any act or acts of any employees.

Nothing is this Article shall abrogate or alter the other Articles of this Agreement.

The working conditions and terms of employment covered in other segments of the *Memphis* contract are:

1. Internal Investigation Procedure—specifies a "Bill of Rights" for officers under internal justice investigation.
2. Seniority Preference—seniority to prevail in "bidding" for job openings.
3. Promotions—specific one-test eligibility.
4. Grievance Procedure—establishes a four-step grievance procedure with advisory arbitration for grievances unresolved at the fourth step.
5. Departmental Disciplinary Procedures—sets limits on disciplinary action and allows for "vocal" representation by a fellow officer when the charges could result in an entry to the accused's personnel file.
6. Rules and Regulations—calls for all orders—written and unwritten—to be in accordance with the intent and language of the contract.
7. Residency Requirement—allows officers to live outside Shelby county (Memphis), but requires them to be able to report for duty within two hours of notification of an emergency.
8. Second Jobs—allows outside employment if it does not affect the employee's attendance, efficiency, or the reputation of city service.
9. Personnel File Review—officers may view contents of their personnel file; arrange for correction of "discrepancies"; and request a "designated union representative," including the "Union Attorney" to accompany them to review such records.
10. Hair Standards—calls for a "hair policy" to be established.
11. Fiscal Year Budget—requires that the union be furnished with a copy of the proposed police budget prior to: (1) submission to administrative hearings; and (2) prior to submission to the City Council.

Management's Rights— Tulsa

Lodge No. 93 of the Fraternal Order of Police, the recognized police union in Tulsa, and the representatives of city management have agreed on "management's rights" and responsibilities as follows:

Lodge No. 93 recognizes the prerogative of Employer to operate and manage its affairs in all respects and in accordance with its responsibilities, and the powers of authority which the Employer has not officially abridged, delegated, granted or modified by this Agreement are retained by the Employer, and all rights, powers and authority the Employer had prior to the signing of this Agreement are retained by the Employer and remain exclusively without limitation within the rights of the Employer.

Except as may be limited herein, the Employer retains the rights in accordance with the Constitution and laws of the State of Oklahoma and the responsibilities and duties contained in the Charter of the City of Tulsa and the ordinances and regulations promulgated thereunder;

A. To determine Police Department policy including the rights to manage the affairs of the Police Department in all respects;

B. To assign working hours, including overtime;

C. To direct the members of the Police Department, including the right to hire, terminate, suspend, discipline, promote, or transfer any Policemen;

D. To determine the table of organization of the Police Department, including the right to organize and reorganize the Police Department and the determination of job classifications and ranks based upon duties assigned;

E. To determine the safety, health and property protection measures for the Police Department;

F. To allocate and assign work to Policemen within the Police Department;

G. To be the sole judge of the qualifications of applicants and training of new employees;

H. To schedule the operations and to determine the number and duration of hours of assigned duty per week; provided that any hours worked in excess of forty (40) hours per week shall be considered overtime;

I. To establish and enforce Police Department rules, regulations and orders;

J. To introduce new, improved or different methods and techniques of operation of the Police Department or change existing methods and techniques;

K. To determine the amount of supervision necessary;

L. To control the departmental budget;

M. To take whatever actions may be necessary to carry out the mission of the Employer in situations of emergency.

The *Tulsa* contract limits the rights of management by covering working conditions and terms of employment in the following areas:

1. Seniority—when other factors (skills, conditions of work) are equal, seniority will be the dominant factor in determining vacation "pick," when compensatory time off will be allowed, regular days off, and shift assignment.

2. Grievance Procedure—described below.
3. Bulletin Boards—calls for the City to allow a bulletin board at each police station or substation for union business.
4. Rules and Regulations—provides for a "Police Officer Bill of Rights," described below.
5. Transfers—requires written notice of intradepartment transfer ten calendar days prior to effective date. (This policy does not apply to promotions, shift changes, temporary job assignments up to 60 days, and "light duty" assignment for partially disabled employees.)

The *Tulsa* contract's segment on handling grievances is both unusual and innovative in its sincere efforts to seek an impartial solution to the disputed issue:

Section 1. A grievance shall be defined as any dispute regarding the meaning, interpretation, application, or alleged violation of the terms and provisions of this Agreement. The Lodge or any employee or employees covered by this Agreement may initiate a grievance within fifteen (15) calendar days of the act or actions giving rise to the grievance, or within fifteen (15) calendar days from the date knowledge is gained of such act or actions in accordance with the following procedure.

Section 2. Any employee or employees who have a grievance may present their grievance in writing to the appropriate Division Commander. A Lodge representative may assist the employee in the presentation to the Division Commander. The Division Commander shall have three (3) working days in which to respond to the grievance. Such response shall be in writing.

Section 3. If the grievance is not resolved to the satisfaction of the employee, it may be submitted in writing to the Chief of Police within three (3) working days from receipt of the response from the Division Commander. The Chief shall respond to the employee in writing within seven (7) calendar days from receipt of such grievance indicating his decision on the issued raised.

Section 4. If the grievance is not resolved by the decision of the Chief of Police, the grievance shall be submitted in writing to the Personnel Director of the City within three (3) working days from receipt of the response from the Chief. The Personnel Director and the Chief of Police, or their designees, shall meet with a grievance committee composed of three (3) members of the Board of Directors of the Fraternal Order of Police within ten (10) calendar days from the receipt of such grievance. The Personnel Director or designee shall notify Lodge No. 93 in writing the answer to the grievance. This response shall be made within seven (7) calendar days from the date of the grievance meeting.

Section 5. If the grievance is unresolved after receipt of the answer from the Personnel Director, the Lodge may request that the matter be submitted to impartial arbitration. This request shall be made in writing to the Personnel Director within ten (10) calendar days from receipt of the answer from the Personnel Director.

Section 6. Within seven (7) calendar days from receipt of the request for arbitration, the parties shall jointly request a panel of seven (7) arbitrators from the Federal Mediation and Conciliation Service.

A. Within seven (7) calendar days from the receipt of such panel, a representative of the Lodge and the City shall meet and alternately strike names until one (1) arbitrator remains who shall be selected as the impartial arbitrator. The party requesting arbitration shall strike the first name.

B. Upon notification to the Federal Mediation and Conciliation Service of the selection of the arbitrator, and the arbitrator is contacted, the date for the Arbitration Hearing shall be set within fifteen (15) calendar days from the date the arbitrator is notified of his selection.

C. Within twenty (20) days after the conclusion of the hearing, the arbitrator shall issue a written opinion containing findings and recommendations with respect to the issues presented. A copy of the opinion shall be mailed or delivered to Lodge No. 93 and the Employer.

D. With respect to the interpretation, enforcement, or application of the provisions of this Agreement, which do not relate to the statutory and Charter authority of the Employer, the decision, findings, and recommendations of the arbitrator shall be final and binding on the parties to this Agreement.

E. The arbitrator's authority shall be limited to the interpretation and application of the terms of this Agreement and/or any supplement thereto. The arbitrator shall have no jurisdiction to establish provisions of a new Agreement or variation of the present Agreement or to arbitrate away, in whole or part, any provision of this Agreement or any supplements thereto or amendments thereof, nor shall any wage structures or structures of job classification be subject to arbitration. This shall not preclude individual wage grievances.

F. The cost of the impartial arbitrator shall be shared equally between Lodge No. 93 and the Employer. If a transcript of the proceedings is requested, then the party so requesting shall pay for it.

Section 7. All time limits set forth in this Article may be extended by mutual consent but if not so extended, they must be strictly observed. If a party fails to pursue any grievance within the time limits provided, he shall have no further right to continue the grievance.

Section 8. Grievances involving discharge or removal from classified service, suspensions, promotions and demotions shall remain under the jurisdiction of the Civil Service Commission.

Section 9. For the purposes of this Article, a "working day" is defined as a scheduled work day of the grievant or the respondent who is responsible for taking the required action to comply with the provisions of Sections 1, 2, 3 and 4 of this Article.

Section 10. It is specifically and expressly understood that filing a grievance under this Article which has as its last step final and binding arbitration, constitutes an election of remedies and a waiver of any and all rights by both parties, the Lodge or other representative of the party, to litigate or otherwise contest the last answer rendered through the Grievance Procedure, in any court or other appeal forum.

The "Police Officer's Bill of Rights" establishes for *Tulsa* police employees under investigation by the police department certain rights similar to those of all citizens in civil proceedings. The fact that Fraternal Order of Police representatives believed this detailing of rights was necessary probably indicates past transgressions during official internal justice investigations. Such a listing limits management's prerogatives during an investigation but also assures officers of fair treatment. The "Bill of Rights" provides:

A. The Chief of Police shall establish and put into operation a system for the receipt, investigation, and determination of complaints against Police Officers received by such Chief of Police from any person.

B. Whenever an Officer is under investigation and is subject to interrogation by members of his agency, for any reason which could lead to disciplinary action, demotion, or dismissal, such interrogation shall be conducted under the following conditions:

1. Interrogation: When an Officer is under investigation by the Tulsa Police Department for a complaint received, and is to be interrogated in respect to such complaint by other members of the department when there is a logical possibility that suspension, demotion, or dismissal may result, such interrogation shall be conducted as follows:

    a) The Officer shall be informed of the name of all complainants, if known. The employee may request to be confronted by the complainants. This shall be allowed where deemed necessary by the employee and the investigating Officer.

    b) Preliminary discussions with supervisory personnel within the Police Department, in relation to a complaint received, shall not be considered as interrogation as used herein.

    c) The Officer under investigation shall be informed of the rank, name, and command of the Officer in charge of the investigation, the interrogating Officer, and all persons present during the interrogation. All questions directed to the Officer under interrogation shall be asked by and through one interrogator at any one time.

    d) The Officer under investigation shall be informed of the nature of the investigation prior to any interrogation.

    e) Interrogating sessions shall be for reasonable periods and shall be timed to allow for such personal necessities and rest periods as are reasonably necessary.

    f) The Officer under interrogation shall not be subjected to offensive language or threatened with transfer, dismissal, or disciplinary action. No promise or reward shall be made as an inducement to obtain testimony or evidence.

g) The Officer under interrogation shall be completely informed of all his rights pursuant to this procedure prior to the commencement of the interrogation and of his responsibility to answer all questions, and this notification shall be included on the tape recording or written record of the session.

h) At the request of any Officer under investigation, he shall have the right to be represented by counsel or any other representative of his choice who may be present at all times during such interrogation.

i) Interrogation of Officers under investigation may be taped or recorded in written form at the discretion of the investigating Officer. Officers under investigation may record the proceedings with their own equipment or record at their own expense. Records and tapes compiled by the department shall be exclusively retained by the department as confidential information, but may be used at the discretion of the City in administrative hearings or for other administrative purposes.

2. An Officer under investigation shall receive written notification from the investigating Officer or the Chief of Police as to the determination of the investigation. Should an Officer be disciplined by suspension, demotion, dismissal, or transfer, or reassignment arising from an investigation, he shall be notified in writing as to the action being taken and the reasons therefor.

3. No Officer shall be discharged, disciplined, demoted, or denied promotion, transfer, or reassignment, or otherwise be discriminated against in regard to his employment, or be threatened with any such treatment, by reason of his exercise of the rights granted by this regulation.

Management's Rights— West Haven

The *West Haven* contract contains a simple statement of management rights, with a similar provision related to areas covered elsewhere in the agreement:

It is agreed that the City maintains and retains all of its rights and they are vested solely and exclusively in the City, unless specifically contracted otherwise by this agreement and further that the enumeration of management rights herein shall not be deemed to exclude any other rights incident to the administration of City management.

Some of the rights "contracted otherwise" are:

1. Seniority—allows for personnel to select their shift and beat by seniority; and for seniority to determine employees to be laid off in the event of a reduction in force, and for any subsequent rehiring.

2. Grievance Procedure—calls for a four-step procedure, with the last step providing for compulsory arbitration (State Board of Mediation and Arbitration) upon the request of the City or the Union.

3. Discipline and Discharge—described below.

4. Extra Police Duty—establishes rules for police work when the employee is paid by some party other than the City.

5. Promotions—requires specified seniority in rank to be eligible for examinations; results of tests to be posted within thirty days after examination; all vacancies to be filled within thirty days; and appointments to be made in numerical order from the eligible list.

6. Physical Fitness—described below.

The "Discipline and Discharge" segment of the *West Haven* contract is unusually comprehensive in marshalling union resources to aid officers ordered to report to the chief for violations of regulations, or otherwise exposed to internal justice administration. It is not as extensive as *Tulsa's* "Bill of Rights", but has many equitable and innovative features to ensure fair treatment for all employees:

1. When an employee is ordered to report to the Chief of Police for any violation of any department rule or regulation, personal or otherwise, such employee shall have the right to be attended by the Local Union if he so chooses. Such persons attending with the employee shall not have the right to enter into the discussion but to appear in body only.

2. The Union shall have the right to be in attendance at all disciplinary hearings before the Board of Police Commissioners. The accused will receive a letter advising him of the date of such hearing and copies of this letter shall be sent to the Union. At such hearings all witnesses shall be sworn. Mechanical equipment can be used to record all testimony. Any cost to be borne by the party requesting same. The accused shall have the right and choice of representation. Such hearings shall be closed to the public and press unless the accused requests an open hearing.

3. Any employee who has been disciplined or discharged and who is subsequently exonerated shall be reinstated with full rights and benefits and without prejudice, and shall be made whole for all losses incurred.

4. Whenever there is a civilian complaint against a member or group of members of the Police Department relating to his or their conduct as an officer or the manner in which such officer discharges his duties, and such complaint results in a hearing or inquiry, said member shall be entitled to be represented by an attorney of his own choosing before the Board of Police Commissioners. The City agrees to pay said attorney according to the schedule established by the New Haven County Bar Association in effect at the time the attorney is engaged. Should the attorney's fee be higher than the aforementioned rate, the employee will assume the difference in cost. The maximum liability to the City will be $500 per case.

5. Employees who are witnesses may be required to attend such hearings when off duty. Said witnesses when on the stand shall be compensated for such appearances by being paid a sum of money that is equal to the

number of hours spent at such hearings. Such pay shall be at the rate of straight time.

A number of police employees objected to the West Haven police chief's physical fitness program, and the police union filed a complaint against the city with the Connecticut State Board of Labor Relations. Subsequently, both the city and the union negotiated this complaint and agreed as follows:

1. That the document designated as "West Haven Police Department Official Weight Chart," hereinafter referred to as Exhibit A, attached hereto and made an integral part hereof, be deemed the official weight chart for all employees within the West Haven Police bargaining unit.
2. That Exhibit A shall list the ideal weight, average weight and maximum acceptable weight, by height.
3. That the maximum acceptable weight shall represent the maximum permissible weight for any employee within the police bargaining unit.
4. That all members of the bargaining unit shall be weighed on or about July 1, 1977, and on or about October 1, 1977, and approximately every 90 days thereafter. However, all present members of the Department, after the initial weigh-in, shall not be subject to punitive action of any kind if their initial weigh-in exceeds the attached chart. Any employee who initially (on or about July 1-77) exceeds the weight chart shall not subsequently exceed that reading at future weigh-ins unless exempted by provisions of Article #14.

   All future employees shall initially and subsequently conform to the weight chart unless exempted by provisions of Article #14.
5. That the weight scale to be utilized for measuring weights in accordance with this Agreement shall be situated in the West Haven Police Department locker room.
6. That a weight chart shall be posted in the locker room with all the police employees' names listed thereon, and their respective weights under measuring dates shall be inscribed adjacent to their names.
7. That all police personnel to be weighed shall be allowed to wear customary police shoes, underwear, pants and shirt.
8. That the column designated maximum acceptable weight incorporates an additional four pounds to compensate for the clothing referred to in paragraph 7 hereinabove.
9. That the City will take no punitive or disciplinary measures against any member of the bargaining unit as a result of the weighing to be performed on or about July 1, 1977.
10. That each member of the bargaining unit whose weight is in excess of the maximum permissible weight on or about July 1, 1977, or exempted by Article 14, shall sustain some weight loss on or before the next measuring date, or on or before October 1, 1977, whichever later occurs. A failure by any member of the bargaining unit to sustain some weight loss as aforesaid shall receive a written letter of reprimand in his official personnel file.

11. That each member of the bargaining unit whose weight is in excess of the maximum permissible weight on or about October 1, 1977, shall sustain some weight loss on or before the second measuring date, or on or before January 1, 1978, whichever later occurs. A failure by any member of the bargaining unit to sustain some weight loss, as aforesaid, shall receive a letter of reprimand in his official personnel file.

12. That all members of the bargaining unit are to reach the level of maximum permissible weight, in accordance with their height as contained in Exhibit A or as recorded on or about July 1–77, and such level shall be recorded on or about July 1–78.

    Failure on the part of any member of the bargaining unit to reach the maximum permissible weight as aforesaid, shall be just cause for suspension of (2) working days.

    Any subsequent infractions of the maximum permissible weight chart shall be just cause for suspension of (1) day.

13. Any member of the bargaining unit who receives a letter or letters of reprimand in accordance with Paragraphs 10 and/or 11, *supra*, shall have such letters removed from his file provided that such member reaches the level of maximum permissible weight on or before July 1, 1978.

    No letters of reprimand, or weight suspensions shall be utilized or evaluated to assess any officer's record insofar as his or her promotion is concerned.

14. That any member of the bargaining unit unable to reach the level of maximum permissible weight in accordance with Exhibit A, on or before July 1, 1978, because of medical reasons shall be exempt from any punitive or disciplinary proceedings, provided, however, that such member furnishes the Chief of the West Haven Police Department, on or before June 15, 1978, a written opinion from a medical doctor supporting such medical reasons.

15. That all such weigh-ins may be conducted by the Chief or any designated subordinate and shall occur immediately prior to or immediately subsequent to a work shift. Weigh-ins shall be conducted so as to cause a minimum of inconvenience to the individual police officer and to the operation of the West Haven Police Department.

16. That subsequent to July 1, 1978, all weigh-ins shall continue on a quarterly basis and, subject to the waiver and exceptions contained in Paragraphs 14 and 4 hereinabove, all members of the bargaining unit shall maintain their weight at the level of maximum permissible weight in accordance with Exhibit A herein attached.

Exhibit A*

Height	Maximum Weight Females	Males
5'0"	146	
5'1"	149	
5'2"	152	
5'3"	155	

Exhibit A* (cont.)

Height	Maximum Females	Weight Males
5'4"	159	171
5'5"	164	176
5'6"	168	181
5'7"	171	186
5'8"	174	191
5'9"	177	197
5'10"	181	202
5'11"	185	207
6'0"	189	212
6'1"		218
6'2"		225
6'3"		232
6'4"		237

*Chart based on "break-off" point for nonmedical insurance applicants

Management's Rights—Concord

The *Concord* Memorandum of Understanding does not contain any provision specifying the rights of management. Areas covered in the other three contracts apparently were not the subject of discussion during the meet and confer sessions leading to this contract. There is a minor segment specifying how seniority will be computed for "step" pay increments ("Anniversary Date of Step Increases"); and another allowing time off with pay for employees involved in grievance hearings scheduled during the employee's work hours.

There is also a section on the "Police Professionalization Program" that may involve some of management's traditional rights, but it merely calls for a good faith review and revision of the existing program to achieve mutually agreeable modifications:

> The City and the Association shall meet and confer regarding the modification of Policy Statement No. 720 titled "Police Professionalization Program" with the intent of reducing the general benefits and financial impact of such a program. The Concord Police Association shall designate its representatives to meet with the City's Management Representative Committee under the conditions set forth under the section entitled *Representation by Employees* of the existing Memorandum of Understanding with the Police Association. Both parties agree to make a diligent good faith effort to arrive at a mutually agreeable plan, prior to May 1, 1978, for modifying the Police Professionalization Program commencing in Fiscal Year 1978-79.

Management's Rights—Overview

Three of the contracts reviewed (Memphis, Tulsa, West Haven) indicate the police union's unhappiness with management's handling of transfers, assignments, internal investigations, and disciplinary procedures. The fourth contract (*Concord*) may be illustrative of employee concern with economic factors, hours of duty, and leaves, rather than satisfaction with other working conditions and terms of employment.

One of the most serious incursions upon management's prerogatives may be the Memphis contract's provision allowing employees to "bid" for jobs. However, this may simply represent the best possible way of handling employee dissatisfaction with a perceived unfair transfer and assignment policy. The Memphis contract's radical innovation provides for a "bid system" for permanent employees:

1. City-wide seniority shall prevail in bidding for job openings within the Memphis Police Division. Job openings in the Organized Crime Bureau are not subject to the bid system.

2. A job is defined for purposes of this Agreement as a working position within a squad, unit, or watch, working a particular shift or rotating shift where applicable, and with a particular set of current days off.

3. Jobs that require specific qualifications must have these qualifications posted on the bid notice. The commander of the unit being bid into may pick from the three (3) most senior qualified applicants. When multiple openings are posted, selections will be made from a list of qualified personnel numbering not more than two (2) times the number of openings to be filled. Employees passed over by seniority for these jobs shall be notified of the specific reasons for their not being selected by the unit commander, which may include attendance and disciplinary patterns, in writing within five (5) days. A copy of this correspondence shall be maintained in the unit commander's precinct or bureau file.

4. Job bids will include job assignment as heretofore defined and date of opening and closing. Bids will remain open five (5) days. This does not restrict management from adding additional qualifications for a specific job where required.

5. Each officer may successfully bid on three (3) jobs per fiscal year.

6. Unsuccessful bids of assignments will not be counted against the member's number of bids per fiscal year.

7. An officer may bid on more than one (1) job, but not more than two (2) jobs simultaneously. In the event an officer bids on two (2) jobs simultaneously, he will list first and second preference, and if successful in both, the officer will be assigned to his first preference. When bidding on two (2) jobs simultaneously and when the officer fails to list a preference, the assignment to one of the two jobs will be at management's prerogative.

8. Upon a job deletion or opening by management after two (2) successful division-wide bids, the most junior officer will be required to fill the open job.

9. Before probationary employees are certified, their jobs will come up for bids and will be restricted to bids from Uniform Patrol, Communications, and Detention.

10. Bids must be posted on all Union bulletin boards and in the Personnel Office for five (5) days. Persons to accept bids will be the Desk Lieutentant at each precinct, Command Duty Officer at Headquarters and Police Personnel Office. Officers must bid for jobs in person by signature and will receive a receipt to show that they placed a bid. The officer will retain the original and the person issuing the receipt will forward the copy along with the bid at the time the bids close to the Personnel Office. An officer may remove his name from the bid by appearing in person at the Personnel Bureau during working hours with his receipt during the five (5) days while the bid is still open.

11. Jobs successfully bid will be filled within twenty (20) days.

12. Commissioned officers regularly assigned to recruiting and training functions may be temporarily assigned, at Mangement's discretion, to various operations within the Criminal Investigation Bureau without being in violation of any clause within the Memorandum of Understanding which relates to the bidding process and job assignments.

The similarities and differences between each of these contracts are of concern to police personnel managers because they indicate areas in police administration that may need correction. Certainly any area that has traditionally come within the scope of management would not be the subject of collective bargaining if employees were not dissatisfied with the procedures and their application.

Prompt and appropriate action by police personnel managers to remediate some of these sore points may help preserve management's traditional areas of unilateral control and keep such issues from reaching the bargaining table. At the least, police personnel managers should give the chief of police an overview of the advantages and disadvantages of proposed union changes before bargaining begins.

Another role of the police personnel officer is to assist the chief of police in administering the provisions of a union contract for its term of years. Again, the police personnel manager can inform the chief of police, prior to contract renewal, of the problems found in working within the various segments of the existing contract and make recommendations for appropriate modifications.

Chapter Review

Summary   We have reviewed police union contracts in four major cities in four distinct geographical areas: West Haven, Connecticut; Memphis, Tennessee; Tulsa, Oklahoma; and Concord, California. All four contracts include sections dealing with the employees represented, economic factors, hours of work, time off, and the rights of management and workers. Among the unusual or uncommon features are absence of a no-strike clause (Concord), merit salary increase (Tulsa), court overtime (Concord), salaries linked to cost-of-living index (Concord), out-of-rank pay (Memphis), maternity leave (Tulsa), 15-minute "relief break" each four-hour work period (Concord), mandatory physical fitness (West Haven).

The provisions of the "management rights" segments of all contracts indicate employee unhappiness with existing procedures on transfers, assignments, discipline, and internal affairs investigation. The Memphis contract, for example, has a "bid system" for job openings based on seniority and demonstration of special qualifications. In effect, then, the Memphis provision restricts managers' rights in the area of transfers and assignments to selecting one from the three most senior qualified applicants to fill each opening.

Critique

Negotiators in collective bargaining recognize the necessity of compromise, but each group seeks the best possible combination of trade-offs. Representatives of the police employee group, for example, may sacrifice one or more demands to gain footing in an area they believe potentially more important; and management's team may agree in one area to gain a concession that will serve them better functionally, fiscally, or politically. Because negotiating strategies commonly involve a good deal of "psychological warfare," no information is available on original demands (labor) or possible concessions (management). Such information would reflect an accurate assessment of employee concerns and the attitudes of management.

Questions for Discussion and Review

1. What job classes are included in the bargaining units of three out of four contracts cited?
2. What is the rationale for no-strike clauses?
3. How do these contracts differ on fringe benefits? Sick leave?
4. Why are provisions as to on-the-job injury included in a contract?
5. Describe the job bid system. What are its implications for management? For police education? For career development?
6. Summarize the trend toward restricting management's rights; toward expanding employee rights.
7. What is the role of the police personnel manager in administering the provisions of labor contracts?

8. Does the fact that these contracts spell out ground rules for various "personnel transactions" indicate gross failure in police personnel management?

Workbook Project   Examine all of the unusual provisions of the contracts cited in this chapter. Develop a list of such terms and conditions of employment.

17

Terminations

Chapter Objectives

- to discuss various termination routes in terms of retaining those employees who perform at a satisfactory or better level
- to explore the role of the police personnel manager in reducing employee turnover

When we speak of "termination," we are referring to several different phenomena. Resignations and regular retirements are voluntary terminations by employees; layoffs, dismissals, and mandatory retirement are voluntary terminations by management; and deaths and disability retirements are involuntary terminations of employment. For a schematic overview, see Figure 17-1.

Prior to the fiscal insolvency of many large cities such as New York and Detroit, layoffs were unheard of in the police field. Now this cause of temporary termination must be recognized as a potential problem and avoided when possible. Dismissals of employees for cause are administrative confessions that all personnel practices have failed. They are both necessary and undesirable. At some point in the employer-employee relationship, an employer may find it necessary to dismiss an employee for good and sufficient cause, yet such actions are undesirable for both business and humanitarian reasons.

On a broad base, terminations must be viewed in relation to the overall cost of training employees. Expenses incurred in recruiting and selecting candidates, in exposing them to basic training, and in maintaining employees on basic salary schedules until they reach peak productivity, all contribute to the employer's investment in human resources. Since this cost factor varies from one employee to another, it is impossible to give an average overall investment

Figure 17-1
Termination Routes

figure. Personnel managers can only note the losses that occur when employees resign, or are killed in the line of duty, retire on a disability, or are discharged.

Resignations

Job disenchantment is the major cause of a high turnover rate; that is, a disproportionate number of resignations. Discrepancies between pre-employment expectations and real-life job experiences are the primary cause of resignations.[1]

Police personnel managers expect some amount of turnover up to the time employees earn a few years seniority and equity in a local pension system. During the initial year or two of employment, dissatisfied employees can find another job to their liking without losing any of these accrued benefits. However, when employees of several years continue to resign in similar numbers, police personnel managers should probe for reasons and take remedial action.

"My job makes me sick" is an increasingly common complaint in all types of work settings. Headaches, back pain, physical exhaustion, insomnia, and all kinds of ills have been traced to job stresses. Fortunately, symptoms of work-related stress that might lead to resignation can be identified and ap-

Paul Pigors and Charles A. Meyers, *Personnel Administration: A Point of View and a Method*, 8th ed. (New York: McGraw-Hill Book Company, 1977), p. 204.

propriate action taken *before* an employee concludes he or she is "sick" of their job.

Exit interviews by police personnel managers can build up a reasonable amount of data on why employees resign, and a growing body of knowledge on job stresses specific to the police workplace will assist them in assigning causes for these job terminations.[2] Once such data have been compiled, line commanders and other concerned personnel can be apprised of the situation and develop programs to combat it. However, it remains the basic responsibility of the police personnel manager to reduce employee turnover. Even a small percentage of turnover signifies a waste of the organization's human resources and justifies an ongoing program to reduce the number of resignations.

One cautionary note: Transfers from one subunit of a police agency to another are not terminations, yet they do indicate dissatisfaction with certain aspects of the work setting that may result in resignation. Police personnel managers should audit all requests for transfers to determine the existence of unsatisfactory work conditions.

This audit may reveal no more than that requests for transfers were motivated by the same dissatisfactions that led to resignations. On the other hand, an alert personnel manager is sensitive to underlying reasons for employees' wanting to get out of a unit, as well as reasons why supervisors are happy to "dump" a member of a work group. Such data can be utilized in any program to reduce employee dissatisfaction, particularly when the dissatisfied employee can ultimately become the worker who resigns.

Layoffs

In industry, layoffs are usually temporary terminations that result from a general reduction in employment, the firm's need to cut costs of production, or the elimination of jobs because of automation. Since these terminations do not result from any dissatisfaction with the employees' work performance, it is reasonable to assume that these workers will be rehired at the employer's first opportunity.

Agencies in a jurisdiction confronting a fiscal crisis usually put a moratorium on entry-level hiring to hold down costs prior to any consideration of layoffs. This is less damaging to the agency because there is no loss of trained personnel. Candidates for appointment are usually already employed elsewhere and must simply wait out the crisis.

In industry, labor relations contracts commonly establish the procedures for layoffs, usually on the basis of seniority in relation to job title. In those

---

[2] See William H. Kroes and Joseph J. Hurrell, Jr., eds., *Job Stress and the Police Officer: Identifying Stress Reduction Techniques* (Washington, D.C.: U.S. Department of Health, Education and Welfare, 1975); see also, William H. Kroes, *Society's Victim—The Policeman: An Analysis of Job Stress in Policing* (Springfield, Ill: Charles C Thomas, 1976).

police agencies which have contracts with police employee groups, the provisions of the contract likewise specify who will be laid off, and again simple equity often dictates "last in, first out."

Periods during which layoffs are made are turbulent times for police personnel managers, and any atempt by line commanders to "manage" layoffs to get rid of less desirable workers should be discouraged. Any management of layoffs must be fair to the employees being terminated. The overriding factor in this decision is the seniority of employees.

Dismissals

There is a known reluctance in police agencies to dismiss sworn personnel. This has been one of the reasons for instituting a period of probationary employment as a part of the selection process. It has long been apparent that this reluctance to terminate sworn police officers goes far beyond any feelings of empathy with the person involved. It is probably a realization of the social stigma involved in being a "dismissed cop," and some latent feelings of fraternity inherent in the organizational socialization process. Whatever the reasoning, it is no more than fair that employees be given every opportunity to change unacceptable behavior patterns prior to dismissal for cause.

Demotion in pay grades has never been utilized to any great extent in police agencies, but police personnel managers should consider such punitive action in lieu of dismissal. One technique that has been utilized is disciplinary probation, but it has the disadvantage of putting the employee under great stress not to overstep the bounds of "good behavior." Disciplinary layoffs, as an action short of dismissal, may bring about the desired and necessary change in a worker's behavior. These suspensions do allow an employee time to reflect upon his or her problems and time to seek help for remedial action. They also have the advantages of packing an economic wallop—as there is likely to be loss of earning capacity for the period of suspension—and of avoiding the daily humiliation of working for less salary or the "good behavior" overtones of probation.

Police personnel managers should be reluctant to use dismissal as a personnel practice until all other possibilities have been ruled out, or unless there are overriding good and sufficient reasons for terminating an employee. Ideally, police personnel managers should subscribe to the philosophy that employees have a proper expectation of continued employment so long as their conduct is within established and appropriate behavioral limits.

Deaths

Deaths from natural causes are act-of-God terminations. Since job stress is now recognized as a precipitating factor in many illnesses, personnel managers should audit these terminations to discover any relationship of the work or work setting to the cause of death. In some states, heart disease has been legally recognized as job-related to the police occupation, and special benefits are forthcoming to victims of heart disease. This official recognition should serve as a goad to personnel managers to probe into the many facets of job-related illnesses and deaths and project appropriate remedial action.

Deaths that occur in the line of duty as a result of accident, misfortune, or attack by an armed opponent are job-related, and personnel managers and line commanders have a joint responsibility to raise safety standards by any means possible. An indispensable first step is to audit the causes of death. Safety programs can be based to some degree on these findings; however, much remains to be done to assure uniformly high levels of safety throughout the profession.[3]

Injury reports give prior notice of areas in which deaths may occur and point out critical areas for implementing special safety programs. Similarly, an audit of violence against police officers in the course of policing events or making arrests serves as a guide to emerging public hostility that could develop into fatal "Target Blue" ambush attacks on police officers.

Like resignations, deaths of police officers represent the untimely termination of an employee's services. The costs of replacing these men and women, and the loss of an unknown number of years of productive service, are out-of-pocket costs to the police agency. In addition, deaths in line of duty often call for the payment of special benefits to a surviving spouse and minor children.

In 1976, the U.S. Congress enacted the Public Safety Officers' Death Benefits Act. Under this legislation the federal government pays $50,000 to the survivors of local public safety officers. The provisions of this federal law apply to cases in which a public safety officer has died as the direct and proximate result of a personal injury sustained in the line of duty. The benefit is paid to surviving family members:

1. If there is no surviving child of such officer, to the surviving spouse of such officer;
2. If there is a surviving child or children and a surviving spouse, one-half [benefit] to the surviving child or children of such officer in equal shares and one-half to the surviving spouse;
3. If there is no surviving spouse, to the child or children of such officer in equal shares; or
4. If none of the above, to the dependent parent or parents of such officer in equal shares.[4]

Suicides of working police officers are a cause for the professional concern of police personnel managers. Obviously, self-inflicted deaths may be

[3] See *Guidelines for Developing an Injury and Damage Reduction Program in Municipal Police Departments* (Washington, D.C.: U.S. Department of Justice, Law Enforcement Assistance Administration, 1973).

[4] Title 42, U.S. Code, Section 3796–96c.

unrelated to the person's public life. On the other hand, some factor in the work setting may have contributed to a suicide decision: Alcoholism or physical illness leading to many suicides is likely to be job-related, and divorce and other family problems leading to depression and suicide of police officers are also known to bear a direct relationship to job stress.[5]

Disability
Retirement

Disability retirement at any time prior to the normal termination by regular retirement is the early and costly loss of a trained and productive employee. The cost of Workmen's Compensation and other disability pension costs, as well as days lost on account of illness and/or injury prior to the disability retirement, all contribute to the employer's loss. Over and beyond these out-of-pocket costs are the personal costs involved in the suffering, anxieties, and depression of the disabled employee.

When an illness or injury warrants serious considerations of disability retirement, there is a great need for a program that is fair to the police officer and to the employer. On the one hand, there is a need for warmth, understanding, and support; on the other, there is the overriding need to serve the public's best interest. Uppermost should be the question, Is the disability job-related? and What is the recuperative diagnosis? Currently, disability pensions are granted as the result of an adversary process in which attorneys on both sides try to determine whether the claimant's injury is job-related.

With respect to disabilities, police personnel managers should seek to implement a program that will (1) reduce injuries and illnesses leading to disability; (2) be supportive of employees removed from work situations because of illness or injury; and (3) lead to timely return to work for disabled officers who desire and are ready for it. When disability retirement is warranted, the role of the personnel manager is to help the employee survive and recover from this difficult termination process.[6]

Any member of a police retirement system is usually retired for disability regardless of age or length of service, if incapacitated for the performance of duty as the result of injury or disease occurring in and arising out of the course of employment. Any member otherwise incapacitated for the performance of duty shall be retired regardless of age, but only for a minimum period of service. Incapacity for performance of duty shall be determined by a board of review, and the minimum period for nonservice-connected injury or illness is generally part of the pension contract.

Police employee groups have been successful in securing state legislation identifying heart disease as a service-connected illness under certain condi-

[5] Jeffrey A. Schwartz and Cynthia B. Schwartz, "The Personal Problems of Police Officers: A Plea for Action," in *Job Stress and the Police Officer*, pp. 130–141.

[6] Jerome H. Jacobs, "Reducing Police Stress: A Psychiatrist's Point of View," in *Job Stress and the Police Officer*, pp. 85–116.

tions. These statutes usually stipulate that after a specified minimum period of service in a police agency, "heart trouble" can be termed an injury or disease occurring in and arising out of employment.

Retirements   Police personnel managers have a dual responsibility with respect to retirements—to process requests for retirement and to advise retirees of their benefits.

Personnel managers at city and county levels should seek to align their pension plan with a sound, statewide police retirement system. State enabling legislation for this purpose accommodates diverse salary plans, assigns an equitable distribution of costs and benefits to participating agencies, and may provide for some carryover of benefits to lateral transferees within the state.[7]

In order to ensure that pension systems are actuarially sound, early retirements are discouraged. Employees do have the option of paying a higher percentage of their salaries to purchase the right to early retirement, but the high cost of these options is prohibitive to most workers.

The normal rates of contribution by employee and employer are determined so as to provide an average annuity equal to one-half of the employee's terminal salary at the minimum age required for service retirement.

Requests for retirement are self-actuating if a review of personnel records indicates the employee has an adequate number of years of service. Usually the minimum term of service is twenty-five years.[8]

The concept of retirement as a personnel practice establishes this form of termination at a time when an employee's peak productivity is likely to decline. In theory, it is an honorable way of making room for younger men, particularly since the police occupation does demand a certain amount of strength and agility. However, police officers do not retire well. Many of them become depressed and there is a known incidence of suicides among retired police officers.[9]

The purpose of mandatory retirement provisions of police pension plans is to protect the public by assuring citizens of the ability of all sworn police personnel to respond to their job demands. The objective of assuring physical fitness in all sworn police personnel is rationally furthered by a maximum age limitation. In rebuttal, opponents of mandatory retirement point out that elderly employees can continue to contribute effective work, and that the substantial economic and psychological effects of premature and compulsory retirement far outweigh possible advantages.

In 1976, the U.S. Supreme Court upheld a Massachusetts law compelling the retirement of a state officer by age fifty. Plaintiff Murgra, a uni-

---

[7] National Advisory Commission on Criminal Justice Standards and Goals, *Report on Police* (Washington, D.C.: U.S. Government Printing Office, 1973), p. 510.

[8] National Advisory Commission, *Report on Police*, p. 511.

[9] See Joseph Wambaugh, *The New Centurions* (Boston: Little, Brown and Co., 1970).

formed member of the Massachusetts state police, brought suit to have the Massachusetts statute declared unconstitutional. The three-judge United States District Court for the District of Massachusetts (376 F. Supp. 753) declared the statute unconstitutional and void, and appeal was taken. In *Massachusetts Board of Retirement* v. *Murgra,* 427 U.S. 307 (1976), the Supreme Court reversed judgment, holding that rationality, rather than strict scrutiny, was the proper standard in determining whether the statute violated equal protection; that the age classification was rationally related to furthering a legitimate state interest—that is, protection of the public by assuring physical preparedness of its uniformed police; and finally that the fact that the state chose not to determine fitness more precisely through individualized testing after age fifty did not mean that the objective of assuring physical fitness was not rationally furthered by the maximum age limitation. In other words, the statute did not deny plaintiff equal protection, notwithstanding that he was physically and mentally capable of performing the duties of a uniformed officer.

Despite this ruling, the high cost of pension plans for both employees and employers may force a reexamination of the concepts of mandatory retirement. Although some elderly persons are less physically fit than younger co-workers, this is not to say that the agency would not profit by using such personnel in limited-duty assignment where their teaching skills and special talents might prove invaluable. The overall costs appear to be less than the cost of mandatory retirement.

Federal legislation in this area indicates a trend against forcing any employee into retirement on the basis of age. While police agencies can always cite physical fitness as a principal qualification for employment, police personnel managers should be aware of all of the many factors in mandatory retirement, from cost to social justice for longtime workers.

In fact, pension systems in some jurisdictions have found it good management policy to encourage workers to postpone retirement even after they have become eligible for benefits. Workers who stay on are rewarded by a small percentage increase in their pensions for each additional year of service.

Chapter Review

Summary The costs of recruiting, selecting, basic training, and duty until the end of the probationary period must be spread over as many years of productive work performance as possible to achieve any reasonable cost-effectiveness ratio. Added to these are the costs of career development, another investment that only proves worthwhile in the long run. Resignations and requests for transfer are warnings and early warnings, respectively, of employee dissatisfaction. Dismissals are failures. It is hard to justify a dismissal unless all other means to correct an employee's performance have been exhausted, and even then disciplinary action must follow a procedure geared to workers' rights.

Layoffs are new to police employment. Since they result from fiscal problems rather than unsatisfactory performance or job dissatisfaction, employing agencies should make every effort to rehire such employees when funds are available.

Deaths are act-of-God terminations. Federal death benefits add to local provisions for surviving families, but these measures miss the mark by overlooking the issue of preventive action. It is up to the local agency to initiate programs to reduce deaths from job-related illnesses, accidents, and line-of-duty injuries. Disability retirements are costly to employers and disabled employees. Again, preventive programs are warranted, as well as assured benefits to disabled employees.

Pension costs and the continued physical ability of workers to meet job demands suggest a program to encourage "late" rather than "early" retirement, and the revision of any rule for the retirement of workers based on age.

Critique

Police personnel managers must be accorded greater authority in effectively blocking resignations, dismissals, early retirements, and disability retirements, and in intiating programs to prevent deaths from job-related illnesses, accidents, or line-of-duty injuries. The present influence of line commanders and other line personnel on factors leading to terminations must be subordinated to the personnel manager's role in retaining as many employees as possible and in averting losses due to preventable deaths, illnesses, and injuries.

Questions for Discussion and Review

1. Define and discuss employee turnover.

2. What routes out of an organization should be audited by personnel managers? Why?

3. What are the problems associated with disability retirements? With line-of-duty deaths?

4. Under what circumstances are federal death benefits awarded to surviving family members of a police employee killed while on duty? While off duty?

5. What are the substitutes for dismissal? Discuss the merit of such substitutes.

6. What are the advantages and disadvantages of mandatory retirement? of "early" retirement?
7. What are the rights of police employees in relation to dismissal?
8. Are line personnel and line commanders more influential than personnel managers in termination decisions or conditions leading to termination?
9. What is the nature and scope of the social stigma allegedly associated with the dismissal of a police employee?

Workbook Project   Examine each of the routes out of a policy agency. For each route, list measures that might be taken to retain employees.

VI

FUTURE
TRENDS

Future Trends   A survey of past and current trends in police personnel management indicates a natural growth process at work enlarging not only the dimensions of personnel management generally, but also extending the horizons of police personnel management.

The increased willingness of police employees to "go public" with demands for improved salaries, hours and other terms and conditions of employment is illustrative of the need for closer examination of all personnel transactions and the need to find out just how imperfect or out of balance contemporary police personnel management might be.

Total personnel management in a police agency means that practitioners in this management area must seize every opportunity to serve more effectively the agency's rank-and-file employees and its supervisors, managers, and executives, and at the same time be responsive to what is happening in courts, legislatures, the central personnel agency, the local market, and the community served. A graphic illustration of the police personnel manager's perspective appears in Figure VI-1 on the next page.

Figure VI-1
Total Police Personnel Management

18

Research
and
Development

Chapter Objectives

- to determine the research needs of the police service and of police personnel management
- to point out the role of organizational socialization in understanding human behavior in the workplace
- to take a look at the promise inherent in the "new professionalism"

Police personnel management is coming into its own as an occupational field. The here-and-now activities and operations of police personnel managers will determine which tasks and responsibilities will constitute the core activities of the field in the future.

Police personnel managers must work toward further clarifying the questions of how, where, when, and under what conditions the human resources of an employing agency will be used. They must also work toward retaining those employees who meaningfully contribute to achieving the objectives of the police service; take significant measures to develop career-oriented employees for jobs of increasing difficulty and greater responsibility; advise and work with the police chief, line commanders, and the public employer to ensure near optimal conditions and terms of employment; and take other appropriate action suggested by research findings and analysis of developmental projects.

Research Design As applied to police personnel management, the purpose of research is to arrive at some propositions about human behavior in a police workplace. The problems are great and the unanswered questions pertain to jobs as well as jobholders.

Field experiments should be conducted in on-the-job settings in which the testing of some hypothesis or the trial of some innovation will produce findings amenable to analysis.

251

Despite the fact that it may be difficult to measure work performance in the police services area, research design must include some technique(s) by which to appraise on-the-job behavior and its results. It is hardly likely that researchers will be able to quantify the effect of police intervention in stemming crime or disorder in a community, but specific measures of productivity, performance, and/or effectiveness can be developed.[1]

The research design should identify and isolate the behavior (or job, or unit) to be studied; establish the research objective(s); set research strategy as to which data are to be collected, when, and how much will be gathered; provide for staffing and funding the project; provide for the application of research findings to work performance and/or work environment; and specify techniques to evaluate those changes made as a result of the research findings. For an outline of these various research stages, see Figure 18-1.

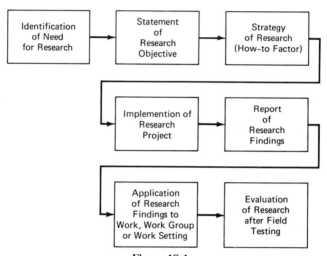

Figure 18-1
The Research and Development Process in Police Personnel Management as Related to Work Performance and Environment

The design of developmental projects depends upon the behavior studied and its relation to police field operations. However, planning for such projects should include a strategy for validating research results and for implementing corrective or ameliorative techniques when these appear warranted.

Research Methods The case method of research is essentially a thorough examination and analysis of one or more individuals (workers, supervisors, or managers/executives) or organizational units (jobs, job classes, work units, or

See *Performance Measurement and the Criminal Justice System: Four Conceptual Approaches* (Washington, D.C.: National Technical Information Service, U.S. Department of Commerce, 1976).

departments). Since this method focuses a large amount of attention upon one small area, its forte is the discovery of useful hypotheses for future field testing and meaningful insights into other areas of rewarding research. The case method of research is particularly appropriate in probing for the overt and covert reasons why individuals behave the way they do in an employee role.

Contract research is often the better choice when a pressing problem requires analysis. In this method the police personnel manager's role is limited to helping establish the research objectives. The other stages of the project are designed and implemented by a team of specialists from an outside firm. This is not to downgrade in-house research—under proper direction and control, police personnel can achieve significant research results.

Personnel assigned to research or professionals hired for this purpose should be able to evaluate information and to recognize and understand relationships among things and people. These individuals should also have the intellectual acuity to draw objective and reasonable conclusions from observed events and learned facts. A final, but no less important qualification is that they be accomplished technical writers. The real worth of a research report is what it communicates about the work done and the research findings.

Research Areas

The most critical need of police agencies today is to measure the level of police effectiveness. The objectives and priorities that guide the delivery of police services in America, and the allocation of resources to and by these agencies, require extensive and probing research. Such research should restate these objectives in quantifiable and measurable terms.

Despite the millions of dollars that have already been expended on delineating the role of police officer, police personnel managers have no specific quantifiable data on the "ideal job applicant," the "ideal police officer," or the "ideal candidate for advancement and promotion." Present research has done little more than detail the various tasks of a police officer and the expectations of management as to role performance. What is required is a more probing analysis of what police officers do and the qualifications and characteristics of those who do it well. With these data in hand, agencies will more easily be able to locate these men and women and bring them into the police occupation.

The area of personnel transactions (acts by management affecting employees) is a primary research area for the study of supervisory and managerial behavior and its impact upon workers. A brief scanning of the police union contracts discussed in Chapter 16 will reveal that most of their provisions came into being as a result of actions on the part of management that alienated a sufficient number of workers. Certainly, when the circumstances of a personnel transaction in one police agency results in union action to overcome unfairness or injustice, researchers in another police agency can justify research examining their practices in similar circumstances.

Another area for research and development from which police personnel managers can profit is the process of socialization within an employing agency. Findings in this area can affect both employee behavior and job satisfaction.

In sum, research should be concerned with all of the foregoing areas as well as the cause-and-effect relationships between them and workers' satisfaction with their jobs. For an overview of the areas for profitable research in police personnel management, see Figure 18-2.

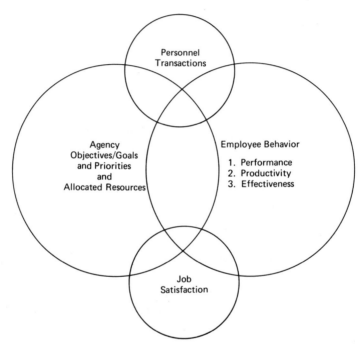

Figure 18-2
Research Areas in Police Personnel Management

Organizational   The process of organizational social-
Socialization   ization communications to new or recently promoted employees what is important in the organization and in the subunit to which they are assigned. Supervisors and co-workers are the "faculty" in this learning process. The so-called "price of membership" requires new or newly promoted employees to learn a complex set of values and behavioral norms:

1. Major goals of organization
2. Preferred means for goal achievement
3. Role responsibility and required role behavior patterns
4. Rules for maintaining the identity and integrity of the organization.[2]

---

[2] Edgar Schein, "Organizational Socialization and the Profession of Management," *Industrial Management Review*, 9, No. 2 (Winter 1968), 1–15.

In police agencies, both police officers at entry level and newly promoted personnel are scheduled for training in the duties of their new jobs. In either case, the primary function of schooling is to initiate the employee into his or her new role. In basic training, civilian ways of thinking and behaving are systematically replaced by the mental attitudes and behavior appropriate to a police officer. In higher training, the title of the new job along with emblems of semi-military rank define the new role as different from past roles.

On the whole, both recruits and candidates for promotion look forward to meeting the anticipated demands of socialization. In a minority of cases, socialization shocks the new or recently promoted worker, and he or she is unable or unwilling to go along with all the demanded patterns of behavior. However, most of these temporarily disillusioned employees are brought by the organizational socialization process, through the support of supervisors and co-workers, to an acceptance of organizational norms and eventually deliver above-average performance. In a good number of cases, the employee finds that one of the "hooks" of the socialization process means loss of benefits in the event of resignation. This is a powerful, although negative device to retain those employees who are otherwise ambivalent about their work.

Such workers have been aptly termed "turn-offs," in contrast to the group of "turn-ons" who are highly motivated to perform at satisfactory levels or above. Turn-offs may present some problems to line commanders, but they are minor problems compared to the loss involved when an employee resigns.

Awareness of the process of organizational socialization will alert police personnel managers to the forces at work upon employees in the early years of a police career and at each promotional step, and should lead to various research projects. There is a great need for data on how best to utilize the socialization process.

The New Professionalism

The continuing struggle of police employees to join the ranks of physicians, engineers, and other professionals promises a great potential for growth in police personnel management. The National Advisory Commission on Criminal Justice Standards and Goals has compiled a body of knowledge that reflects the prevailing practices, standards, and goals of police in the United States, and police agencies and employees all across the country have contributed to and extended this body of knowledge. All of these data point toward more stringent educational and on-the-job performance standards, which in turn foreshadow a credentialing of police not only for entry-levels jobs but for all positions, including that of police chief.

Public reluctance to pay a premium for less than adequate police service, and strong disapproval of any hint of police corruption or coercive interrogation practices, will certainly support the objectives of these new professionals.

At this point, the changes that need to be made in the dimensions of police personnel management may be nebulous, dependent as they are upon the results of future research and trial-and-error development of emerging ideas.

However, we can expect these new professionals to support promising research projects and to initiate collateral efforts to discover better ways of finding, utilizing, and keeping the human resources of management.

Chapter Review

Summary　　　　　　　　　　Contemporary developments in police personnel management clearly affect the direction in which the field will grow. New directions and dimensions should be based on research into the full range of human behavior in the work setting of the police agency.

Research design should probe cause-and-effect relationships, and experimental projects should utilize the results of research in an innovative way. Of course, all research findings should be challenged by evaluation and field testing. All researchers, whether personnel department employees or professional consultants, must have the technical know-how to cope with assigned tasks and to report results simply and clearly. Research areas of particular importance to police personnel management include (1) how to measure police effectiveness, (2) qualifications and characteristics of the "ideal" police officer, and (3) the relationships of employer to employee and supervisor to subordinate. The study of police union contracts on a statewide or nationwide basis is an area of potential research that relates personnel transactions to potential job dissatisfaction.

Organizational socialization is described as a process by which the organization (police agency) and its membership assimilate new employees. Because of its relationship to job satisfaction, this process is also a prime research area. "New professionals" are presented as career police employees intent on upgrading police services and, therefore, supportive of research and development efforts to yield new perspectives on recruiting, utilizing, and retaining men and women who will perform well at police work and find meaning and satisfaction doing it.

Critique　　　　　　　　　　Research into any form of human behavior often seems to add to the complexity of known problems, while at the same time raising a number of more troublesome questions. For this reason, funds for research and development are often diverted to field operations. However, the growth of police personnel management will depend upon the findings of future research, its testing in the field, and the corrections and improvement of existing practices concerned with personnel transactions of all kinds.

1. What are the elements of total police personnel management?
2. Describe the case method of research as it applies to the field of personnel.
3. Why is technical writing ability a must for researchers?
4. How can research help to quantify the objectives and goals of a police agency?
5. How do police union contracts help pinpoint topics appropriate for future research? Why are they useful to police personnel managers?
6. Define organizational socialization.
7. Why is organizational socialization an area that can yield worthwhile findings about employee behavior?
8. Who are the "new professionals"?

Workbook Project

Develop a list of qualifications and characteristics that describes—in your opinion—the "ideal" police officer.

Selected
Bibliography

ASSOCIATES, Office of Military Leadership, U.S. Military Academy (eds.). *A Study of Organizational Leadership.* Harrisburg, Pa.: Stackpole Books, 1976.

BENT, ALAN EDWARD. *The Politics of Law Enforcement—Conflict and Power in Urban Communities.* Lexington, Mass.: Lexington Books, D.C. Healh and Company, 1974.

CROUCH, WINSTON, W. *Local Government Personnel Administration.* Washington, D.C.: International City Management Association, 1976.

LUTHANS, FRED. *Organizational Behavior.* 2nd ed. New York: McGraw-Hill Company, 1977.

MADDOX, CHARLES W. *Collective Bargaining in Law Enforcement:* Springfield, Ill.: Charles C Thomas, 1975.

PIGORS, PAUL, and CHARLES A. MYERS, *Personnel Administration: A Point of View and A Method.* 7th ed. New York: McGraw-Hill Book Company, 1977.

STRAUSS, GEORGE and LEONARD R. SAYLES, *Personnel—The Human Problems of Management.* 3rd ed. Englewood Cliffs, N.J.: Prentice-Hall, Inc., 1972.

Index